FINISH STRONG

RESISTANCE TRAINING
FOR ENDURANCE ATHLETES

BLOOMSBURY SPORT
Bloomsbury Publishing Plc
50 Bedford Square, London, WC1B 3DP, UK
29 Earlsfort Terrace, Dublin 2, Ireland

BLOOMSBURY, BLOOMSBURY SPORT and the Diana logo
are trademarks of Bloomsbury Publishing Plc

First published in Great Britain 2021

Bloomsbury Publishing Plc does not have any control over, or
responsibility for, any third-party websites referred to or in this
book. All internet addresses given in this book were correct at
the time of going to press. The author and publisher regret any
inconvenience caused if addresses have changed or sites have ceased
to exist, but can accept no responsibility for any such changes

A catalogue record for this book is available from the British Library
Library of Congress Cataloguing-in-Publication data has been applied for

ISBN: PB: 978-1-4729-7743-4; eBook: 978-1-4729-7744-1

2 4 6 8 10 9 7 5 3 1

Typeset in Noto Serif by Lee-May Lim.
Printed and bound in Great Britain by CPI Group (UK) Ltd. Croydon, CR0 4YY

To find out more about our authors and books visit www.bloomsbury.com
and sign up for our newsletters

FINISH STRONG

RESISTANCE TRAINING FOR ENDURANCE ATHLETES

RICHARD (RJ) BOERGERS AND ANGELO GINGERELLI

BLOOMSBURY SPORT

LONDON · OXFORD · NEW YORK · NEW DELHI · SYDNEY

CONTENTS

1

INTRODUCTION

We are endurance sports athletes just like you. Between us, we have completed three IRONMANs, 15 half IRONMANs, six marathons, 20 half marathons, 10 open water swim (OWS) races, five off-road cycling events, including X-terras, and countless other shorter-distance swims, bikes, runs and multisport events. You might say we've been building our aerobic bases over the last 10 years. Just like you, we enjoy training and racing and pushing ourselves to try to achieve a better placing or a new personal best (PB). While we are not elite athletes, we certainly aren't bringing up the rear at our races, typically finishing in the top 20 percent and occasionally grabbing a podium finish at some smaller events.

As a couple of self-coached athletes, one thing that keeps us motivated is that we are still seeing improvements. Both of us have actually achieved personal bests in events as recent as last year. At the end of a season, we plan our race calendars for the next year and begin setting goals and go to work on our training plans. Lather, rinse, repeat.

We also happen to be qualified healthcare, wellness and fitness professionals and have been helping athletes attain their goals for decades. Richard (RJ) Boergers obtained a BS in Health Science and Athletic Training, an MS in Human Performance (Biomechanics and Exercise Physiology) and a PhD in Human Movement Science. He is a licensed athletic trainer and is an Associate Professor in the Master of Science in Athletic Training program at Seton Hall University. Angelo Gingerelli earned a BS in Exercise Science, an MS in Education and also possesses an MBA. He is a certified strength and conditioning specialist and is a strength and conditioning coach at Seton Hall University.

Strength coaches, athletic trainers and other members of a sports performance team need to work together closely to optimize the performance of their athletes and clients. We have developed a close working relationship over the years because we both believe in the power of resistance training to improve endurance sport performance, practice it regularly in our training and preach it to anyone who will listen. What's more, we both have the same end goals in mind for incorporating regular resistance training with our aerobic sport training – improving athletic performance, injury prevention and career longevity. Sometimes, we have slightly different reasons for doing an exercise or selecting a particular training modality, but we are in total agreement that adding this resistance training program to your regimen will only help you Finish Strong.

The long (like ultramarathon-level long) list of benefits of regular resistance and mobility training includes increased muscular strength, improved balance, decreased risk of injury, better flexibility, improved functional movement patterns, more efficient mechanics and a more efficient energy metabolism due to increased muscle mass. In addition to these physical components, lifting weights is often accompanied by mental benefits, such as improved self-esteem, feeling younger or more athletic, and increased confidence.

Whether training for a 5K or IRONMAN, all endurance athletes can benefit from some form of resistance training. This training manual outlines exactly *how* to incorporate strength and mobility training into a weekly schedule in ways that are practical and effective for both novices and experienced racers. We will introduce the principles of resistance training to all forms of endurance athletes – runners, cyclists, swimmers and triathletes – in a way that will optimize their training and allow them to compete at a higher level.

Most athletes realize that strength training is a vital part of a comprehensive training program, but many are unsure about where to start or how to integrate lifting weights into their already packed training schedule. If you fall into this category, you are getting a starting point and a blueprint for how to structure training plans to maximize results and minimize injuries. The information and programs presented in this book will give you the knowledge and the information necessary to take your training to new levels.

TRY IT OUR WAY

You've heard the saying that the definition of insanity is doing the same thing over and over and expecting to get a different result. If this represents your training for endurance sports then maybe it's time to think about doing things differently.

One of the things that makes us different from many endurance athletes is our insistence on combining regular, planned resistance training and mobility work with aerobic sport training. We believe that doing this with *purpose*, to achieve maximal results, can help you reach your next personal best, keep you free from injury and extend your career!

Resistance training can be performed using a number of modalities that provide external force to the muscles – bodyweight, resistance bands, dumbbells, barbells and gym machines. In short, the muscles are "challenged" throughout a range of motion by the external force, which will result in stronger muscles. After all, Newton's Third Law states that for every action there is an equal and opposite reaction. When thinking about this, the muscles are providing a reactive force to move the external force.

We realized that both types of workouts (aerobic endurance training and resistance training) were important to overall athletic development and worked together to devise training plans that would help our athletes and ourselves continue to improve performance at endurance events.

As the years passed and the miles piled up, so did the medals as we both continued to improve our personal bests and compete in increasingly prestigious events. Let's be honest, world records were not being broken and companies were not beating down our

What is "resistance training"?

For the purpose of this book, "resistance training" will be defined as any stimulus that forces the muscles to work through a range of motion that is challenging enough to elicit the eventual strengthening of the muscle tissue. The key word is "challenging"; the body must be challenged in order to adapt. Sure, you can do endless "Runner's Curls" with 5lb (2.3kg) dumbbells, but unless you are challenging your body with progressively more taxing tasks (in this case, making the jump to 10lb/4.5kg dumbbells), you can't expect much strengthening to really happen.

doors with endorsement opportunities, but we were both getting progressively better by using our method, and we were having fun doing it.

While training together, a common topic of conversation (there's a lot of time to talk when you're running for hours) was the lack of knowledge most endurance athletes had about resistance training. Many of the coaches we dealt with knew a huge amount about training the cardiovascular system for a particular sport, but virtually nothing about resistance training. We found ourselves constantly educating other endurance athletes about why the weight room doesn't make people slower, why muscle mass is not always detrimental to speed and how general strength and muscular endurance would actually help movement mechanics and injury prevention.

These conversations eventually resulted in us writing this book. We figured out that we could inform more coaches and help more athletes by researching, writing and publishing a resource that could reach more people than any lecture we could deliver to our students or meeting we could have with a coaching staff. So here it is.

Finish Strong is the direct result of a lot of research, writing and program design, and the indirect product of decades of running, cycling, swimming, coaching, lifting, training, experimenting and competing by both authors that will hopefully change the way you train for your next event. We have developed these ideas and this training plan over years of trial and error, training cycles that ended in great triumphs and crushing disappointments, workouts that were just right and sessions that ended up being too long, too intense or too difficult. We have read, researched, lectured, presented and implemented the ideas in this book with both ourselves and the students and athletes we are responsible for educating and training. We believe that the implementation of these lessons on proper resistance training will potentially subtract minutes from your next finish time and add years to your endurance career.

This book will provide a roadmap for endurance athletes to:

» prevent injuries;
» create balance within their bodies through a combination of strength and mobility;
» build muscular strength;
» enhance athletic performance;
» find the confidence to Finish Strong.

Let's face it, there is an overwhelming amount of information about training the human body available right now. From peer-reviewed research journals to social media accounts and from books to podcasts, there has never been more to read, watch, hear, discuss and experiment with. That said, surprisingly, a relatively low percentage of this information is dedicated to helping *endurance athletes* achieve their goals of better times, longer careers and consistently setting new personal bests. This is an odd void in the marketplace because the idea of participating in resistance training to improve sports performance has been commonly accepted for decades, yet very little has been written about adapting this training for the men and women who run dozens of miles in pouring rain, bike hundreds of miles in blistering heat and swim thousands of yards before sunrise.

Endurance athletes are not the typical "I don't have time to train" excuse-makers or the "I'm too sore every time I go to the gym" complainers. Generally, they are the exact opposite.

Men and women who voluntarily commit thousands of hours per year to pushing their bodies to the absolute physical limit in pursuit of faster times, qualifying for more prestigious events and putting together a successful endurance career résumé are some of the toughest and most excuse-free people on the planet. When it rains, they train. When it's hot, they train. When they have a full day of school, work, meetings, etc ... they train! This is a cohort who is committed to achieving the absolute best version of themselves that's humanly possible, but for many, the lack of strength, muscular endurance and structural integrity is the limiting factor in this peak performance equation.

This led to us asking the crucial question: "Why aren't endurance athletes incorporating resistance training into their training programs?" After a lot of unofficial polling and discussions, we found that there were three major prevailing themes that presented themselves when answering this question:

1) lack of knowledge by endurance coaches regarding strength training;
2) lack of role models in endurance sports;
3) general lack of knowledge about how to start a resistance training program.

LACK OF KNOWLEDGEABLE COACHES

Lifting weights to improve performance has been commonly accepted in most sports for several decades. Sports such as American football and baseball were early adopters and resistance training has become entrenched in the culture of the games themselves. Today, even sports that were slower to embrace this kind of training, such as soccer and basketball, have fully committed to the importance of strength and conditioning. However, endurance events, like the marathon, open water swims, cycling and triathlons, have been some of the last sports to embrace strength training as a vital component of a comprehensive program and have only recently been open to experimenting with this type of training stimulus.

The fact that many distance coaches have limited strength training backgrounds has created a situation whereby endurance training sessions involve meticulously planned rest/ work ratios, periodized intensity intervals and calculated target heart rates, yet end with the directive "Go to the weight room!" with limited instructions about what to do once athletes arrive there. What exactly happens in the weight room and how it adds to the athlete's overall performance is rarely discussed... Until now!

This situation has become common because while most track trainers, swim coaches and distance gurus recognize the vague concept that "getting stronger" is important to endurance sport performance, most have very little knowledge about how to optimize the time and effort spent in the weight room. Some programs involve strength coaches or consultants who attempt to guide the training, but unfortunately many of these have extensive backgrounds in training sports such as American football, basketball and baseball but very little experience with long-duration aerobic events. Also, there is so little written about the topic that even extremely dedicated and diligent fitness professionals have trouble finding quality information. Sure, there are a few social media accounts that mention doing some calisthenics on lighter running days and a few blogs will post the occasional video about how "Runner's Curls" will help upper-body running mechanics, but the resources for coaches and athletes truly interested in finishing races strong, fast and injury free have been very limited.

If you purchase a training plan on TrainingPeaks for your next half marathon, Fondo, OWS or IRONMAN, trust us, you won't find a program with enough detail about the strength and mobility work you need to be doing to keep your body in top shape. These plans are awesome for preparing your cardiovascular system for your upcoming race – we've used them plenty of times; the problem is that the focus and detail is on making you a cardiovascular beast ready to conquer your "A" race. The strength and mobility sessions (if there are any) are simply window dressings or afterthoughts. The other thing to remember is that these plans are usually limited to a three- to five-month training period. Our goal is to get you to adopt good habits and perform dedicated strength and mobility exercises *throughout the year*. The training plans in this book therefore follow a periodized yearly format that addresses all phases of training and preparation for all major events.

LACK OF ENDURANCE SPORTS ROLE MODELS WHO STRENGTH TRAIN

We all have sports heroes whom we follow and hope to emulate. These heroes are commonly what keep athletes interested in the sport, and we often imitate their training or racing style either consciously or subconsciously. Unfortunately, though, it really is quite hard to find one of our heroes touting the benefits of strength and mobility training. If you've ever read a book by Chrissie Wellington or Chris "Macca" McCormack, two of triathlon's biggest stars, you won't find any great detail on how much strength training they did in their career. That said, Macca did write that as he got older, resistance training was important to keep his body injury free, but there's very little information available about exactly what he did. Strength and mobility training can be the fountain of youth. For those of you entering the 40+ age bracket like us, be like Macca and use resistance training to stay competitive or even get progressively better as you age.

Ryan Hall, arguably one of the best distance runners in the USA, retired at the age of 33 because he was injured so often, having never lifted a weight during his stellar running career. Since then, he has turned to regularly participating in strength training, is throwing down some serious speed and there has even been talk of a comeback. Did we mention that he looks *strong*? For those of you who haven't been doing regular strength and mobility work and are often sidelined by injury, be like Ryan Hall.

US Olympic swimmer Michael Phelps is the most decorated Olympian of all time! In his book *No Limits,* he touted the importance of regular strength training when he was training for his second, third and fourth Olympic games. His greatest feat came in 2008 at the Beijing Olympics, where he won eight gold medals. He stated that when you are striving to get faster by fractions of a second, there is just no way to do it without getting stronger and more powerful. Do you want to beat some of your rivals and perhaps land a podium finish? For those of you looking for that performance edge, be like Michael Phelps and add regular resistance training to your program.

In our opinion, there's nothing worse than

It's not too late

Long-distance running is one of the few sports where real improvement is possible well into middle age. Nobody is better at basketball, baseball or American football when they are 50 than when they were 20 years old, but a lot of people run their best races when they are "old" by conventional sports standards. There are a lot of reasons for this, but keep in mind that it's never too late to improve your training to improve your performance.

seeing someone with vast potential never make it to the starting line because of injury, or never hit that personal goal they want to achieve. Simply put, we believe in Finishing Strong!

LACK OF KNOWLEDGE ABOUT WHERE TO START

We've heard countless stories of athletes who just didn't know where to start when it comes to strength training, or who have been doing the wrong things when they actually did make it to the gym. This is troubling for us to hear. As endurance athletes, one thing we have in common is that Type A personality and mindset to strive to always get better. Newbies, seasoned veterans, elites and professionals all share one goal: *to get faster.*

There are almost countless variables that we monitor and manipulate in our aerobic sport training to help improve our performance. Unfortunately, many leave out key ingredients to success by ignoring strength and mobility or by forcing themselves to work through a plan that *lacks purpose.* Going into the gym without goals and a plan is the equivalent of running junk miles (and we hope you've been coached to avoid those). We spend time in this book explaining which exercises you should be doing, how to properly perform them, and how to adapt and progress them. Aside from seeing people execute strength exercises with poor form, one of our other main pet peeves is seeing an overall lack of creativity. We get it, the gym isn't a comfortable place for everyone. We always say, it's better that someone develops a good habit of getting to the gym regularly, even if they are doing the same routine every day, but this isn't actually necessary – it should be varied.

For a guy like Angelo who's been a strength and conditioning coach for 20 years, progressing or regressing an exercise doesn't take much thought since he has done it countless times with his athletes. This book will empower you to be able to think through the idea of progressing exercises as you get stronger, or need to regress because of an injury (hopefully not) before progressing again. What's more, performing planned progressive resistance and mobility exercise from the programs that this book provides will help you unlock your potential. We have no doubt that you're willing to make the sacrifices and put the time in training for your sport; it's our hope that now you're ready to join us in adding resistance and mobility training into your training program so that you can Finish Strong.

TOO MUCH FATIGUE AND TOO LITTLE TIME

Training for endurance events requires the manipulation of dozens of variables, including distance, pace, heart rate, recovery, rest intervals, hydration, nutrition, and many others to be able to continue training at a high level without exhaustion or overtraining. Even a novice preparing for their first 5K needs to plan out some rest days in order to successfully finish the event.

Two variables that impact all endurance athletes are fatigue and time; too much of the former, too little of the latter. Training for these events takes several hours a day and the overwhelming majority of athletes still have "life commitments", such as careers, families, school and relationships that also require their time. Statistically, most endurance athletes are not independently wealthy or professional athletes who can spend all day training while a group of corporate sponsors pays for their lifestyle, so making the absolute most of the time spent in the gym is incredibly important.

We are sensitive to these facts and we've designed a program made for endurance athletes who live real lives in the real world. We aren't like the typical college strength coach telling a cross-country runner who just finished a hilly 10-mile (16km) loop to do 5 sets of 3 reps each max effort Back Squats before they go to class. We also aren't like a stereotypical you-can-do-anything-you-set-your-mind-to motivational speaker telling you that you could spend two hours a day in the gym if you had your priorities straight. We're providing practical advice that can be applied in the real world because it was written by guys who practice this advice while living in the real world.

HOW TO USE THE BOOK

Finish Strong is divided into two overarching parts. The first section of the book details *why* endurance athletes should perform some kind of strength training. If you are reading this book, chances are you already see some value in resistance training, but this part will answer any lingering questions you may have as well as dispelling some common myths, such as that lifting weights leads to a lack of flexibility and all strength training is accompanied by a massive increase in muscle mass. It also explains why some weight lifting is ineffective and how novices can avoid the pitfalls that often affect endurance athletes when they are new to the weight room. If you are a personal trainer, strength coach or even a track/cross-country/swim coach, this section will give you the ammunition you need to convince clients/athletes/parents/coaches that the program is solid and will help them reach their maximum potential. The research has been done, the terms have been defined and the data has been compiled for you. If you can read this section and apply it to your daily training and coaching, you will already be on the road to getting better.

The second section deals with *how* to implement these principles into a comprehensive training program. The yearly training calendar has been broken down into four phases and there are guidelines and parameters for how to add strength training to each one, based on the desired effects of each and how much time/effort is being dedicated to endurance training. For example, the strength sessions during a period when an athlete is running 50 miles (80km) per month are radically different than when they are running 50 miles (80km) per week. The section also includes detailed descriptions of the six 'Foundation Exercises' that are valuable for all endurance athletes, the 'Top 10' exercises for each discipline (swim, bike and run) and progressions/regressions for each exercise based on time and fatigue. Each discipline-specific chapter contains exercises tailored to the sport based on common movement and postural dysfunctions caused by repetitive motions in the sport and the neuromuscular demands placed on key body parts (for example, a swimmer will need to focus on more specific shoulder strength compared to a runner). Triathletes will be able to use parts of each of these discipline-specific chapters to build the plan that's right for them.

Our inclusion of progressions/regressions comes after years of noticing that people do the same exercises in a gym – over and over. Our hope is that this empowers you to progress when a movement has become too easy or use the regressions when you are working through an injury. This section gives you everything you need to implement a yearly resistance training plan for either yourself or your athletes.

What is sport specificity?

"Sport specificity" is a common term in the strength and conditioning world and basically means training in a specific way to maximize performance in a specific sport. Improving general strength and mobility is beneficial to overall health, but when training for specific activities, it's best to follow a training plan that is designed for that activity. Keep this in mind when it's time to put the book down and hit the gym.

Both sections are important in providing a comprehensive explanation of why and how to add resistance training to an already packed training calendar, and when understood and implemented will have a definitive and positive effect on athletes who put in the work and commit to the process.

AUTHOR BIOGRAPHIES

Richard ('RJ') Boergers is a certified athletic trainer who worked in sports medicine at the collegiate level for many years before becoming a full-time professor. He has been a serious endurance athlete since 2007 and has competed in various events covering running, cycling and swimming in multiple countries, including finishing three IRONMAN triathlons and more than 15 IRONMAN 70.3 races. Throughout his training for these prestigious events he has always applied general strength and conditioning principles, such as progressive overload, general adaptation syndrome and basic periodization to continue to stimulate his body to improve and handle training at consistently higher levels.

Angelo Gingerelli has been a strength and conditioning coach for two decades and has worked with youth, collegiate and professional athletes. Gingerelli's background in powerlifting and Olympic weightlifting combined with his academic pursuits provided him with a solid background to work with traditional power sport athletes but was lacking when it came to training athletes specializing in longer-duration activities for the first decade of his coaching career. In 2010, he began running road races and ran his first marathon in 2011, where he promptly caught the "marathon bug" and has since run several similar races. During this period, he became interested in applying resistance training principles to endurance sports in an effort to better serve the swimmers and cross-country athletes he was training and in order to improve his own marathon performance.

SECTION I

THE LOWDOWN

2

THE IMPORTANCE OF RESISTANCE TRAINING

RJ fondly remembers his IRONMAN 70.3 personal best in 2019, which was at IRONMAN 70.3 Connecticut (the old Rev3 Quassy). Anyone who has done this race knows that there is a killer hill to climb out of for the last ½ mile (800m) on the run course (we all have had that hill in a race that breaks our hopes and dreams – well, this is that hill). In a previous race on this same course, RJ found himself deflated and walking in this very spot. On the day of his personal best, he was able to put together a great swim, bike and run, as well as conquer that dreaded hill, running the entire way. Just where did this strong finish come from? Was it the favorable weather conditions? Was it the execution of the nutrition plan? Was it the hill repeat runs in training? Was it mental toughness? Was it familiarity with the course? Was it the year-round strength training? The answer is that it was *all* of these. Failure to have hit on *all* of these things would not have yielded the PB.

Many triathletes will talk about the "fourth discipline", which requires practice and training. To some, these are the transitions – placing an emphasis on speed moving from one discipline to another; to others, it is the execution of the hydration/nutrition plan; while some consider mindfulness to be this key important ingredient. For RJ, regular strength and mobility training done year round is his fourth discipline. We both believe that implementing this fourth discipline will not only allow you to achieve peak performance, but it can also keep you free from injury and extend your athletic career. We will share our tips for how often you should strength train, how the sessions should be structured, and cover the different types of strength and mobility training that are out there for you to choose from. We want you to have an understanding of the impact that resistance training can have on your sports performance and adopt good habits that will allow you to reach a new personal best and Finish Strong!

The majority of major college cross-country and swim coaches, world-class running clubs and books on peak endurance performance (including Joe Friel's *The Triathlete's Training Bible* [1] and Jack Daniels' hugely influential *Daniels' Running Formula* [2]) advocate for some kind of resistance training when training for endurance events. The reasons for this include decreased risk of injury, increased work capacity, more efficient movement patterns, improved muscular physiology and a longer/healthier running career. When applied properly to an endurance training regime, resistance training can be the difference between merely surviving and actually thriving when training for an event or season.

As in most sports, a stronger athlete is better positioned for long-term success than a weaker one, and endurance sports are no different. Now, there are some obvious differences between competing in marathons or triathlons and sports with much higher power requirements, like American football, or muscle mass requirements, such as bodybuilding, but the prescribed training will also differ from that advocated for those kinds of sports. It also takes into account the fact that actually training to run a marathon is in itself a figurative marathon. It involves months of training, hundreds of miles run and thousands of calories burned. To expect the body to respond positively to this level of training without the strength, structural integrity or muscle mass to endure that much activity is somewhat foolish. By making the body structurally sound, strong and flexible, an athlete has much improved chances of having a successful, injury-free and enjoyable training/competition cycle. Without this baseline strength development, many runners/cyclists/swimmers end up feeling drained, looking emaciated and performing worse than they did at earlier points in their training.

THE BODY IS ALWAYS OVERCOMING RESISTANCE

Another key element that is often overlooked in the Resistance Training vs. Endurance Sports debate is that the human body is constantly working against resistance. Whether we are overcoming gravity to sit up from our bed, running up a steep incline, pedaling into a strong headwind or swimming against water resistance, our skeletal musculature is always fighting to move our bodies from Point A to Point B. If we can accept this fact, it becomes apparent why strength development is an important component of peak endurance performance.

What's more, increased strength is also an asset when a kick or push is required at the end of an event. A strong finish is often the difference between a personal best and just another race. Having the muscular endurance to "sprint through the finish line" (cliché alert!) is a big part of having enough "in the tank" (keep the clichés coming!) to establish new personal bests. We often see men and women finishing events looking like they are dragging their bodies across the line by the sheer force of their will. While it is compelling drama to watch people complete an event physically, mentally and emotionally drained, it normally means there was some flaw in their training or preparation that could have possibly been avoided. One potential training issue during these dramatic finishes is the lack of resistance training that may otherwise have made the athlete's body strong enough to finish the event without the histrionics.

IT DOESN'T HAVE TO TAKE ALL DAY

One of the biggest misconceptions about resistance training is that it is the polar opposite of endurance training. The idea that developing endurance requires long bouts of steady state exercise and developing strength requires max effort sets with long rest intervals in between is not entirely true. Yes, if you want to be successful at endurance events you have to put in the time, effort and mileage to steadily tax your cardiovascular system over prolonged periods of time. It's also true that to get bigger/stronger you must move enough weight to elicit a breakdown of muscle fibers that will be bigger and stronger once they rebuild themselves, and to some extent this type of training requires prolonged rest intervals. According to the American College of Sports Medicine (ACSM) *each muscle group* should be trained 2–4 sessions per week for at least 2–4 sets of 8–12 repetitions per set to cause strength improvements.[3] While this volume of training is still required for endurance athletes, if we are training for a marathon or IRONMAN there is a way to stress the body in the gym in a more specific manner that matches the demands of the sport and will be more beneficial in the long run (in both the literal and figurative senses).

> ## Scheduled resistance training
>
> Having predetermined dates and times for incorporating resistance training into your weekly schedule will help improve accountability. You are already used to doing this for your aerobic endurance training. When it's on the schedule, you're less likely to skip it or forget about it. If you use TrainingPeaks like we do, you'll also get the satisfaction of seeing a "green" completion on the calendar once you finish.

Decreasing rest intervals or moving between exercises and sets with very little time in between is a more sport-specific way for endurance athletes to hit the gym. Sitting around in between sets, checking your phone or making small talk with training partners while your body fully recovers between sets is fine for powerlifters or Olympic weightlifters who require full central nervous system activation and muscles firing from an almost completely resting state in order to move the most weight possible. For endurance athletes, though, this model should be altered to encourage moving quickly between different exercises or sets of the same exercise in order to keep the heart rate, respiration rate and core body temperature elevated while the skeletal musculature is firing, which mimics the way the body must operate during endurance sports.

In addition to the physiological advantages of training in this manner, the amount of time saved is also a huge practical bonus. Runners, cyclists, swimmers and triathletes spend huge amounts of time on their chosen discipline(s) throughout the year and even more time when preparing for a big event. Considering that most competitors are not professional athletes and have to find ways to train at a high level while having multiple other responsibilities (career, family, social life, etc.), spending less time in the gym while getting results is a good thing.

There are several ways to put this idea into practice, but one of the easiest is performing exercises in super sets[4] or mini-circuits with minimal rest in between sets. One key component of this will be understanding opposing muscle groups[4] and taxing one while the other recovers. For instance, an opposing muscle group super set of Push-ups for the chest and Pull-ups for the back is ideal because the back muscles are recovering while the chest muscles are performing Push-ups, and vice versa. There are some nuances to this that will be discussed later, but for now this is a sufficient explanation. The same concept can be applied to upper vs. lower body movements. After a set of Squats has been performed for the lower extremity, an upper extremity exercise like Dumbbell Row or Shoulder Press should be done while the legs recover for the next set of Squats.

"Circuit training"[3] has seen a resurgence in popularity recently through programs such as CrossFit, Orangetheory Fitness and F45 Training, among others. Doing several exercises in a row with very little rest is a good method to stress the body in a way similar to endurance events, but it should be noted that the majority of circuit training programs like these incorporate some kind of cardiovascular or "conditioning" component that is not necessary for most endurance athletes. While this mixture of strength and cardio training is perfect for the general population, who want a great workout in a limited amount of time, they are not nearly as effective for people who are already covering hundreds of miles a month in other aspects of their training. That said, circuit training combining both types of training is a good way to stay in shape during the off-season and give the body a chance to recover from the rigors of running, cycling or swimming, but during more intense periods of training the majority of cardiovascular training should come from the track, bike or pool and not the gym.

DEVELOPING STRENGTH WHILE MAINTAINING FLEXIBILITY

The stereotypical muscle-bound bodybuilder has become a largely antiquated idea. Sprinters, Olympic weightlifters and even competitive bodybuilders have proven for decades that the human body can be packed with skeletal muscle and still be fast, functional and flexible. These are athletes who dedicate a very large percentage of their training time to lifting weights and building muscle mass and even they don't see a significant reduction in flexibility when training is planned properly. Also, considering the much lower optimal level of resistance training for endurance athletes and that most don't have a genetic predisposition to "get jacked", the idea of getting "too big" or muscle-bound is not a realistic concern for most men and women.

To prevent a loss of flexibility or range of motion, the resistance training program should include daily mobility exercises that will maintain or improve movement quality while the body becomes bigger and stronger. Every strength training session should start with a generalized warm-up that raises the core body temperature, heart rate and respiration rate. This can be done by jogging, using cardio machines, jumping rope or doing light calisthenics. This prepares the body for activity in the same way that letting a car "warm up" before driving will improve the engine's performance. You wouldn't jump out of bed from a sound sleep and immediately start sprinting at full speed, and you shouldn't do it in training, either. Once you are primed for activity, some combination of self-massage, mobility and activation drills should be used. Detailed explanations of these drills will be provided later.

DYNAMIC WARM-UP/FLEXIBILITY/MUSCLE ACTIVATIONS

The National Strength and Conditioning Association (NSCA) defines "dynamic flexibility" as the available range of motion during active movements that require voluntary muscular actions. Put simply, this is how far the body can move during activity, which is a more accurate way to assess movement than static measures, such as the traditional sit-and-reach. Being able to squat properly, lunge to full depth or press a bar overhead with good posture are all ways to measure the body's dynamic flexibility. These basic dynamic flexibility exercises are important because they stress the various soft tissues of each joint in a similar way to actual physical activity.[5]

Much like strength, dynamic flexibility falls in the "if you don't use it, you lose it" category. So, once movements like Overhead Squats, Hip Openers and Lunges have been mastered, they must be constantly utilized to maintain the flexibility required to do them properly. The body naturally gets less pliable with age – just watch older sedentary people getting out of cars – but with consistent, progressive dynamic stretching, flexibility can be maintained or improved. The best time to schedule these movements is during the warm-up period before resistance training. When performed on resistance training days, they will also help flush out the soreness following long swims/rides/runs. Generally speaking, it is also good to perform dynamic flexibility drills prior to starting your endurance workouts.

Another way to prep the body before endurance training sessions or resistance training is by performing muscle activations. While the role of the dynamic warm-up is to keep the muscles pliable to help the joints move through their functional end ranges, the role of muscle activations is to "wake up" and recruit muscles for complex movements. Swimming, biking and running all require synchronization of several muscles. Muscle activation exercises are meant to target important muscles that are sometimes under-recruited. By proactively prepping these muscles prior to activity, you will improve the synchronization of the muscles in each of the kinetic chains and allow for improved performance. Activation exercises typically just involve bodyweight and most often target the core.

FLEXIBILITY IN TRAINING

Maintaining or increasing flexibility goes beyond simply stretching before or after a training session. There are measures that can be taken *during* training that can potentially make an even bigger impact than the traditional pre/post stretch.

PARTIAL REPS FOR PARTIAL RESULTS!

Like most gym clichés, "partial reps for partial results" has some element of truth. While doing sets to failure with partial reps tacked on at the end has a place in the pursuit of pure hypertrophy (bodybuilders chasing a pump), there is really no use for partial reps for most endurance athletes. In general, weights that can be lifted properly through a full range of motion should be lifted for an appropriate number of reps so that entire sets can be performed fully.

Exceptions to this rule are injury, imbalances or immobility limiting the range of motion on a particular movement. However, while partial or shortened movements may be used until a full range of motion can be performed properly, the goal should always be to attain full movement as soon as possible. For example, if squatting until the thighs are parallel to the floor is impossible when training begins, doing Box Squats with progressively lower boxes is a good way to safely increase range of motion.

For athletes with extreme restrictions it may be necessary to continue to work on unresisted versions of certain movements until range of motion improves, while getting the majority of actual strength development from simpler movements. For example, if an athlete is struggling to do Romanian Deadlifts (RDLs) properly, they can work on their RDL technique with a dowel or PVC pipe while they are warming up, but then get the majority of their hamstring work by doing Machine or Physioball Leg Curls. This allows the athlete a chance to get better at the movement with very little resistance and then stimulate strength/growth with another exercise that is not as technique intensive. The goal should be for all athletes to properly perform all Foundation Exercises, but if the body is just not cooperating with certain exercises, there are multiple options that can be used until they get more proficient at more challenging movements.

The following table illustrates some of the progressions and regressions for the Foundation Exercises that will be discussed later in Section 2. These are the exercises that will be the cornerstones of your program. Understanding how and when to push to the next level, maintain your current level or temporarily regress a level will be important to your overall success.

PROGRESSIONS AND REGRESSIONS FOR FOUNDATION EXERCISES						
SQUATS						
Bodyweight Squat	Goblet Squat with kettlebell, dumbbell or medicine ball	Dumbbell Squat	Barbell Back Squat	Barbell Front Squat	Barbell Overhead Squat	
LUNGES						
Walking Lunge	Resisted Lunge dumbbells, kettlebells, medicine ball or weighted vest	Resisted Walking Lunge dumbbells, kettlebells, medicine ball or weighted vest	Barbell Stationary Lunge	Barbell Walking Lunge	Barbell Front Position Lunge	Barbell Overhead Lunge
ROMANIAN DEADLIFTS (RDL)						
	Dumbbell RDL	Single Leg Dumbbell RDL	Barbell RDL	Hip hinge		
PUSH-UPS						
Hands Elevated Push-up	Push-up	Dumbbell Chest Press	Barbell Bench Press	Push-up	Dumbbell Alternating Chest Press	Unstable Surface Chest Press
PULL-UPS						
Suspension Trainer Inverted Row	Barbell Inverted Row	Pull-up palms in	Pull-up palms out	Resisted Pull-up with hanging plates/ dumbbells, bands, chains, etc.		
HIP BRIDGES						
Hip Bridge	Banded Hip Bridge	Elevated Hip Bridge	Resisted Hip Bridge	Single Leg Hip Bridge	Hip Thrust March	Resisted Hip Thrust March

Table 2.1

STATIC STRETCH AND COOL-DOWN

The NSCA defines 'static flexibility' as the range of possible movement about a joint and its surrounding muscles during a passive movement.[4] Examples of static stretches are holding the sit-and-reach position or the touch-your-toes position while standing up. In recent years, static stretching has got a bad reputation as being antiquated, useless and basically the VHS player of the stretching world. In reality, this kind of stretching is valuable for extended muscle elongation and long-term flexibility, and can be used to great effect as part of the cool-down segment of most training sessions. A post-workout static stretch is a great way to lengthen the muscles that have just been forcefully contracting while the body cools down from the arousal of the training session. Most static stretch positions should be held for 20–30 seconds and a gentle stretch should be felt throughout the duration. It should not be a painful or an "I can't hold this any longer!" situation. Individual stretch selection will be based on areas of necessity and personal preference, but in general some of the old-school stretches we have been doing since junior high phys-ed are still good for us today.

YOGA

Yoga is a great way to develop flexibility as well as aid in recovery, improve balance and strengthen the core. It's been embraced by some of the top riders in the pro tour, including 2012 Tour de France General Classification winner Bradley Wiggins. Attending in-person yoga classes with an attentive instructor who helps adjust your position through the poses is the best way to get started. It's true that these can be expensive and time-consuming, but there's no doubt that a series of Downward Dogs and Sun Salutations can do wonders to make the body feel better and extend your endurance career.

When searching for yoga classes in your area, look for a practice geared toward "sports" or "active people" to ensure it's going to involve more physical activity than just breathing and meditation. While there's absolutely a place for that kind of practice, it might not be mid-week during a very intense training period. Also, hot yoga has become an increasingly popular way to increase range of motion by performing a series of poses in a room heated to well over 100°F (38°C). Endurance athletes should be cautious of doing this during weeks when they are already traversing hundreds of miles because of the potential for extreme dehydration, and everyone should be mindful of overextension.

For best results, match the style, teacher, class schedule and effort level to where you are in your physical development and training plan. We were both "late adopters" of incorporating yoga into our weekly resistance training and we are kicking ourselves for not being receptive to it sooner! But at least those kicks are being performed with perfect technique and a full range of motion because of all the positive impact yoga has had on our bodies!

Once you've gained some experience and understand how the flows work, it would be more than fine to use a subscription-based program like Peloton or the Down Dog App, or just purchase a few DVDs that you can rotate through on your own.

We've given you a lot to think about and consider. Hopefully, we've eased some of your concerns about adding in resistance training and mobility exercises to your regular training program. It doesn't have to be time-consuming and it doesn't necessarily require expensive equipment or gym memberships. By making your body stronger and more flexible, you will be a more powerful athlete and less prone to injury. Don't make the same mistake that some of your competition is making ... become more powerful and start smashing personal bests!

So, are you one of us now? Are you a believer in incorporating resistance training into your weekly training regimen to become a better, stronger endurance athlete?

1. Friel, J., *The Triathlete's Training Bible*, 4th ed. (VeloPress, 2016)
2. Daniels, J., *Daniels' Running Formula*, 2nd ed. (Human Kinetics, 2005)
3. *ACSM's Guidelines for Exercise Testing and Prescription*, 10th ed. (Wolters Kluwer, 2018)
4. Earle, R., *Essentials of Strength Training and Conditioning*, 4th ed. (Human Kinetics, 2016)
5. Starrett, K., *Becoming a Supple Leopard*, 2nd ed. (Victory Belt; 2015)

3

HOW TO AVOID CHRONIC AND OVERUSE INJURIES

Remember this one thing: the human body thrives when it is balanced. That is, when balanced, it will achieve optimal performance while being at the lowest risk for overuse and chronic injuries. Keep this in mind when you are developing your resistance and mobility training program! You are ripe for an overuse injury once you ignore this important principle. A couple of examples include choosing to have more focus on chest strength while ignoring back strength, resulting in an imbalance, or having a good deal of trunk mobility to the left with limited mobility to the right, which would also be troublesome.

Are these imbalances simply caused by the repetitive motions of our favorite endurance sport (swimming, cycling, running)? The answer to this is yes and no. There is such a thing as training error, which would be increasing volume and intensity too quickly, before your body is ready. However, the SAID principle (specific adaptations for imposed demands) (McArdle, 2010)[1] helps us understand that as we continually add training intensity and volume at a reasonable rate, our body will respond and will be able to manage the workload. I'm sure we all remember when we first started our training for our endurance sport and a half marathon or 30-mile (48km) bike ride seemed to be unachievable. However, soon after we began a regular training regime, our bodies adapted and we could accomplish that workload with relative ease. There doesn't appear to be a set workload that is definitively too much. How else would you explain Tour de France riders being able to cover more than 2,000 miles (3,200km) in 21 stages with many having significant elevation gain; transAmerican runners like Marshall Ulrich; or the Iron Cowboy, who did 101 IRONMAN distance "races" over 101 days?

It therefore appears that the "wear and tear" theory seems to have been debunked and that the SAID principle prevails. However, we do have to discuss the negative effects of the repetitive motions we perform in our endurance sports. Doing the same action over and over can affect our muscular strength and endurance, create scar tissue buildup in our joints and cause adhesions in our fascia. All of these things can lead to imbalances, which may result in injury. Specifically, we may notice that postural syndromes or movement dysfunctions start to appear, and these may be the predisposing factor for the development of an overuse or chronic injury.

The occurrence of overuse and chronic injuries is well explained using envelope of function (EOF) theory (Dye, 1996).[2] Dye's theory finds that there are four main factors that affect function: anatomic, physiologic, kinematic and treatment.

1. Anatomically, we all have our individualized genetic code. This governs our bone density, bone and joint shapes, soft tissue make-up, and overall alignment. Some people may have conditions like a femoral anteversion (internal rotation of the leg at the hip) or genu valgum (knock-knees), which would predispose them to greater stress on their knees during weight bearing. Some people may have connective tissue that is really loose, which could make a joint unstable and vulnerable to injury. Whether or not we can do something to combat the negative effects of the anatomic factor is somewhat debatable. Certain corrective exercises can be done to place the body in a more favorable alignment (i.e. keeping the knees in line with the hip and foot), but sometimes we are stuck with what we've got.

2. The physiologic factor takes into account training errors and the SAID principle. If we ramp up intensity and volume of our training appropriately, as in the "10 percent rule"[3] we should avoid overtaxing our bodies. Failure to gradually increase demands on our bodies will likely result in injury. Over the years, we've seen countless incidents when an athlete gets too aggressive with their training in the pre-season after having taken nearly the entire summer off, and their body simply revolts. Physiologic factors are easy to eliminate with simple planning and a smart progression of training loads.

3. The kinematic factor explains the importance of proper form. Hopefully, you've achieved a proper fit on your bike, and have received a reasonable level of coaching on your swim stroke, running gait and pedaling. Failure to have good mechanics is a major reason why we get hurt. Overstriding when running can lead to knee problems for runners; cycling in too aggressive a position may round out the lower back, leaving it vulnerable to injury; and having your arm pull across the midline of the body while swimming will place a great deal of stress on the shoulder. These are just a few of the many mechanical flaws that need to be diligently avoided. If you know your form needs work, invest in some coaching so you can eliminate the kinematic factor as a possible cause of injury.

4. The final factor of Dye's envelope of function principle revolves around treatment. This speaks to the amount of self-care we give ourselves as athletes. Hopefully, you've taken adequate time to perform an active warm-up prior to exercising and usually take time to stretch and foam roll afterward. Some of us will require more body maintenance in the form of massage and other bodywork. One other major way that an athlete can provide quality self-care, and the premise of this book, is taking time to do regular resistance training and mobility work to avoid imbalances. If we want our body to help us achieve success, we have to take care of it.

Each of us has an individualized envelope of function. We all have that friend whose body can get away with murder: they never warm up, never stretch, never strength train and have the ugliest form/mechanics, yet they are still a good athlete. These people are frustrating to have as friends. They are the lucky ones who have really large envelopes of function. Then we may have that friend who always seems to be injured and is never able to make it to the starting line of a race. They do everything by the book: they follow a strict training plan, they

Ready to race

Your body is the "vehicle" that will get you across the finish line and it needs to be cared for. To avoid overuse/chronic injuries, take time to properly warm up prior to training, and perform regularly planned resistance and mobility training that targets common problem areas for your sport. Getting proper rest and adequate nutrition and staying hydrated are other key ingredients to keeping your body ready to race.

warm up, they strength train, they work on form with coaches, they go to physical therapy to do corrective exercises, and they get the additional bodywork/massages. These poor folks have a very small envelope of function. Once their body becomes even slightly imbalanced, their body reacts negatively with pain and pathology.

If our body falls out of optimal alignment for any large period of time, creep will set into the tissues (muscles, fascia, capsules) and a postural syndrome will set in. The repetitive nature of our sport may leave us somewhat vulnerable to these unwanted postures and it can be further complicated by our occupation (i.e. desk jobs). Phil Page[4] explains Dr. Vladimir Janda's approach to postural syndromes. He says these are a result of muscle imbalances where the muscles on one side

> ## Common overuse/ chronic injuries
>
> Postural syndromes and movement dysfunctions go hand in hand with overuse/chronic injuries. Failure to perform self-care via resistance and mobility training will allow these problems to linger. Common postural syndromes and movement dysfunctions include: forward head, forward shoulder, kyphosis (curving of the spine), anterior or posterior pelvic tilt, knee valgus (knock-knees) and flat feet.

are long, weak and inhibited, while the muscles on the other side are short and facilitated. These muscle imbalances create faulty force couples, which leave us vulnerable to injury. Addressing the postural syndromes with corrective resistance exercises and mobility work is vital to restore proper alignment. The National Academy of Sports Medicine[5] describes movement dysfunction as being a result of poor length/tension relationship of the muscles, altered joint motion and inadequate muscle control. Clearly, there is overlap with these two models that explains why we have overuse/chronic injuries.

Wow, that was a lot to unpack! One thing is for sure, being sidelined by overuse/chronic injury is no fun. Hopefully, it prompted you to start thinking about the changes you can make that will prevent the injury cascade from occurring so you can continue to train for and race the events that you love. There are definitely a lot of factors you can control. If you have poor form or haven't had a bike fit, get some coaching and get the fit. If you haven't done much self-care beyond eating well and getting some sleep – *change* that. It should be clear to you by now that regularly performing resistance training and mobility work will help keep the postural syndromes at bay and allow your body to achieve balance. A balanced body is a more powerful body that will allow us to continue training and racing. What's more, in addition to the injury prevention and career longevity benefits, having stronger muscles will result in improved finish times and hopefully yield new personal bests.

1. McArdle, W. D., Katch, F. I. and Katch, V. L., *Exercise Physiology: Nutrition, Energy, and Human Performance* (Williams & Wilkins, 2010)

2. Dye, S. F., 'The knee as a biologic transmission with an envelope of function: a theory', *Clinical Orthopaedics and Related Research*, 325 (1996), pp. 10–18

3. Nielsen, R. O., Parner, E. T., Nohr, E. A., Sorensen, H., Lind, M. and Rasmussen, S., 'Excessive progression in weekly running distance and risk of running-related injuries: an association which varies according to type of injury', *The Journal of Orthopaedic and Sports Physical Therapy*, 44(10) (2014), pp. 739–747

4. Page, P., Frank, C. C. and Lardner, R., *Assessment and Treatment of Muscle Imbalance: The Janda Approach* (Human Kinetics, 2010)

5. Clark, M. A., Lucett, S., Sutton, B.G., *NASM Essentials of Personal Fitness Training* (Williams & Wilkins, 2008)

4

IDENTIFYING PROBLEMS THROUGH MOVEMENT ASSESSMENTS

For years, pro and elite endurance athletes have had more training and recovery "tools" available to them to help them succeed in swimming, cycling, running or multisport. One tool or service provided by rehabilitation clinicians and many fitness professionals is a movement assessment. We're going to share the secrets of how these can help improve your performance, decrease your incidence of injury and essentially improve your career longevity. We've performed countless movement assessments on different athletes with the goal of "plugging the leak" in their kinetic chains. By plugging these leaks, we create more power through the muscles, which results in improved performance (and we love getting faster). Our movement assessments have also often revealed dysfunctions that put the athlete at risk of overuse/chronic injury. By identifying these dysfunctions and plugging the leaks proactively, you will surely spend less time on the treatment table and more time training, racing and attaining new personal bests. We encourage you to treat yourself like an elite athlete, get a movement assessment, and get a tailor-made plan to address your dysfunctions so that you can Finish Strong!

Earlier, we explained that when the body is balanced it has the opportunity to reach peak performance while mitigating risk of overuse/chronic injuries. Due to our participation in endurance sports, the repetitive motions often create postural syndromes that may affect your normal functional movement. Instead of having smooth, clean movements, the body may have adapted to this faulty posture and some compensations may have set in that have the potential to result in injury. Continually moving with compensatory motions will only reinforce a poor motor program and lead to more dysfunctional movement.

The problem with letting compensations occur is that the body is resilient and will find a way to accomplish a task. Therefore it will *steal* motion from another spot, which then creates an overuse/chronic injury. A great example of this occurs in

Stolen movements

Neighboring joints or regions in the body that don't produce a normal range of motion "steal" motion from adjacent areas. A decrease in thoracic spine (upper back) and hip mobility creates excess stress on the lumbar spine (lower back). A decrease in shoulder mobility will cause excessive movement of the shoulder blades, which may then create a limit of motion at the neck. Remember, the human body is resilient and will find a way to complete a task (even if it has to occur through compensation). It's one giant vicious cycle.

the lower extremity kinetic chain, and is a common problem for runners. When there is poor dorsiflexion range of motion (ROM) at the ankle, it forces larger motions at the hip and knee, which may place greater stress on structures in those areas. The same thing can occur in the upper extremity and may be problematic for a swimmer. If a swimmer lacks flexion at the wrist or pronation in the forearm, it may have to borrow or steal some extra motion from the shoulder, which might put it in a vulnerable position for getting hurt. It's therefore extremely important that each of our joints function properly so it won't create havoc down a kinetic chain. To this end, Gray Cook introduced the 'joint-by-joint' concept in his book *Movement*[1] and it is a great road map to keeping the body balanced, and thus preventing us from being sidelined by injuries.

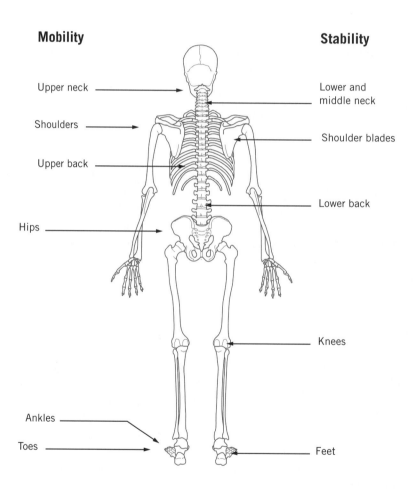

Figure 4.1 Joint by joint concept

TYPES OF MOVEMENT ASSESSMENT

There are many different types of movement assessment that have been developed for rehab clinicians (certified athletic trainers and physical therapists), strength and conditioning specialists and personal trainers to use to identify postural syndromes and movement dysfunctions. These professionals can take additional certification courses that help train them to recognize and treat dysfunctional movement. Some of these certifications include the National Academy of Sports Medicine's Corrective Exercise Specialist and Functional Movement Screen to name a few. These programs feature key functional movements that the client performs in front of the rehab or fitness professional. The quality and symmetry of the movements are noted and are compared to what would be considered normal, to allow the rehab or fitness professional to figure out what structures aren't balanced. Once the movement dysfunction and postural syndromes have been identified, corrective exercises that feature mobility or strengthening are deployed to get the body balanced again. This helps the rehab or fitness professional tailor your program to meet your exact needs. If you've struggled with overuse/chronic injuries in the past, or just don't know where to start when it comes to resistance and mobility training, we encourage you to seek out someone who can perform a movement assessment, so they can identify your problem areas.

One tool that rehab clinicians use to help guide their treatment plans after performing the movement assessment is the 4 x 4 matrix (Table 4.1 on p.28). We are not sharing this information with you expecting you to create treatment plans for yourself, but we want to explain a few key concepts of the 4 x 4 matrix that may help you: 1) determine whether you are ready for progressions and 2) know how and when to use some common assistive exercise tools.

The left-hand column refers to your body position. In general, greater contact with the ground or a bench will increase your base of support, which should make the exercise easier. An example of a glute/ham exercise done as a beginner exercise is a (1) Double Leg Glute Bridge with (1) bodyweight. Once that person stands up (4) and performs a Barbell Deadlift (4), the activity becomes a 4 x 4, reducing the stability and increasing the load. Position the body wisely as you attempt progressions.

The right-hand column refers to the load. 'Unloaded' refers to simple bodyweight. The part of the right-hand column on loading that we'd like to discuss in detail is the 'use of assistance' (seen in 1 and 3). There are many great assistive devices that you will see people using in the gym. The purpose of these is to: 1) apply tactile feedback, 2) help build muscle tension, 3) aid with proper motor recruitment or 4) assist motion.

Mini bands are small resistance loops that apply tactile feedback so that you get your body in correct alignment when performing an exercise. A classic example of this is a mini band around your thighs while performing a Squat to ensure you create glute recruitment

Full body tension

Learning how to create full body tension when performing resistance training is a critical skill. Perform a Standing Dumbbell Biceps Curl while only focusing on using your biceps. We bet your lower back rounded and your shoulders came forward. In a nutshell, your body made compensations because you had "leaks" in your kinetic chain. Now create full body tension: plant your feet to grip the floor, hold your core tight, engage the muscles of your scapula and perform the same Biceps Curl. It was easier with full body tension, right? You've plugged those leaks, which put you in an optimal athletic position and made you more powerful. Always perform resistance exercise while creating full body tension.

STABILITY	LOADING
1. Supine or prone	1. Assisted/unloaded
2. Quadruped	2. Unloaded
3. Half or tall kneeling	3. Assisted/loaded
4. Standing	4. Loaded

Table 4.1 4x4 matrix

to correct for knee valgus. Heavy resistance bands can be used to help build tension in your body and also to assist motion. It is common for people to hold heavy resistance bands in their hands to build tension in their core and upper extremity while performing a Hip Thrust, which helps take out the compensations in the trunk often seen when no tension is built. An example of the heavy resistance band assisting motion is in a Band-assisted Pull-up. The athlete might not be able to use a full range of motion without the band, but since they will have assistance, they are able to fully extend their arms and shoulders and complete the exercise in the full range of motion.

Another example of a heavy resistance band being used to aid mobility is when they provide distraction at a joint (i.e. hips and ankles). Sometimes, placing a foam roller along the spine while performing Quadruped Bird Dogs can be enough to provide tactile feedback that enables you to be aware when you have too much motion and are making compensatory movements. We encourage you to purchase these simple tools for your home gym so that you can effectively progress/regress exercises and use them to help fix the common compensations that your body may make while performing resistance training.

Training for endurance sports can be hard on our bodies. The repetitive motions and spending relatively long times in certain positions can leave us vulnerable to postural syndromes and movement dysfunctions that can derail our training. Hopefully, you've had that "aha!" moment and realized that resistance and mobility training is the self-care you *need* to be doing to get your body balanced. Having strong muscles that function optimally will keep you training and racing and chasing down those personal bests.

To recap: the first step to making improvements is getting a movement screening so you're aware of the dysfunctions within the kinetic chains of your body; the second step is performing very targeted strength and mobility exercises to "plug the leaks" in those kinetic chains and fix those dysfunctions. Fixing dysfunctions won't happen overnight; it's like training for an endurance event – it takes time and patience. We do promise it's one of the best things you can do to enhance your career longevity – you won't regret it! Taking the time to get your body balanced will not only keep you from being a frequent flyer with the physical therapist, but it will also make you a stronger athlete and help you to improve your performances on race day.

---

1. Cook, G., Burton, L., Kiesel, K., Rose, G. and Bryant, M., *Movement: Functional Movement Systems – Screening, Assessment, and Corrective Strategies* (On Target Publications, 2010)

5

FIXING MOVEMENT DYSFUNCTIONS WITH RESISTANCE AND MOBILITY TRAINING

One of our guilty pleasures while we are out training (and sometimes even while racing if we lack focus that day) is watching how other athletes move. Some have perfect form and move through space like a gazelle, while others have a herky-jerky movement that looks awkward and sometimes even painful. Being a couple of nerds, we like to hypothesize what the underlying causes of these poor movement patterns could possibly be. We are fortunate that one of us lives in an urban environment and the other in a beach community, so there's never a shortage of endurance sports athletes out running or biking. Perhaps you've taken notice of some "odd" movements or postures by others when you were training. Whether it's the triathlete riding in perfect aero position with their neck craned back so they can see the road, the runner with knees falling inward at foot strike or the swimmer who is a unilateral breather ... all of these are indicators or predictors of faulty movement patterns or postural syndromes. Some of us are lucky and can get away with these for a while, but surely at some point the body falls out of balance, breaks down and succumbs to an overuse/chronic injury, potentially shortening our athletic careers. The last thing we want is to lose the opportunity to compete in the sport that we love. The good news is that we can "fix" these problems through resistance and mobility training!

By now we've emphasized the importance of strength/mobility training for keeping our bodies balanced. You understand that as soon as one area becomes too tight or too weak, the body falls out of balance (for example, tight groin musculature pulling the leg inward and weak glute muscles that can't stop it), we start to see injuries creep in and we stop reaching our full potential. Over the course of many years of performing movement assessments to identify movement dysfunctions and postural syndromes, we've noticed some common findings. Once again, please remember that we are all individualized so if these don't hold true for you, don't be frustrated. Males are notorious for having a lack of hip and thoracic spine mobility, so usually greatly benefit from mobility work that addresses these areas. Females are notorious for having core and hip abductor weakness. A program directed at activating glutes and core musculature helps to address these issues. Below, we will identify the common movement dysfunctions and postural syndromes most associated with the specific disciplines.

SWIMMING ISSUES

Both of us learned how to swim as adults ... and we both consider it one of our biggest accomplishments. To say our stroke form is pretty is a giant overstatement. Learning how to be comfortable in the water after 30 years of being terrestrial humans was hard. Because of this, we both started by breathing in only one direction. We were creating dysfunction in our bodies and knew it, but we were just happy that we were successfully swimming laps. Fortunately, we were still performing resistance training and mobility exercises to help limit the dysfunction. For RJ, though, after a triathlon season where he battled through some minor shoulder and sacroiliac (SI) joint injuries, enough was enough. It was time to put an end to the underlying cause of the muscle imbalance and learn how to breathe bilaterally.

Unfortunately, in this book we won't be delving into how improper swim form contributes to overuse/chronic injuries. Certainly, proper stroke mechanics do play a role and we always support seeking out the advice of a coach to make form improvements. Similar to running track in one direction, only breathing to one side in swimming will lead to muscle imbalance, and therefore we recommend becoming a bilateral breather as soon as you learn to swim.

What's more, using a *targeted* approach to fix the postural syndromes and dysfunctions common to swimmers can help to reduce your incidence of injury and allow you to keep staring at that little black line at the bottom of the pool that brings you so much joy.

SWIMMING INJURIES

Some common overuse/chronic injuries that swimmers often suffer from are shoulder impingement syndrome, rotator cuff tendinitis, biceps tendinitis, thoracic outlet syndrome, SI joint dysfunction and general neck and lower back pain. As you've probably guessed by now, we're going to tell you that these all stem from imbalances. Shoulder impingement and rotator cuff or biceps tendinitis often come together and can be painful and difficult to deal with. Failure to address these issues can lead to a number of other shoulder conditions that may require surgical intervention. An irritation to the brachial plexus (the bundle of nerves near the neck and shoulder) can cause a peripheralization of symptoms down the arm, leading to a heaviness or altered sensation in the form of thoracic outlet syndrome. Pain from this will impede performance and may irritate other structures in the body. Additionally, the SI joint (where the lower back meets the pelvis) can become stuck and painful – especially in unilateral breathers.

MOVEMENT DYSFUNCTION IN SWIMMERS

Some common postural syndromes seen in swimmers are forward head and forward shoulder posture. The two go hand in hand. The imbalances can be characterized by the muscles of the chest being much stronger than the muscles of the upper back. This is simply a result of the freestyle swimming motion relying heavily on the large chest muscles to propel us through the water. You can typically notice a long-time swimmer when they walk through the door because of their forward shoulder posture.

Another common issue that many swimmers present with is a kyphotic (rounded) thoracic spine (middle back) posture. This will simply exacerbate the forward shoulder posture since it places the scapulae in a poor position to function correctly, thus decreasing the mechanical advantages of the back musculature.

Some swimmers may also have a glute dysfunction if they have a dominant side or preferred side for breathing. If you've ever noticed that someone stops their kick when they breathe to a particular side it's an indication that there is a breakdown in the kinetic chain that connects the glute to the contralateral shoulder.

The best way to address these imbalances is through targeted resistance and mobility exercises. Strengthening the muscles of the upper back (scapular stabilizers) and the external rotators of the shoulder will help to fix the forward shoulder posture. Performing external rotation exercises with a resistance band while standing with the shoulder in a neutral position will help to keep the rotator cuff muscles balanced as well as help position the shoulder. After performing the corrective exercises over time, the body will achieve the optimal alignment that will not only help decrease the risk of injuries, but also aid in making you a faster swimmer.

CYCLING ISSUES

One way to look like a competent rider out on group rides is to have a fancy bike (but then you have to ride it). The most impressive riders (regardless of the bike) have a perfectly symmetrical and efficient pedal stroke and awesome positioning on the bike (aero if you're a triathlete) and are fast. Have you been out on a training ride and seen a rider whose knees track close to the bike frame, or out wide? Perhaps you've seen someone with a really aggressive fit (or maybe a lack of fit) whose lower back is dramatically rounded. Or possibly you've come upon a triathlete riding in aero position with their neck painfully craned back to see the road. There are a number of muscle imbalances and movement dysfunctions that cause these unfortunate positions. Taking a targeted approach to strengthening or lengthening the muscles involved will help you come closer to being the envied impressive rider who is fast and efficient.

Certainly, proper bike size and fit play a role in proper cycling mechanics and we support seeing an experienced bike fitter to ensure that it isn't a contributing factor for your overuse/ chronic injuries. Getting into the specifics on how improper bike sizing and poor bike fit contribute to overuse/chronic injuries goes beyond the scope of this book, but we acknowledge that certain bike positions may leave you more vulnerable to different types of injuries. Additionally, whether you ride a mountain bike (MTB), road or time trial/triathlon, there are specific pedaling tips that may help you improve your cycling performance. If you have experienced some injuries while riding or are looking to make improvements in your performance, seek out the help of a fit specialist and a cycling coach. Cycling coaches will be able to assist you with all ride-related tips.

CYCLING INJURIES

Some common overuse/chronic injuries that cyclists often suffer from are neuropathies in their hands, disc herniation (lumbar and cervical), upper cervical spine dysfunction (headaches) and scapular pain. Neuropathies in the hands involve paresthesia and potentially some decreased grip strength, and are typically due to peripheral nerve entrapments of the ulnar, median or radial nerve – which can happen at the wrist or elbow. Simply changing gloves may help, but it likely comes down to a weakness and muscle imbalance. This is most common in MTB because of the stresses placed on the arms when navigating uneven terrain. The most serious of the injuries listed involves the intervertebral discs in your spine (lumbar – lower back) and (cervical – neck). Herniated discs place pressure on nerve roots and cause radiating pain down the extremity (lumbar – down the leg; cervical – down the arm). The pain may have associated weakness and can be debilitating.

Unfortunately, riding for long periods of time can be a predisposing factor for this – especially if the muscles that should stabilize that area are fatigued and can no longer hold an optimal position. Time trial/triathlon riders who spend a great deal of time in the aero position are likely to experience tension headaches as a result of extending their neck thanks to the riding position. In this case, the suboccipital muscles (at the base of the skull) become shortened and develop trigger points that cause referred pain in the form of headaches.

Some of these injuries can be nagging, while others can actually prevent you from cycling. Using targeted strength and mobility exercises will help to achieve balance in the body, avoid overuse/chronic injuries and improve cycling performance.

MOVEMENT DYSFUNCTION IN CYCLISTS

Some common postural syndromes seen in cyclists are forward head and forward shoulder posture, rounded lumbar spine (lower back) posture while riding, and kyphotic (rounded) thoracic spine (middle back). A proper bike fit can minimize the degree to which these may be seen, but unfortunately for triathletes, getting into an aggressive aero position may exacerbate these conditions. In most situations, comfort is key for the fit. Perhaps you'll sacrifice a few watts that could be gained from an aggressive position, but your body will thank you.

Reaching for the handlebars (whether riding the tops, the hoods or the drops) causes the upper back (thoracic spine) to round and the shoulder blades to slide outward (protraction). Prolonged riding in this position will elongate the back muscles, which over time creates an imbalance – unless of course the rider is doing regular resistance training exercises to strengthen those muscles. The lack of stability at the scapulae can then create poor stability down the arms, which may contribute to the paresthesia in the hands.

All riders, but especially triathletes, are also susceptible to the forward head posture since some of the muscles of the shoulders and upper back are shared with the neck. The aero position requires the cyclist to extend their upper neck quite a bit, which contributes to the imbalance. The neck extension causes tightness in the suboccipital muscles and underactivity in the deep cervical flexor muscles, possibly leading to headaches.

All riders also have to have a rounded lumbar spine (flexion) to some extent due to the nature of the riding position. Unless you're racing on a beach cruiser (and we hope you aren't), the lower back will be stressed because it will have to sustain the flexed position for long periods. The more aggressive the aero position the rider is trying to achieve, the more of a problem this becomes. Unfortunately, the rounded lumbar spine (flexion) is a position of vulnerability with major implications for disc herniations. Having strong core stabilizing muscles and trying to achieve a neutral pelvic position is important for mitigating the risk of injury.

A resistance training and mobility exercise program can help to provide stability and mobility to the appropriate areas as suggested by the joint-by-joint concept.

RUNNING ISSUES

Think of a training partner or your favorite pro with great running form. It's elegant, easy, economical. Now contrast that with the biggest disaster you've seen lately out on a training run. Maybe you've seen the egg-beater legs, or the knee falling painfully inward, or the person who lands awkwardly on the inside of their heel. Have you ever looked around at your fellow racers before a marathon and realized that many of them have heads that jut forward like a giraffe? There are a number of muscle imbalances and movement dysfunctions that cause these unfortunate positions.

Getting into how improper running form contributes to overuse/chronic injuries falls beyond the purview of this book. Certainly, proper mechanics do play a role and we highly recommend seeking out the advice of a coach to make improvements if your form could use some work. A couple of things that runners need to be vigilant about that may be pulling their body out of balance are running in the street against traffic, and track workouts. The problem with running in the street is that roads have a camber or are dome shaped to promote drainage. Therefore, if you are running in the street against traffic, the surface will be in slightly closer contact with the foot nearer the middle of the road than the foot nearer the edge of the road. For an endurance athlete logging long miles every week, this can take a toll and lead to compensations. Similarly, running on a track can have this effect. Track workouts, while helpful, can lead to imbalances since we only run in the counterclockwise direction during races. To help prevent these issues from happening, consider switching it up from time to time when picking which side of the road you run on (keeping traffic and safety in mind!) and at least do some warm-up and cool-down laps at the track in a clockwise fashion.

RUNNING INJURIES

Some common overuse/chronic injuries that runners often struggle with are shin splints, stress fractures, knee pain, IT band syndrome and all of the "itis"s. Tendinitis lasting longer than a couple weeks is no longer considered acute and would fall under the category of what rehab clinicians and physicians call tendinopathies. These can be nagging and tough to deal with and can occur anywhere we have tendons in the lower extremity (patella, Achilles tendon, plantar fascia). You already know the secret of why those injuries occurred – the body isn't balanced any more! Interestingly, the body structures that are hurt and painful often aren't the structures responsible for creating the problem. Finding the region that is actually responsible and addressing it is the key to overcoming the injury. An example of this might be a case of plantar fasciitis where underactive glutes on one side cause extra stress on the plantar fascia because the overall leg mechanics have changed (remember, if you have a small envelope of function, it just takes a minor change to create the problem). It should also come as no surprise to you that *rest alone will not fix that problem*. Targeted resistance and mobility training is the key!

MOVEMENT DYSFUNCTION IN RUNNERS

Some of the common postural syndromes seen in runners are pronated feet (low arch due to underactive foot intrinsic muscles), dorsiflexion restriction at the ankle (due to tight gastrocnemius/soleus muscles), valgus knee collapse (knee falls inward due to underactive glutes), anterior pelvic tilt (due to underactive hamstrings and core, and tight hip flexors) and forward head/neck posture (due to underactive use of diaphragmatic breathing).

In the book *Born to Run*[1], Chris McDougall talks about the negative effects of footwear on foot intrinsic muscles. No, we're not barefoot runners, but we certainly like some of the theories behind the barefoot movement. The barefoot running craze is founded on the idea that you will actually have stronger feet if you run barefoot, and that you'll run with a more natural form and therefore be less prone to injuries. Believe it or not, the flat foot can negatively affect the positioning of the knee up the kinetic chain. By activating the foot intrinsic muscles, we are able to "build an arch", which puts the foot in a favorable position and thus keeps the rest of the body positioned in correct alignment.

Dorsiflexion of the ankle is the movement whereby the toes come upward. The repetitive running motion causes the calf muscles (gastrocnemius and soleus) to tighten up, thus limiting dorsiflexion. As endurance athletes, we're logging significant miles, which means lots of foot strikes, which will make these muscles tight. Lack of dorsiflexion motion has been linked to knee pain since the disrupted motion at the ankle is forced to 'steal' motion from the knee.[2]

Decreased dorsiflexion may seem benign, but it will adversely affect what happens up the kinetic chain.

The knee is in a bit of a pickle thanks to its location in the kinetic chain, and it's unfortunately one of the more common areas in which runners experience pain. Any faulty positions of the foot/ankle (decreased arch, decreased dorsiflexion) or hip (internal rotation) will affect the positioning of the knee. We might see the valgus collapse when the foot is pronated if we have weak glute musculature. Interestingly enough, typically the fixes come from work done at the foot/ankle complex or at the hip.

When we run, the trunk segment rotates on the pelvis segment. Inability to keep the pelvis in a neutral alignment will place stress on many structures, including the lower back. Weakness or underactivation in the core musculature and hamstrings, along with tightness in the hip flexors (iliopsoas) will cause the pelvis to tilt anteriorly, which will then change the length-tension relationship of so many muscles up and down the kinetic chain. Keeping these structures balanced through resistance training and mobility exercises can help keep the pelvis neutral and hold off a number of injuries that could otherwise occur.

Endurance runners will often have a forward head posture as a result of using accessory neck muscles (scalene and sternocleidomastoid) to assist with breathing, rather than using a proper belly breath (diaphragm). The accessory neck muscles become tight and there is also an underactive deep neck muscle that can be stimulated with Chin Tuck exercises. Chin tucks are simply performed while seated and involve moving the base of the scull upward while pulling the chin inward. Breathing exercises fall beyond the purview of this book, so if you'd like assistance with this, you should see a rehabilitation clinician. To keep things simple, we're going to provide strengthening exercises for underactive/weak muscles, and mobility exercises for tight and restricted muscles.

THE FIX

Earlier, we indicated that there isn't a one-size-fits-all approach to resistance/mobility training because each of us is highly *individualized*. We have also explained how movement dysfunctions and postural syndromes can lead us to develop overuse/chronic injuries that will inhibit our performance, and detailed which movement dysfunctions or postural syndromes are commonly associated with injuries seen in each of the three disciplines. We now present to you the shortcut or cheater's approach to managing these issues, by following the joint-by-joint concept.[3] We have developed something we refer to as Frank's Red Hot Exercises (like the famous hot sauce), for the mere fact that you can put that s*^t on everything! As much as we are highly individualized as athletes, addressing these main areas is a safe bet for *most* of us. You can pretty much never go wrong by using any of these exercises. Don't worry, we will describe all of them in detail in Section 2, so you'll be ready to go.

If you're like us, and we think you are, there's nothing more satisfying than nailing a long training session or achieving a hard-earned personal best at your "A" race. We simply don't have time to be sidelined by injuries because we need to get ready for the next race, and so do you.

Unfortunately though, in endurance sports, as the miles pile up, sometimes our bodies start to break down and revolt. Perhaps you can relate to some of the injuries/conditions that we've outlined in this chapter? It can be downright frustrating when you can't go out of the door and do the thing you love. Taking a proactive approach to keeping the body balanced will keep you off the treatment table, extend your career and help you perform better. We've outlined the postural syndromes and common dysfunctions for each of the three disciplines, and we've given you the formula to address these common problems with Frank's Red Hot Exercises in the table below, so now you know which strength and mobility exercises you need to combat them. Use this new knowledge to stay healthy, keep training and chase your goals!

ISSUE TO ADDRESS	SPECIFIC EXERCISE(S)
Poor ankle dorsiflexion	Static stretching of calves (gastrocnemius and soleus)
Underactive foot intrinsic muscles	Short Foot Exercises
Poor hip mobility	Band-assisted mobilizations
Underactive glute muscles	All progressions of Hip Bridges; Clam Shells
Underactive core muscles	All progressions of Dead Bug, Bird Dog and Plank
Decreased balance	Any exercises in single leg stance
Decreased thoracic extension and rotation	Foam Roller Back Extension; Book Openers
Underactive scapular stabilizing muscles	Rows; Cable Cross-pulls
Underactive shoulder external rotator muscles	Resistance Band External Rotation
Forward shoulder	Doorway Stretch
Poor shoulder joint mobility	Cross-body Stretch; Sleeper Stretch
Forward head	Chin Tucks

Table 5.1 Frank's Red Hot Exercises

1. McDougall, C., *Born to Run* (Vintage, 2011)
2. Backman, L. J. and Danielson, P. 'Low range of ankle dorsiflexion predisposes for patellar tendinopathy in junior elite basketball players: a 1-year prospective study', *The American Journal of Sports Medicine*, 39(12) (2011), pp. 2626–2633
3. Cook, G., Burton, L., Kiesel, K., Rose, G. and Bryant, M., *Movement: Functional Movement Systems – Screening, Assessment, and Corrective Strategies* (On Target Publications, 2010)

6

COMMON QUESTIONS
AND CONCERNS

As athletes and health professionals we get asked a lot of questions about our approach to resistance training for endurance athletes. A few of these questions are very specific. (Example: "I have incredibly limited ankle mobility, are there any alternatives to Barbell Back Squats?"'Answer: "Yes, there are alternatives. Yes, there are ways to increase your ankle mobility. Yes, you should pursue both.") However, there are some common questions and themes that consistently arise whether we are training athletes, teaching classes or presenting at conferences. From concerns about increased bodyweight due to muscle mass to what type of equipment should be used, these queries all come from a place of wanting to improve performance and get the absolute most out of the training plan. Our goal is to answer these questions to the best of our ability so athletes can fully commit to the importance of resistance training without any doubt about its efficacy or safety. Also, these are generalized answers that apply to a large cross-section of athletes who are relatively healthy, have some experience with endurance training and do not have pre-existing conditions that would prevent them from safely implementing resistance training into their routine.

If you need a more specific response to a question because of your particular circumstances (such as that you live in a very remote place miles away from the nearest gym), feel free to reach out on social media and we will try to help you find an answer that applies to you. If your concerns are health related, you should consult a doctor or sports medicine professional to find out how this information can be implemented safely for your current condition.

A quick note on how to use this section: the "short answer" to each question is great if you are skimming the chapter and want to get started training right away; the "slightly longer answer" digs deeper to explain the "short answer". Both are valuable and depending on how much proof/reasoning/explanation you need to believe an answer to your question, both can be useful.

Q) Will I gain bodyweight?
A) Short answer: Possibly.
Slightly longer answer: Most people know that muscle weighs more than fat and they are more than willing to share that information with anyone who will listen every time the number on the scale rises. While this statement is technically true, few men and even fewer women pack on enough muscle mass to really affect their bodyweight. This number is even lower for people participating in rigorous endurance training, who burn hundreds to thousands of

calories daily. When an athlete begins a training program there will most likely be a period where body fat decreases and bodyweight remains relatively constant due to a slight increase in muscle mass. When an untrained, sedentary or overweight person begins training, they should see a decrease in overall bodyweight due to a loss of body fat.

Gaining enough muscle mass to see it on the scale requires incredible amounts of effort in the gym (heavy weights, long hours, sets to failure, etc.), at the table (eating every few hours, protein supplements, copious amounts of water, etc.) and in life in general (meal prep, sleeping eight-plus hours a night, avoiding stress, etc.). Even under ideal training conditions, most men/women can't look like an action figure without drug use. Sure, there are "genetic freaks" out there, but most people simply don't have the body type, metabolism or lifestyle to gain a ton of muscle. Combine this with the fact that most endurance athletes struggle to consume enough calories to maintain their bodyweight during heavy training periods and you can see that gaining enough bodyweight to negatively affect performance is almost an impossibility.

The exception is very thin men and women, who may see a slight increase in bodyweight due to increased muscle mass, but this will be a small price to pay for the reward of a stronger and more structurally sound body that will be more durable over the course of a career that lasts for decades.

Q) Will I become "inflexible" or "tight"?
A) Short answer: Not if you do it right.
Slightly longer answer: Losing flexibility is not a side effect of getting stronger! Training mistakes like not performing reps through a full range of motion, insufficient mobility work before/after workouts and improper recovery techniques lead to inflexibility. Training properly and placing a premium on doing movements correctly and taking the time to develop/maintain flexibility is the key to being both strong and flexible.

Q) How will I fit resistance training into my already busy schedule?
A) Short answer: Figure it out!
Slightly longer answer: Everybody has a busy schedule and the fact that you are making time to train/compete is awesome. You are already doing better than a lot of people out there. Now, if you want to really throw your hat in the ring (in reality you should hold on to your hat because it's super valuable when training outside) and compete with your previous best times and other racers, finding the time to add resistance training to your already packed schedule might be a game changer. Also, if you plan on being in this for the long haul, there are few things you can add to your training program that will positively impact your long-term success as much as weight training.

It doesn't have to take forever

Resistance training sessions don't have to be marathons! Long hours in the gym are not necessary to make significant strength and mobility improvements. Doing two to three sessions per week for about 45 minutes each will be more than enough to see improvements. That's literally less time than most people spend on social media per week to get on the way to realizing your body's potential.

There are multiple ways to make your schedule work outlined in this book. Experiment with a few and see how your body reacts. Once you have got into a groove, try to stick to it as closely as possible and make appropriate modifications as they become necessary.

Q) How do I structure my resistance workouts around my endurance training?

A) **Short answer:** Do as much resistance training as possible without negatively affecting endurance workouts.

Slightly longer answer: Different times of the year bring different goals and training should be scheduled to achieve those goals. During the off-season, strength workouts can be done on three to four days a week with much more volume and intensity because the endurance components have been reduced and there is no need to manage soreness to be ready for competition. When building an aerobic base or covering peak mileage, resistance training should be built around the more important endurance workouts. When training tapers for big events, weight training should taper as well. In short, then, during various training phases, resistance training must be altered and scheduled to meet the demands of the road/track/pool. See Chapter 16 for details.

20 percent rule

This doesn't have to be rocket science! If your endurance work is reduced by 20 percent during your taper period, decrease your resistance work by 20 percent as well. For example, if your normal training plan would have been a 10-mile (16km) run followed by 3 sets of 10 reps at 100lb (45kg) of Bench Press and your plan requires you to reduce your mileage to 8 miles (13km), go ahead and reduce the number of reps per set from 10 to 8 and reduce the weight on the bar from 100lb (45kg) to 80lb (35kg) This is an easy rule of thumb that allows you to maintain strength and mobility while preparing for big events.

Q) How do I handle resistance training when I'm tapering for a big event?

A) **Short answer:** Taper everything!

Slightly longer answer: In general, tapering in the weight room should follow the same model as tapering for endurance events. Please see Chapter 16 for more information on how to maintain strength and muscle mass, but still show up rested and prepared on race day.

Q) Do I need a lot of specialized equipment?

A) **Short answer:** No!

Slightly longer answer: Implements such as barbells, dumbbells, kettlebells and certain machines are valuable for gaining muscular strength/endurance but are by no means necessary. For most endurance athletes, particularly those new to resistance training, bodyweight resisted exercises like Push-ups, Squats and Lunges combined with basic "playground equipment" for Pull-ups and similar movements are a great place to start. Eventually, as athletes get stronger and more proficient at basic exercises, some equipment will become useful, but there's no rush to buy a lot of gear or join a gym. The most important thing is to start strength training and getting acclimated to the new style of training and then decide how to invest your money (gym membership, home equipment, personal trainer, etc.) when necessary.

No equipment, no excuses

The best example of how a lack of equipment doesn't have to result in a lack of strength is the situation caused by the Covid-19 pandemic. When gyms, health clubs and personal training studios shut down, we used what was available to stay as strong as possible. Exercises using bodyweight (Push-ups, Bodyweight Squats, Lunges), playground equipment (Pull-ups, Dips, etc.) and basic training equipment (TRX suspension trainers, resistance bands, floor slides) allowed us to maintain a reasonable level of strength while traditional strength training equipment was not available. A weak athlete often blames their lack of equipment, the same way a bad workman blames his tools. Not having a home gym is no excuse for not getting stronger.

Q) On what days should I train each body part?

A) Short answer: Train the whole body, two to four times per week.

Slightly longer answer: Training the upper body one day and the lower body another day, or training one body part per day, isn't conducive to endurance training. Endurance events are total body ordeals, and weight training should emulate the way the body is stressed during competition in the gym. Also, if you're covering large distances during endurance workouts, it is nearly impossible to schedule enough productive strength training sessions per week if only one body part is being trained at a time, and still have any kind of life outside of running and lifting.

A better way to approach this scheduling issue is to plan for two to four total body sessions per week. Sure, one day might be more upper body dominant (the day after a long run), or lower body dominant (a mid-week session when you've recovered from a long run, but are not quite getting ready for the next one yet), but in general, total body workouts will make the best use of your time, energy and muscular development. See the section on periodization in Chapter 8 for suggestions for optimal ways to do this during various phases of training.

These are the questions we get asked the most and the answers that apply to most of the people asking them. Sure, there are exceptions to common rules and circumstances where these answers will not apply, but for most people, these responses are comprehensive enough to start training and feeling good about the decision to take your body, fitness and performance to the next level. If you do have a unique set of circumstances where these answers do not apply, please seek specialized guidance before starting a new exercise program.

SECTION 2

THE MOVES

7

FROM SEA TO LAND – GENERAL STRENGTH-TRAINING PRINCIPLES

The week after Angelo ran the 2018 New Jersey Marathon, he decided it was time to make a change to his training routine. It was the third time he had run in the event and he finished a few minutes away from a personal best. Overall, it had been an incredibly productive season that yielded positive results. After a few days of recovery, he began swimming to give his body a break from pounding out so many miles on the Jersey streets. He jumped in the pool and quickly realized that it was possible to simultaneously be a decent marathoner and one of the world's worst swimmers. His technique was terrible, his breath control was horrendous and despite being in great cardiovascular condition (remember, he had run 26.2 miles /42.2km about 100 hours before this happened), a few laps in a 25-yard (25m) pool was exhausting. It would have been easy to give up, decide he wasn't cut out for "that swim life", put his running shoes on and go for a run. Instead, he kept coming back to the pool every Tuesday and Thursday for the next several months. He had some great workouts and some where the kids taking swimming lessons in the shallow end couldn't understand how an adult could be that bad at swimming, but he kept doing the work, improving his technique and forcing his body to adapt to this new stimulus. Over time … a *lot* of time … he eventually was able to swim a mile in one session.

Angelo's road from being exhausted after a few laps to being able to swim a few thousand yards each session was paved by a plan of progressively challenging himself to swim more laps each session, which forced his body to make the necessary adaptations to become more proficient at propelling itself through the water. While this journey did not transform him into Michael Phelps, it illustrates how the body responds to new training tactics if the stimulus is introduced systematically and proper care is taken to avoid overtraining and other possible negative outcomes.

Different people respond to training in different ways. A slender marathon runner, a hulking bodybuilder and a towering basketball player will all react in a unique way to any training stimulus. This is due to their individual body types, energy metabolism, amount of muscle mass, aerobic conditioning level, nutrition/hydration status, muscle fiber breakdown and countless other factors. However, the general way the body responds to resistance training is standard for all human beings. If you are new to resistance training or are combining it with endurance training for the first time then you may be more fatigued, experience more soreness or require more recovery time than more experienced athletes, but rest assured that your body is adapting to the increased demands and will soon be strong enough to withstand increased training loads. Getting through this initial period in which the body is shocked to be challenged in new ways is instrumental to building the foundation to long-term improved performance.

In order to adapt and improve, the body must be "overloaded" or asked to do more than normal, and in order to make constant progress the body must be "progressively overloaded", which we'll take a look at next.

PROGRESSIVE OVERLOAD

All athletes, coaches and trainers eventually have some variation of this conversation when people find out what we do...

Them: "I've been working out, I just can't seem to get stronger (or faster, leaner, etc.)."
Us: "What are you doing now?"
Them: "Well, I usually..."

What follows "Well, I usually..." can be literally anything. Whether they usually run 3 miles (4.8km) on the treadmill, bench press 135lb (60kg) for 3 sets of 10 reps or swim 550 yards (500m), if they are "usually" doing anything with no progression, they can't be shocked that their body is never progressing beyond what they "usually" do.

The key to progress in resistance training, endurance training and arguably anything else in life is what the NSCA calls "progressive overload" – in other words, purposely placing greater than normal demands on the exercising musculature.[1] In the same way a swimmer must continuously swim more laps to keep improving, an endurance athlete needs to take the same approach in the weight room by constantly demanding more of their body and forcing it to respond by getting stronger.

However, the swimmer has more options than simply swimming more laps to overload their body. Otherwise, the only way world-class swimmers could train effectively would be to swim literally all day. In addition to simply increasing distance during each workout, swimmers can add resistance in the form of swim paddles or parachutes, perform drill work to slightly alter stroke mechanics or manipulate interval times to make shorter workouts more physiologically taxing. The same idea applies in the gym.

Too many people think that the only way to get stronger is to steadily increase the amount of weight being lifted until there are 45lb (20kg) plates stacked to the very ends of the bar. While this kind of lifting will garner a solid social media following, looks impressive in the gym and absolutely has a value for certain kinds of athletes (bodybuilders, powerlifters, Olympic weightlifters, etc.), it's simply not necessary for the overwhelming majority of endurance athletes. So, while anybody who participates in resistance training needs to push their body to get stronger, there are multiple ways to do it that don't involve steadily increasing training loads until the body is too sore, fatigued or depleted to perform quality endurance training sessions.

Resistance training should be a supplement that

Art and science

Coaching is often called "an art and a science" and this idea absolutely applies to strength coaches and personal trainers. Anybody can mindlessly keep adding weight or resistance to an exercise until they reach failure. It takes knowledge and experience to effectively manipulate load, volume, intensity and other factors to optimize the time spent in the gym.

aids in race preparation in the same way a dietary supplement should aid in overall nutrition. If you were to buy a multivitamin that made you sick, you would rightfully stop taking it, but hopefully you would look for another product that provided your body with what it needs without the side effects. Resistance training should be looked at in the same way. If you try a training program that makes your body feel worse and doesn't add to your long-term development as an athlete then you should absolutely stop doing it. But you should also look for another training protocol that will get the desired effects of a stronger body, increased muscular endurance and better resistance to injury without the negative repercussions.

There are multiple options. From increasing the difficulty of individual exercises to creative set/rep schemes, there are almost limitless ways to progressively overload the body and force it to respond with increased strength and structural integrity. These methods should be used with a somewhat conservative approach and care that basic exercises are mastered before attempting more complex variations, but there must be progress and planned overloading for the body to improve in any capacity.

GENERAL ADAPTATION SYNDROME

The human body has an incredible facility to adapt to its circumstances. Nobody is born with the ability to run an ultramarathon, deadlift more than 750lb (340kg) or swim from Cuba to Florida like Diana Nyad, but with a systematic approach to increasing the amount of work required by the body, humans can accomplish extraordinary feats of strength, power and endurance. The way our bodies respond to increased training loads is a product of how we physiologically adapt to being asked to perform increasingly difficult tasks like running faster, swimming further or lifting heavier weights.

According to the NSCA, "general adaptation syndrome" is defined as the human body's three-stage response to stress. These stages are: 1) stress, 2) resistance and 3) exhaustion. The concept explains the body's natural reaction to various kinds of stress and has become one of the key pillars of designing resistance training programs over the last several decades.[1]

When we introduce a new stimulus, it produces a stress response because our body is shocked to be doing something new. Resistance training is hard and the associated stress response is tough on the body, which is why New Year's Resolutioners are often nowhere to be found by early February and your gym is a lot emptier by Valentine's Day.

The next phase in the process of introducing new stimuli is resistance. This is characterized by the body adapting to the new stimulus (weight training, increased mileage, faster paces, etc.) and beginning to develop the means to deal with this new version of "normal". The best example of this is someone who goes from being sedentary to becoming a runner. When an individual is not engaged in any physical activity, the natural state of things in their body is inactivity. Their muscles, cardiovascular system, energy metabolism, skeleton, etc. are used to doing the bare minimum to keep them alive in this inactive state. When they start running, a trip around their block might be an epic undertaking, but if they push themselves to make it around their block once and then rest/recover properly before doing subsequent runs, they will eventually make it around their block twice. If they continue pushing themselves in an organized and systematic manner and take care of their body between training sessions, they will eventually turn a few trips around their block into a 5K and then a half-marathon and eventually a marathon.

This ability for the body to adjust to new stimuli and new standards of performance is called "super compensation" (as in the body compensates for new stresses by improving itself to meet those stresses) by the NSCA. This concept is the main physiological reason we see/hear inspiring stories about men and women who go from being sedentary, overweight and out-of-shape to being competitive endurance athletes.

The third and ideally avoidable phase of the general adaptation syndrome is exhaustion. While most adults have experienced some level of exhaustion during their lives, this is the kind of physical exhaustion caused by repeated bouts of intense physical activity without adequate rest or recovery between sessions. It is characterized by extreme fatigue, soreness and stiffness. While some level of soreness is a positive sign that we are training hard enough to improve the body, extended periods of extreme discomfort or a general feeling that we are progressively wearing the body down instead of building it up during training are bad signs. Happily, this is largely avoidable with proper planning and something known in strength training circles as "periodization", which we'll talk about in the next chapter.

> ## No turning back
>
> Avoiding chronic exhaustion and overtraining is one of the keys to long-term development in any sport. Being conservative when introducing new training methods or increasing total work is the best way to ensure continued improvement. If you are performing too little work, it's fairly easy to increase the total workload and keep making improvements. Once too much work has been done, and the body has responded poorly, it is much more difficult to deal with the detrimental effects of overtraining.

Generally, preparing for an event should be a positive experience, yet endurance athletes often feel worn down, beat-up or physically, mentally and emotionally exhausted in the final days/weeks before a big event. There are multiple reasons for this, including insufficient recovery time, sub-par nutrition, overtraining and lack of physical preparedness for the chosen level of training. While resistance training may not be able to prevent all of these factors from having an impact on the athlete's physical state, performance and overall health, it can absolutely aid in the body being more resistant to injury and more resilient to higher volumes of training.

It is important here to understand what we mean by "resistance training". For many, the idea of "going to the gym" or "lifting weights" conjures images of hulking men and women stacking plates on barbells, throwing around massive dumbbells and doing sets to failure as a spotter or training partner yells words of encouragement. In reality, this type of training is not necessary for endurance athletes. In the same way we wouldn't ask a bodybuilder to run 10 miles (16km) or do mile repeats, we wouldn't ask a marathoner to max out their Back Squat or perform a grueling Bench Press drop set.

Proper training for people who are traversing dozens or even hundreds of miles a week and sometimes on various modalities (a triathlete might run, bike and swim well over 50 miles/ 80km on a single day) should be focused on preparing their body for the stress of the endurance training and aiding them in staying strong, healthy and moving with good biomechanics throughout their training program.

This is where general adaptation syndrome comes into play for endurance athletes in the weight room. During most training protocols, total mileage increases on a weekly basis until the taper period during the few weeks right before the event. These periods of increasing mileage bring many positive physiological effects to the body, including increased cardiovascular functioning, improved lung capacity and better oxygen exchange. However, if rest/recovery is not a priority, the athlete fails to focus on proper nutrition or an effort is not made to maintain a general level of strength, these periods of high-mileage training are often accompanied by atrophy of the skeletal muscle responsible for not only locomotion but also the structural integrity of the body itself.

The idea of the body adapting to whatever stimuli we introduce is valuable here because it means that the athlete's body will eventually change to meet the demands of whatever stress we place on it during resistance training. So, if we gradually increase our resistance training, the body will gradually get stronger to rise to the occasion. In the gym rat or traditional strength training world, this means putting extra 45lb (20kg) plates on the bar, picking up heavier dumbbells or moving the pin lower on the weight stack. When training for endurance events, this might mean progressing from Push-ups to Dumbbell Alternating Chest Presses, adding reps of Glute-ham Raises or incorporating new kinds of resistance like bands, kettlebells or sandbags.

The progressive and systematic introduction of new and more challenging types of resistance training and the body's increased muscular strength, size and endurance in response to those changes is the basis for incorporating resistance training in a comprehensive training plan for endurance events.

1. Earle, R. *Essentials of Strength Training and Conditioning*, 4th ed. (Human Kinetics, 2016)

8

THERE IS NO OFF-SEASON!*

(*Well, technically there is an off-season, but it's an opportunity to work hard and get better!)

Most sports have delineated phases throughout the year: team sports have clearly defined off-seasons, pre-seasons and start/end dates that dictate when training, competitions and championships will happen. The endurance sports are somewhat different. For examples of how important yearly planning is for peak performance, look at 2020, a year when most major endurance events were cancelled or postponed due to the Covid-19 pandemic. The rescheduling of events caused some of the best endurance athletes in the world to perform below expectations and below their normal standards of excellence because of the disruption to their training plans.

Sure, at the high school or college level, formal practice starts on a specific date and the competition schedule is finalized before training starts, but for most adults this is not the case.

For the majority of "regular people" trying to fit endurance training and competition into their already busy lives, the most practical way to devise a yearly plan is to decide early in the year what races/events are feasible, pick a few that will be treated with the most importance and plan training around those tentpole events. Many triathletes will pick an "A" race (aka their most important event) and plan all yearly training and competition around that one main event, and this method can be valuable for athletes of all levels.

Deciding when to start training, total mileage and weekly scheduling will be a process of trial and error that will improve the more you compete and get to know your body. Fitting resistance training into the various periods of the year can be done successfully if care is taken to manage time, fatigue and recovery. Planning training to manipulate these factors in a manner that maximizes progress and minimizes potential negative side effects such as excessive soreness, prolonged recovery time and overtraining is what periodization isall about.

PERIODIZATION

The best way to avoid exhaustion when introducing new components to a training program is periodization. According to the NSCA, periodization is the manipulation of training factors like volume, intensity, rest intervals, exercise choice and overall training load to allow the body to adapt to higher levels of training without ever reaching the state of exhaustion that is detrimental to not only training outcomes but also overall health.[1] Put simply, periodization is planning training sessions that are appropriate for the time of year and fitness level of the person working out. Even world-class marathoners don't run 26.2 miles (42.2km) every day.

Sometimes they run a few easy miles, sometimes they do speed work on a track, sometimes they crush miles at race pace and sometimes they take a day off completely. Proper planning of work and recovery facilitates constant improvement in novices, elite athletes and everybody in between.

In many endurance training circles, this is known as "base & build", and it entails periods of establishing an aerobic base alternated with periods of building proficiency for specific events or distances. For example, a swimmer might spend the early part of a season swimming a steadily increasing number of laps at a steady pace before transitioning to specific strokes, distances and intervals that will prepare them for upcoming races. In the same way, if we are periodizing our aerobic endurance sport training then we need to periodize our planned resistance training as well.

Modern periodization has been developed by dozens of scientists and practitioners over the last several decades and while there is a never-ending number of theories that appear to have merit in the strength and conditioning world, there are a few key concepts that hold true for basic human responses to training that should be applied to almost all types of resistance training.

When resistance training is properly periodized, athletes should see increased strength, muscular endurance, flexibility and durability during most phases of their training. During periods of extreme endurance training, such as the final few weeks of marathon preparation or the highest-volume weeks of IRONMAN training, the goal of resistance training should shift slightly to maintaining the improvements made during the earlier stages of training. Adjusting a resistance training program during periods of high-volume endurance work – by decreasing intensity (less weight on the bar)[1], lowering volume (fewer overall sets and reps)[1] or modifying exercises (replacing Barbell Back Squats with a less intense lower body exercise like Dumbbell Goblet Squats or Bodyweight Step-ups) – is a fine way to keep the body healthy and maintain some level of strength during these incredibly taxing periods.

The key to properly periodizing a resistance training program is realistic consistency. Athletes and coaches should be realistic about how many times per week they will train, how much volume/intensity they can handle at various times throughout the year and how efficiently they will recover from bouts of training. If a runner plans to do heavy Squats every Monday, but every Sunday is their longest run of the week and on most Mondays they are too exhausted from the run to do quality work in the squat rack, they are setting themselves up for failure. However, if that same athlete plans long runs on Sundays, recovery drills such as foam rolling and some light Bodyweight or Medicine Ball Squats on Monday and saves the heavier leg work for Wednesdays or Thursdays, when they are in a much better state to push their body, they may be able to maintain that program for the duration of their season and not see the decreases in strength common in endurance athletes when training for long events.

Trial and error

There will be an element of trial and error when strength training is first introduced. Some sessions will make you more fatigued than expected. Some will be easier than you thought, and some exercises will need to be modified so they can be performed regularly. Like any other new training technique, it's important to introduce lifting weights gradually and with caution until you determine how your body feels and how long it takes to recover after typical lifting sessions.

Lack of periodization can result in extreme soreness, stiffness, inflexibility, limited range of motion and eventually the medical condition known as "overtraining".[1] To put this in perspective for runners, implementing resistance training without some level of periodization would be like someone who is marathon training doing a "long run" every day for weeks at a time instead of doing a few short runs and speed sessions during the week with a long run every weekend. While there are absolutely people out there who can handle this kind of training – such as the legendary Dean Karnazes, who voluntarily runs ultramarathons in blistering desert heat, people who run across the USA (giving new meaning to the term "cross country") and people who run a marathon every day for several weeks in a row – they are few and far between. If the average endurance athlete were to follow this training methodology, they would not only be exhausted, but probably emaciated, dehydrated, injured and hating life in just about every way imaginable.

Yet this failure to periodize resistance training is a big reason why so many endurance athletes have a difficult time implementing a consistent training program and sticking to a routine once they get started. However, with proper planning, commitment and consistency, endurance athletes can achieve new PBs while feeling better than ever and extending their careers by years or even decades.

PHASES OF TRAINING

While there are almost countless approaches to periodization available, and many have been proven effective both in the lab and in practical settings, we will keep this simple, practical and realistic so it can be implemented by athletes who are running/swimming/biking hundreds of miles a month while maintaining lives outside of training. Too often, periodization is presented as an overly complicated and numbers-driven approach with no room for human factors like fatigue, physical state or relationship to other training activities.

Most collegiate and professional strength coaches will admit that while there is absolutely a value in understanding the "textbook" reasoning of why the human body responds one way when performing 3 sets of 10 reps of Back Squats, but a completely different way when performing 10 sets of 3 reps of Back Squats, these theories and studies don't account for real-life scenarios such as losing streaks, slumps, celebrating after wins, hangovers, travel complications, bad practices, sleep disturbances and poor nutrition.

While understanding how the human body functions and responds to various types of stimuli is imperative to getting the most out of your athletes or yourself, coaches or trainers and you must also understand the other factors that determine the right times to push harder, stay the course or possibly pull back on training loads. Also, a basic understanding of the various factors that can be manipulated (volume, intensity, frequency, etc.) is valuable in tailoring a program to individual athletes or events. Too many athletes get sore and stop resistance training completely because they believe it will negatively impact their endurance training, or they actually plan to stop lifting as their total mileage increases as they get closer to a big event. While there is unquestionably a value in tapering training before the biggest events of the year, ceasing all weight training is one of the worst ways to handle this and will negatively impact performance, the structural integrity of the body and overall health.

For most endurance athletes, breaking training down into four main phases is sufficient to adequately coordinate a resistance training program that will help instead of hinder the other aspects of training. These phases are:

1. off-season
2. base & build
3. peak mileage
4. taper

Each phase has distinct characteristics and demands a specific type of training to be optimally effective, but there are some principles and movements that can be utilized year round with a few tweaks that will aid in the overall development of the body. For example, the Squat is a great total body exercise that develops musculature and motor patterns that are valuable for pretty much anyone who can do them safely. During the off-season phase, they might be done with a barbell and heavier loads to increase strength, but during the taper phase they might be done with bodyweight or light kettlebells to maintain flexibility, proper biomechanics and range of motion.

OFF-SEASON

Whether we are discussing marathoners, criterium racing cyclists, masters swimming competitors or IRONMAN distance triathletes, most novice and experienced race participants have an "off-season". This is probably not as clearly defined for these sports as it is for collegiate or professional athletics, which have start and end dates predetermined years in advance by a governing body, but once an event/race schedule is decided, the yearly training program can be devised for most "regular people".

The off-season is the time of year when there is no event in the immediate future that requires structured training. For people living in variable climates, this may be the winter months when very few events are scheduled in their area due to weather concerns. For people with somewhat seasonal work schedules, such as accountants who work 80-plus hours per week during tax season or people in the tourism industry who might have incredibly busy summers, this would be the time of the year when their professional lives prevent them from training and competing at a high level.

We are going to call this time of the year the off-season but it's really not a time to take "off" from training, but rather an opportunity to make the body stronger, more resilient and durable enough to push through the hard mileage and set new personal bests when normal training gets underway.

TRAINING EMPHASIS

The emphasis during the off-season should be placed on getting stronger and improving the body's resistance to injury by addressing known issues such as inflexibility, poor posture or muscle imbalances and weaknesses. There are multiple ways these issues can be addressed and it's important to remember that not all people will respond to a particular training protocol in exactly the same way. Even with all the research available and all the "experts"

Active rest

The off-season is the perfect time to try new activities. When he's not training for a marathon, Angelo experiments with swimming, CrossFit, yoga and Pilates and brushes up on his Olympic weightlifting technique so he can demonstrate it properly to his athletes. This gives his body and mind a much-needed break and allows him to stay active. We suggest picking activities that have a different movement pattern from your sport, to stress the muscles and joints in other ways.

(including the ones who wrote this book) making statements like "The research shows that all swimmers should do … (insert hot new training program here)", it's really impossible to say what is best for each athlete without a decent amount of trial and error. The bad news is that most people will eventually try an exercise or program that isn't right for them. The good news is that as long as it's performed safely and an injury doesn't occur, these minor bumps in the road occur during a time of the year when they won't affect races, long training runs or other important events.

The off-season is therefore the perfect time to experiment in the gym and see how the body responds to different training stimuli. If the athlete is proficient at Barbell Back Squats, introduce variations such as Barbell Front Squats, Box Squats, Pause Squats or contrast training like Squats and Box Jumps performed with very little rest in between. We will address the ways to progress from basic or foundational movements at various points throughout the book, but remember that the off-season is the best time to introduce new exercises, tempos and rep schemes and become proficient at them so they can be used during other phases of training. Some ways we can introduce these progressions are outlined below.

EXERCISE SELECTION

Once the athlete is good at the "basics", such as Squats, Lunges, Push-ups and Pull-ups, and has enough strength to consistently perform those exercises well, it's time to introduce more demanding movements. There are multiple ways to make basic movements more demanding, including placement of resistance, isolateral (aka single limb) versions of familiar movements and doing basic exercises on unstable surfaces.

Altering the placement of resistance drastically changes the way an exercise or movement affects the body. To put this in perspective, think about carrying a backpack loaded with a few thick books, a full water bottle, a laptop and a couple of changes of clothes. If the backpack is strapped to your back, you can walk around with it all day with little to no discomfort or fatigue. However, if you hold that same backpack in front of your chest with your arms stretched out, it feels much heavier and can be held comfortably for a much shorter period of time. Now take that backpack and lift it overhead with your arms extended. Your upper body muscles will fatigue within seconds instead of hours.

The same principle applies to strength training. Once key movements have been mastered, changing the position of the resistance (barbell, dumbbells, sandbags, etc.) can make an exercise radically more challenging and cause the body to develop in new ways. One of the most basic lower body exercise progressions that will benefit almost all endurance athletes is the Squat. The progression is as follows:

Bodyweight Squat ◆Goblet Squat ◆ Barbell Back Squat ◆ Barbell Front Squat ◆ Overhead Squat

All of these variations make one of the most basic lower body exercises more difficult and tax the body in new ways by simply changing where the resistance is placed. See also Table 2.1 on p.20 for more progressions and regressions.

The off-season is also a great time to introduce isolateral moves to develop muscular strength in a way that more closely resembles how the body functions during most endurance activities. Let's keep it real: Squats are great, but if you are pushing off both legs with equal force during any point in your running stride, you are definitely doing something wrong! In addition to adding variety to training sessions, isolateral movements such as Single Leg Squats, Lunges or Dumbbell Alternating Chest Presses/Pulls force the body to stabilize one side while dynamically exerting force against external resistance on the other side. This is similar to how the body works during running or swimming as one side of the body is propelling the body forward through space while the opposite side is trying to maintain stability during the recovery phase and prepare itself to start the next propulsion cycle. Once the basic or foundational exercises have been mastered, most can be performed isolaterally, as long as a few key concepts are kept in mind.

Be overly cautious

When a lifter is good at bilateral movements such as Squats, Bench Presses and Romanian Deadlifts, it's easy to get overconfident and try to rush into doing those movements with one arm/leg at a time. The trick is to be conscious of what your body doesn't yet know how to do and plan accordingly by gradually implementing these new movements into your training program. For example, if Monday is your regular day for heavier upper body training, pick one exercise to try with this new approach and perform the rest of the workout normally. This will allow you to gauge how your body responds to the new movement without excessive soreness.

Also, be conservative when selecting weights the first few times these exercise variations are added to the program. There is a huge difference between moving one object that weighs 100lb (45kg) and two objects that each weigh 50lb (22.5kg). While the total amount of resistance is exactly the same, the body must work harder to control, balance and manipulate the resistance while keeping itself in a safe position when dealing with multiple objects. An easy way to think about this is the Bench Press. If a person can bench press a 100lb (45kg) barbell for 10 reps, it doesn't necessarily mean they can chest press two 50lb (22.5kg) dumbbells for 10 reps. If they are doing those Chest Presses with one arm at a time, there's almost no way they can safely use 50lb (22.5kg) dumbbells.

A good starting point for most people when working unilaterally is to use roughly 50 percent of the total weight you used for the bilateral version of the exercise. So, in the Bench Press example, a person who can handle a 100lb (45kg) barbell for 10 reps in the Bench Press, 25lb (11.25kg) dumbbells would be a good place to start Dumbbell Alternating Chest Presses. Depending on your strength and build, this may be a pretty conservative estimate, but it's better to start lighter and gradually progress to heavier loads than to start too heavy and perform the exercise incorrectly, which can possibly lead to injury. Also, these movements should eventually become staples in the program, so there will be plenty of time to move more weight once technique has been mastered.

Examples:
Squat ✦ Single Leg Squat to Bench ✦ Single Leg Squat
Split Squat ✦ Lunge ✦ Step-up ✦ Reverse Lunge to Step-up
Romanian Deadlift ✦ Single Leg Romanian Deadlift
Push-ups ✦ Bench Press ✦ Dumbbell Alternating Chest Press
Inverted Row ✦ Single Arm Dumbbell Row
Plank ✦ Side Plank

PROGRAM INTEGRATION

Even though isolateral movements are a great addition to any training program and they stress the body in similar ways to locomotion, bilateral exercises should not be totally removed from the program. Basic movements like Squats, Bench Presses and Pull-ups should continue to be performed bilaterally even when more complex movements are integrated, because they provide the foundation of the program. These exercises require the least balance, proprioception and central nervous system activation, which means the most weight can be moved and the most muscle fibers can be recruited. From a strictly strength and size perspective, these exercises are still extremely important for building a strong and stable body.

One simple way to integrate isolateral movements into your weekly programming is to pick one day per week for bilateral upper body exercises such as Bench Presses, Pull-downs and Inverted Rows and to save single-arm movements like Dumbbell Alternating Chest Press, Dumbbell Rows and Single Arm Kettlebell work for the other day of the week. A similar plan can be used for lower body movements.
Example:
Day 1: Lower body bilateral/upper body bilateral
Day 2: Lower body isolateral/lower body isolateral
Day 3: Mixed

Be advised that in general, isolateral versions of exercises create fewer residual effects (soreness, muscle damage, prolonged recovery time, etc.) than bilateral versions of the same exercises because the former involve decreased loads and a lower number of muscle fibers are recruited. For practical proof of this, ask any lifter if they are more sore after a day with multiple sets of fairly heavy Squats or a session with a lot of single-leg movements and the overwhelming majority of people will respond that the Squat day was tougher on their body. One way to work with this principle instead of against it is to alternate sessions that focus on upper or lower body exercises and single- or double-extremity movements.
Example:
Day 1: Lower body bilateral/upper body isolateral
Day 2: Lower body isolateral/upper body bilateral
Day 3: Mixed

This allows for one day with heavier and more taxing lower body movements that will enable the body to respond with increased strength and hypertrophy while working on the balance, proprioception and body control that come with isolateral movements for the upper body. On the second day of training that week, the same principle is at play with the upper and lower body being reversed. A sample training week might look like this:

Day 1:
Barbell Back Squats
Barbell Romanian Deadlifts
Prone Leg Curls
Dumbbell Alternating Chest Presses
Isolateral Dumbbell Rows
Single Arm biceps and triceps work

Day 2:
Barbell Bench Presses
Pull-ups or Lat Pull-downs
Inverted Rows
Dumbbell Step-ups
Single Leg Dumbbell Romanian Deadlifts
Single Leg Standing Calf Raises

Day 3:
Incline Dumbbell Alternating Chest Presses
Push-ups
Pull-ups (palms in) or Inverted Rows
Goblet Squats
Kettlebell Swings
Hip Bridges

This week of training has three total body lifts, which would be optimal either during the off-season or peak mileage phases of training. It also features a heavier lower body session on Day 1, a heavier upper body session on Day 2 and a moderate total body session on Day 3. These sessions are somewhat interchangeable and can be manipulated to fit your schedule with very little effect on overall development. For example, if you must change the day of your long ride or run because of personal responsibilities or weather, you can easily change the day of the heavier leg work (Day 1) to a time that will not affect your performance on that important training day.

See Chapter 16 for examples of how to put these exercises together into effective and efficient training sessions.

MAINTAINING A HEALTHY BALANCE

Another training tool to implement during the off-season is doing basic exercises in an unbalanced position. This requires the body to balance and stabilize itself in awkward positions that more closely mimic the way it functions during trail running or mountain biking. Once the athlete is proficient in these variations, they can definitely be included during other phases of the year, but because there is a learning curve and some potential for injury (probably nothing major, but enough to derail a week of training due to a mild injury sustained after falling off a balance board, unstable surface pad or physioball), they should be introduced during the off-season.

There are several ways to incorporate a balance component into most exercises. The following are the most common and will be sufficient for most endurance athletes to attain the desired effect. Most exercises can be tweaked in small ways to improve the body's balance and proprioception without being dangerous or looking like they should be done in a circus between the trapeze act and 50 clowns getting out of the same compact car.

Standing vs. seated

Several upper body exercises can be performed in either the standing or seated position with minimal changes to the targeted musculature. Shoulder Presses, most Rows, biceps/triceps work and Delt Raises can be done effectively in both positions. The deciding factor should be what the lifter hopes to get out of the exercise. If we are interested in building absolute upper body strength, we should do the exercise seated because if our body and nervous system are less concerned with keeping the body upright and maintaining proper lifting posture, we are stronger and can move more resistance with the intended muscles, which will result in bigger/stronger muscles. If we are more concerned with overall athletic development, though, standing is usually a better option. This upright position causes all of the body's muscles to function together to keep the body in the proper posture to perform the exercise and continues to develop balance and proprioceptive functions in a fatigued state.

It was said that "fatigue makes cowards of us all" by either General George Patton or American football coach Vince Lombardi (it wasn't said that long ago, but for some reason nobody remembers who made the statement!). It can also be argued that "fatigue makes people with poor biomechanics out of all of us". Think about the opening miles of a race. At first glance, most people have pretty decent running mechanics. If you were to break down a stop-motion video of a starting line, you might find some poor body positioning, but for the most part, people with a decent level of experience and training will look pretty solid during the first few miles. Fast-forward to the finish line, though, and runners are hopefully in the state that's a mixture of euphoria and exhaustion that comes with pushing their bodies to the physical limits. While this type of effort is awesome to witness, it often features poor running mechanics because some runners are simply not strong enough to maintain efficient movement for the duration of the event.

The same applies to completing reps or sets in the gym. If a set of Standing Shoulder Presses starts with feet flat on the floor, knees slightly bent, hips right under the shoulders, core tight and full range of motion with the dumbbells being fully extended directly overhead, the set should end with the body in the exact same position. This ability to repeat quality reps in the weight room or maintain body positioning while training/racing is often the difference between steadily improving performance and plateauing or getting injured.

Once the exercise can be performed correctly and the athlete is strong enough to hold the desired body position for the required number of reps, exercises should be done standing whenever possible. This engages the entire body and is more like actually running, swimming or cycling.

Single leg vs. double leg

Performing standing exercises while balancing on one leg is a way to add another component of maintaining balance to standard resistance training exercises. While this will greatly decrease the amount of weight that can be handled, it will add an element of balance that is not possible while standing on two legs. Obviously, we are not as strong standing in this "flamingo position" because the body is being forced to stabilize, balance and push/pull at the same time in a somewhat similar fashion to what happens during locomotion.

Like most new modalities, doing even basic exercises like Cable Rows, Triceps Extensions or Dumbbell Curls while balanced on one leg should be introduced with minimal weight and during the off-season so the body can adapt accordingly. Also, this concept should be used for upper body exercises only, because changing the foot positioning for lower body exercises or doing them isolaterally completely changes the movement and training effect. By contrast, doing upper body exercises while balancing on one foot/leg/side of the body keeps the exercise fundamentally the same while adding a balance component.

Unstable surface training

There is no shortage of products that claim to aid in balance training. Like most products, some of these are great and do what they claim while others are not so great and are ineffective or even potentially dangerous. Let's look at some of the best devices available right now and see how and why they are effective.

(Airex®) pads/mats

There is a range of pads/mats on the market that provide various levels of instability for the person standing on them while exercising. These are relatively affordable, easy to transport and are a good place to start this type of training. Doing upper body training while standing on one of these pads will provide a slightly unstable surface and require the body to balance itself enough to perform the exercise properly, similar to the way that the body must find balance during a trail run or all-terrain bike ride and continue performing. In addition to balance training, these types of pads are also useful for glute/hamstring work, core exercises and limiting range of motion during certain exercises for people dealing with injuries.

The only real negative with pads/mats is that a very low level of balance is necessary to excel while using them. This means that they are great for people new to this kind of training, but they will be mastered quickly and more advanced equipment will soon be needed to achieve the same effects.

Balance boards

From placing a piece of wood on a dowel to incredibly elaborate apparatuses that produce tons of data about the subject's balance and weight distribution, the term "balance board" can mean a lot of different things. Most of the commercially available balance boards are good products that do a decent job of disrupting the body's natural state of equilibrium. The questions here are basically: "How much is too much?", "How much data do you need and what are you going to do with it?", and finally "How much is this training/information worth to you?"

Basic balance boards are a natural progression from pads/mats and provide a more unstable surface for training. Upper body exercises such as Push-ups and Biceps Curls or lower body exercises such as Squats and Lunges can be done on balance boards as long as care is taken to use proper technique and resistance is adjusted for the new unstable surface.

Unless you are really interested in amassing and interpreting the information you can get from more expensive balance boards in a way that will be meaningful to your future training, these systems are probably too sophisticated and not worth the cost for the typical endurance athlete trying to finish local or regional events stronger. However, if there is an issue that is causing pain or discomfort while training, having a professional evaluation on this kind of device might aid in determining what's wrong and how to fix it.

BOSU balls

BOSU balls or "half balls" are circular platforms on top of half of a physioball. These can be used on either side, hence the acronym "BOSU" or "BOth Sides Up". In general, it is more difficult to perform exercises while standing on the platform with the ball side on the floor because it is a less stable base. However, if ankle stability is a priority (think trail or sand running), it is better to train with the feet on the ball side because it forces the lower extremity to control plantar flexion, dorsiflexion, inversion and eversion while keeping the rest of the body stable enough to perform the exercise.

BOSU balls are the next logical progression from basic balance boards, are widely available and there are tons of exercises that can be done while standing on them that will improve balance. While buying one might not be a financially viable decision for everyone, incorporating them into training sessions when they are available is a good idea.

DON'T BE SCARED TO GET STRONG

There are multiple reasons why competitive or recreational endurance athletes may not be proficient in the gym. Factors such as lack of experience, poor or no coaching and less than ideal body types to develop absolute strength all play a role. One of the biggest issues with many runners/cyclists/swimmers is often the mental block of intimidation. Too many men and women who absolutely crush it in their chosen discipline are hamstrung with fear when it comes to basic weight room exercises. Let's be honest, while the typical triathlete might not look like Mr. or Mrs. Olympia, nobody who runs 100 miles (160km) a week or can swim 11,000 yards (10,000m) at a time should be panic-stricken at the sight of a Lat Pull-down machine!

During the off-season, the focus of training should be on getting stronger and preparing the body to be efficient and injury resistant when mileage is increased to get ready for bigger events. This requires a similar level of commitment to resistance training during this time of the year as endurance training during other times. Also, simply "punching the clock" and going through the motions of the prescribed workout *will not work!* To actually see changes in strength, body composition and muscle mass, the body must be stressed in ways that demand it adapts to the stresses we place on it.

Walking into the gym for the first time is a good starting point, but that's exactly what it is ... a starting point! If you continually do the *same* weights for the *same* reps of the *same* exercises, you can't be surprised when you get the *same* results! To make progress, you must progress!

If the goal is getting stronger, heavier loads must be lifted. If the goals increased range of motion, exercises must be performed with increasing ranges of motion. If the goal is better coordination, body control exercises must be performed in increasingly difficult variations by changing the positioning of the resistance, doing them with one arm/leg at a time or standing on an unstable surface. Just as running an increasing number of miles in a planned and systematic approach prepares the body to run longer distances, pushing the body to move increasing loads in increasingly difficult ways makes the body stronger.

Also, this is not a green light to fall into the "if a little of something is good, a whole lot must always be better" approach to resistance training. In the same way that there's a limit to how much you can run/cycle/swim and keep seeing positive results, there's a limit to how much resistance training the body can handle before states of exhaustion and overtraining become inevitable. Proper rest/recovery

Proper fueling

Most endurance athletes put a lot of time and effort into planning pre-event meals and hydration. From pasta dinners to expensive water bottles, they realize the importance of proper fueling on race day. Nutrition and hydration are equally important during other times of the year if real progress is to be made. Adequate calories, macronutrients and water are just as critical when you are training for strength gains as when training for a big race.

is imperative and the program must be properly devised and adhered to for the body to continue to improve over periods of intense weight training.

So, we know that the program must be well planned and rest/recovery/nutrition/hydration must be prioritized, but there is simply no way to get stronger without effort and intensity. This is particularly true during the off-season phase of training when the body is not being asked to cover nearly as many miles in event preparation. To see real improvement, being afraid of heavier dumbbells, 45lb (20kg) plates and big kettlebells must become a thing of the past. Remember, there was a time when running the mileage you are running right now seemed impossible. The same is true in the gym!

MAINTAINING AN AEROBIC BASE DURING THE OFF-SEASON

Most endurance athletes will not take long periods of time away from cardiovascular conditioning. It's simply not in their blood, both literally and figuratively, to "do nothing" for weeks or months. The off-season is therefore a great time to experiment with other types of cardio that will require increased heart/lung functioning without the pounding of running or repetitive motions of cycling and swimming. There is an almost endless variety of cardiovascular options and while not every activity or class will be for everyone, there is probably something that you will enjoy when you are not training seriously. Also, there is not a lot to lose by trying something new and giving your body a break from your normal training methods. In the best-case scenario, you will discover an activity that you can use throughout the year to improve your body's cardiovascular fitness in a new way. In the worst-case scenario, you spent a few bucks, figured out what you *don't* like and have a funny story to tell.

Spinning, dance-based classes, combat sport training, boot camps, CrossFit, cardio machines and boutique personal training studios all offer options that will keep athletes "in shape" (whatever that means to you) while stimulating the body in new ways. This is the best way to "take a break" from serious training because it allows the athlete to maintain a level of fitness while also giving the body a chance to recover after the high mileage and heavy training of race season.

The NSCA refers to this idea of continuing to train during various parts of the year while using alternative modalities as "active rest"[1] and advises that most of the training should be focused on addressing injuries, muscle imbalances, areas of weakness and maintaining a reasonable body composition. Athletes who choose to do absolutely nothing during their off-season are always starting at the proverbial "square one" when they resume training after the extended break. This constant restarting prevents them from ever making real physical progress because they are always fighting to get to "square two" instead of being able to progress to "squares three, four and five" by coming into a season in shape and prepared to continue their development.

The off-season is therefore absolutely a time to celebrate the previous year's competitive season and let the body recover from intense training, but it is *not* a time to completely stop training and start earning rewards as a frequent shopper at the local doughnut shop! By continuing to train, staying in decent shape, getting stronger and addressing anything that might be hindering training (flexibility, range of motion, imbalances, etc.), athletes should enter their next serious training period in a solid physical, mental and emotional state and be primed to take their training and results to the next level.

BASE & BUILD

In most race preparation programs, the first few weeks or months (depending on the duration of the event) are dedicated to developing a cardiovascular or aerobic base that will allow the athlete to endure more intense training during later stages. This normally involves gradually increasing the total mileage covered per week with the emphasis placed on reacclimating the body to coving longer distances without injury or technique breakdown. While there may be some element of speed development, interval training or other more advanced concepts, most of this period is spent building basic aerobic fitness so the body can continue to perform at a high level when more intense training loads are required.

To keep it simple, consider any weeks of training where your longest session of the week is under 10 miles (16km) running, 50 miles (80km) biking or 5,500 yards (5,000m) swimming to be the base & build stage of resistance training. During these weeks, the training emphasis will shift to quality distance workouts and building an aerobic base, but consistent resistance training is still incredibly important. This is because most training programs will require resistance training to become less of a priority as distances continue to get longer and events get closer. Realistically, unless you have unlimited time in your day and the body of a superhero that recovers incredibly quickly from activity, productive weight training is really difficult when you're covering dozens or hundreds of miles. For this reason, we want to continue to gain strength, muscle mass and stability during these first few weeks, with the idea that it will be difficult to maintain the same level of weight training down the line.

TRAINING EMPHASIS

Workouts during the base & build phase should consist mainly of the Foundation Exercises that are beneficial for almost everyone, plus the more advanced variations we introduced during the off-season. Carefully selecting reps/sets/weights is important during this phase because the resistance training must be properly balanced with the increased total mileage taking place during the endurance component of the program. If weights are too heavy or volume is too high, it will result in soreness and decreased performance during endurance sessions. If too little overall work is done, the positive effects of off-season training (muscle mass, strength, muscular endurance, etc.) will be lost before the hardest training period of the year even starts. If the goal is to maintain strength while logging enough miles to prepare for an endurance event, it is absolutely necessary to properly plan workouts during the early phases of training.

The main goal of this training period is to continue the muscular adaptations that occurred during the off-season and continue to get stronger as total mileage steadily increases. This will not always be an easy task as there will be days when the body is fatigued, sore or depleted from swimming, running or cycling and it will be tasked with fairly intense resistance training. The keys to progress here are to mentally and physically prepare yourself for the increased training load and to put yourself in a position to succeed.

Some coaches like to "keep athletes on their toes" by making every workout a complete surprise every time practice starts. While this "be ready for anything" approach to training probably has a place in team sports such as baseball or soccer where literally anything can happen and players must react accordingly, it doesn't work nearly as well for endurance sports. There are high school and even college cross-country coaches who will have their team run through a difficult workout and when they are stretching say "Good work! Now, everybody go to the weight room to lift!" There are few things in life worse than seeing the light at the end of the tunnel and then having someone abruptly make the tunnel longer!

This isn't to say there's not a value in surprising yourself or your athletes with "gut check"-type training sessions, but doing this consistently without the bigger picture in mind is a recipe for failure. It is better to have your resistance training sessions planned in advance and placed strategically on days that will not negatively affect endurance sessions, but will rather positively impact muscle development and allow for optimal recovery time. Knowing what each day/session will entail and what you hope to accomplish during each is a recipe for success.

Having a concrete plan and only deviating from it during extreme circumstances (bad weather, gym closing unexpectedly, family emergency, etc.) will also allow athletes to mentally prepare for what every day brings. Knowing you are going to the gym after a run puts you in a much better mental state to tackle the "double session". A lot of these post-run training sessions can quickly degenerate into walking around aimlessly, relaxing on foam rollers and feeling sorry for yourself (as in "I just ran 10 miles, there's no way my body can throw a medicine ball right now.") if they are not carefully planned and athletes are not mentally prepared.

In addition to mental preparation, having a properly designed program with clear goals and objectives that is implemented in a way to put the athlete in a position to succeed is extremely important during this time of the year. If you plan heavy Squats and Romanian Deadlifts right after each week's longest run, there is almost zero chance your body will respond positively. In reality, there's a much higher likelihood that you will end up overtrained, fatigued and completely miserable way before your big event. The weekly schedule during this phase will be somewhat individualized and largely dependent on factors such as total mileage, available time and personal preference. Unfortunately, if you are new to strength training, a lot of this will be trial and error because it's nearly impossible to predict how everyone will respond to different training methods. The important thing here is to get this experimentation done early in the training program when mileage is still relatively low and there is no danger of being sore/fatigued/tight during major events. Once resistance training becomes a regular component of your training program and lifestyle, it will be easier to determine when to train each week, but until that level of comfort is attained, be overly cautious until you can gauge how your body will respond each week.

EXERCISE SELECTION

Resistance training during the base & build stage of training should consist predominantly of the Foundation Exercises that are the cornerstone of the training program, plus the more advanced variations that were learned during the off-season. "Big exercises", such as Squats, Romanian Deadlifts, Bench Presses, Dumbbell Rows and Pull-ups, are essential as performing them will continue to make the body bigger and stronger during this time of increased endurance activity. These movements use large portions of muscle mass across multiple joints and trigger the release of testosterone, which is responsible for the hypertrophy and increased strength associated with lifting weights. If these exercises are abandoned when endurance training is increased, most of the gains (#GAINS for all the social media people out there!) made during the off-season will evaporate and the body will return to pre-training levels. Also, the increased caloric expenditure required to cover the additional mileage will make retaining muscle mass difficult for most people, and if this is combined with lack of "real" strength training, the negative effects will increase exponentially.

This effect can be seen in athletes who have very different bodyweights based on the time of the year. In certain team sports, such as baseball or basketball, where the season is a figurative "marathon" of practices, games, travel, missed meals, poor sleep habits, etc., bodyweights can easily decrease 5–10 percent over the course of the season. While some players might actually be dropping body fat and improving body composition during the season, the overwhelming majority are losing muscle mass due to the rigors of a long season that puts resistance training and good nutrition firmly on the back burner. This also happens in individual endurance sports where men and women lose sometimes incredible amounts of bodyweight while training for events. Keep in mind that this isn't always a bad thing. If somebody starts off overweight and with excess body fat then a good training program should decrease their bodyweight and improve their body composition. However, if the person starts off relatively fit with a decent percentage of body fat, training for an event should make them stronger, faster and healthier overall instead of worn out, weak and emaciated. This pattern is common in high school and college cross-country where programs are often not individualized and student-athletes are tasked with very high mileage at very fast paces while juggling academics, travel, questionable nutrition options, social lives and the other aspects of being a teenager or young adult. Some of this gradual wearing down of the body can be prevented or at least slowed by commitment to resistance training and the basic exercises that help the body maintain muscle mass and strength.

There are almost countless ways to implement these exercises into the weekly programming leading up to the peak mileage stage of training, but the most important factor is to continue taxing the body with enough intensity to stimulate the muscles to respond with increased size and strength. This means at least two to three sessions per week and 2–4 sets of 8–12 reps per exercise, according to the American College of Sports Medicine.[2] Second, using a variety of movements that both develop strength and force the body to work in a somewhat similar fashion to how it functions while running, cycling or swimming is vital to preparing the body to Finish Strong as mileage is steadily increasing.

Below are some options to structure this phase of training. There will be an element of trial and error to see how each individual athlete responds to the training load, but for most endurance athletes, one of these basic templates should work reasonably well as a starting place, with the option of making small tweaks as needed.

PROGRAM INTEGRATION

Below are examples of base & build training weeks. Note: This example is for runners. The same concepts apply to cyclists, swimmers and triathletes and can be implemented with very few changes.

Option 1
Sunday – long run (endurance)
Monday – recovery/resistance session
Tuesday – mid-distance run (tempo)
Wednesday – total body lift (lower body focus)
Thursday – speed development (interval)
Friday – total body lift (upper body focus)
Saturday – rest/prep for long run

Definitions

Long run

This is fairly self-explanatory. Depending on the level of training, the long run can be from 3 to 25-plus miles (5 to 40km-plus). It is the focal point of the week when you're training for longer endurance events. It's the longest, hardest and most important session of the week and the clearest indicator that your training is moving in the right direction. If your long runs aren't going well, there's a pretty good chance there are flaws in your training plan that need to be addressed if you are going to salvage the season and perform well in competition.

Recovery/resistance session

This workout is devoted to helping the body recover from the long run and get ready for the rest of the training week. There can be some productive strength training, but the major focus should be placed on flexibility, moving through full ranges of motion and bodyweight exercises. Tools like foam rollers, intermittent compression, cold tubs and massage are invaluable in helping the body bounce back and get ready for more training. These can be used whenever needed, of course, but scheduling them following each week's longest run will ensure they get done and prepare the body for success the rest of the week.

Training on this day can be limited to bodyweight exercises like Squats, Lunges, Push-ups and Pull-ups with an emphasis on quality reps and full range of motion. This will help the body recover by stimulating blood flow to potentially sore areas, maintaining flexibility during fatigue and helping maintain some level of strength. These sessions don't have to be very long or physically taxing and can consist of a generalized warm-up, dynamic and static stretching, a few sets of bodyweight exercises and some recovery work. This is a good thing because you probably dedicated several hours to the long run on the previous day and now you will have a few extra hours to catch up on life!

The exact stretches and recovery techniques you choose should be based on your particular body and situation (although we have identified the common problem areas for each sport). If you have tight hip flexors, spending more time on hip flexor stretching and foam rolling will be beneficial. If you are experiencing overall fatigue and soreness, spending that time in a cold tub might be a better option. This part of the plan is highly dependent on how you feel and can change from week to week depending on how your body is responding to the training.

Mid-distance or tempo

Again, this is pretty self-explanatory, but it will mean different things to different people based on experience, fitness level, training program and whether they are running, swimming or cycling. It should produce some level of fatigue if a decent pace is maintained but should not produce as much soreness as a speed/strength session or the same energy expenditure as a long run.

Total body lift – lower body focus

Sets, reps and intensity will vary based on multiple factors, but in general there should be enough volume (total number of reps) and intensity (total weight lifted) to stimulate gains in both muscle mass and strength. This will be somewhat challenging because the body will also be experiencing residual fatigue from the increased mileage, but athletes who are able to push through this discomfort will see big dividends when they are stronger during later phases of training.

Speed development – track workouts and intervals

Most race preparation programs have at least one day a week dedicated to getting faster. This might include sprinting on a track, maintaining a specific pace or alternating intense efforts with slower intervals. These days should be planned well in advance and done when the body is not fatigued and is able to achieve and maintain the effort level necessary to elicit the desired effects.

Whatever your speed days look like, plan your resistance training around them so you can attack speed training and lifting weights with the intensity they deserve.

Total body lift – upper body focus

Again, sets, reps and intensity will vary based on multiple factors, but in general there should be enough volume and intensity to stimulate gains in muscle mass and strength. As mileage increases, this will become more challenging as the body will be somewhat fatigued. By pushing through some of the mental and physical discomfort, your body will be strong and prepared for when your mileage really starts to increase.

Rest/prepare for the long run

There are as many ways to prepare for a long run as there are people who run road races, but in general ... get some sleep, drink plenty of water and eat a few carbs if you are into that kind of thing. Do whatever is necessary to wake up primed and ready for a great endurance session that will set the tone for the rest of your training week.

Sample session for Option 1

- Stationary bike, jump rope, light jog jump rope or rowing machine – 10 minutes at moderate pace
- Foam roll or other self-massage option – 10 minutes
- Dynamic stretch – 10 minutes

(*Note:* All exercises should be performed on both sides of the body.)

Standing Leg Swings – 1 set of 10 reps
- Stand perpendicular to a wall and use the arm closest to the wall for balance. Swing each leg forward while extending the knee and then behind the body by flexing the knee. The range of motion should steadily increase throughout the set.

Standing Lateral Leg Swings – 1 set of 10 reps
- Stand facing a wall with both hands flat against the wall at shoulder height for balance. Keep the leg straight and swing it across the body as far as comfortably possible in both directions. Keep the upper body still and the head neutral.

Standing Knee Hugs – 1 set of 10 reps
- While standing, flex the right knee so the quad moves toward the upper body. Grasp the shin right below the knee with both hands and pull the knee into the chest while rising on to the ball of the left foot. This will make the stretch effective on both sides of the body.

Standing Lateral Knee Hugs – 1 set of 10 reps
- While standing, flex the right knee and then grasp the leg under the knee with the right

hand and over the ankle with the left hand to create a "cradle" position. Pull the knee out and away from the midline of the body while rising up on the ball of the left foot.

Standing Straight Leg Kick – 1 set of 10 reps
- Extend both arms in front of you so they are parallel with the ground and in line with the shoulders. Flex the hip while keeping the leg straight to bring the leg as high as possible. The goal is to kick your fingertips with the hip flexing to 90 degrees, but achieving this may take some time. The upper body remains upright and the majority of the stretch should be felt in the hamstrings.

Reaching Lunge – 1 set of 10 reps
- Stand with legs hip-width apart and start by stepping out far enough with your right leg that when you complete the Lunge your right shin will be perpendicular to the ground. Sink into the Lunge position until your left knee is about 1 inch (2.5cm) from the floor. Extend both arms overhead until the elbows are straightened and the biceps are in line with the ears. Maintain a strong Lunge position and lean back to emphasize the left-side hip flexor stretch.

Reverse Lunge with Rotation – 1 set of 10 reps
- Stand with legs hip-width apart and step back with the right leg far enough that when the Lunge is completed the left shin will be perpendicular to the floor. Sink into the Lunge position until the right knee is about 1 inch (2.5cm) from the floor and raise the left arm straight up. Reach across the back with the left arm in an effort to touch the right ankle. Actually achieving this may be hard for less flexible people, but getting steadily closer still represents quality improvement and it is a great stretch.

Mountain Climber Stretch – 1 set of 10 reps
- Start in Push-up position and step the right foot outside the right hand. Shift your bodyweight forward while keeping the back leg fully extended and palms flat on the floor. This should be felt throughout the entire lower extremity.

Leg Over – 1 set of 10 reps
- Lie on the floor with both legs straight and both arms extended to the sides with palms facing up (aka the Iron Cross position). Raise the right leg straight up at the hip while keeping the knee fully extended. Drop the leg across the body in an effort to put your right foot in your left hand while keeping the entire back in contact with the floor.

Lying Leg Swings – 1 set of 10 reps
- Lie on the floor with the right leg fully extended and the left knee bent with the left foot flat on the floor. Swing the right leg up and back toward your body at the hip while keeping the knee extended. Try to increase the range of motion with each rep.

• Bodyweight circuit
(*Note:* All exercise descriptions are available in the Foundation Exercises and sport-specific exercise chapters.)

- Bodyweight Squats – 3 sets of 10 reps
- Push-ups or variations – 3 sets of 10 reps
- Bodyweight Lunges – 3 sets of 10 reps
- Pull-ups or variations – 3 sets of 10 reps
- Calf Raises – 3 sets of 15 reps
- Core exercise of your choice – 3 sets of 15 reps

- Total body lift – lower body focus sample session

(*Note:* All exercise descriptions are available in the Foundation Exercises and sport-specific exercise chapters.)

- Barbell Back Squat – 4 sets of 8 reps
- Barbell Romanian Deadlift – 4 sets of 8 reps
- Calf Raises – 3 sets of 15 reps
- Dumbbell Bench Press – 4 sets of 8 reps
- Dumbbell Row – 4 sets of 8 reps
- Dumbbell Shoulder Press – 4 sets of 8 reps
- Core exercise of your choice – 100 reps

- Total body lift – upper body focus sample session

(*Note:* All exercise descriptions are available in the Foundation Exercises and sport-specific exercise chapters.)

- Barbell Bench Press – 4 sets of 8 reps
- Pull-ups or Lat Pull-downs – 4 sets of 8 reps
- Inverted Rows – 3 sets of 10 reps
- Lunges or Step-ups – 4 sets of 8 reps
- Leg Curls, Glute-ham Raises or Partner Leg Curls – 3 sets of 10 reps
- Calf Raises and Dorsiflexion – 3 sets of 15 reps
- Core exercise of your choice – 100 reps

Option 2: less time to train

Mixing any kind of athletic pursuit with 'real life' is challenging to say the least. Sure, if you had unlimited resources and limitless time you would meticulously plan every session, carefully prepare each meal and routinely get your optimal amount of sleep. In reality, workouts must be scheduled around your job, meals can be chaotic and sleep schedules are often based more around your kids' internal clocks than your own.

Ideal conditions thus rarely exist for endurance athletes who have numerous other responsibilities, but with proper planning, resistance training can be added to a training program and have a massive impact on health and performance while requiring minimal amounts of time. Your schedule may look like this if you're pressed for time:

Sunday – recovery/resistance session
Monday – mid-distance run and total body lift (lower body emphasis)
Tuesday – off
Wednesday – speed development and total body lift (upper body emphasis)

Thursday – off
Friday – rest/prepare for long run
Saturday – long run

Option 3: more time to train

Perhaps you're the lucky one with the cushy job and no extra responsibilities and a totally Type A approach to training and racing – we're jealous. This means you've got time to treat yourself like a professional endurance athlete and hopefully achieve the results that someone who has endless time to train should.

Sunday – long run
Monday – recovery/resistance session
   and mid-distance run
Tuesday – total body lift (lower body emphasis)
Wednesday – speed development
Thursday – total body lift (upper body emphasis)
Friday – mid-distance run or speed development
Saturday – rest/prepare for long run

> ### Make time!
>
> Everybody is busy. There are 24 hours in a day and we make time for what we value. If you value training and peak performance, you will make time to train. If you don't, you will make time for other things like watching television, browsing social media and explaining to people why you are struggling to post a new personal best. Make time. Be smart about it. Get better.

PEAK MILEAGE

All endurance sport training programs will have a period of "peak mileage". This is the few weeks or months when the most overall mileage is being covered. The exact duration of this period will vary based on training program and event, but to keep it simple, any weeks where the total distance is more than 30 miles (50km) of running, 125 miles (200km) of biking or 27,340 yards (25,000m) of swimming can be considered peak mileage.

Endurance training and event-specific preparation (running hills if the race will have elevation changes or ocean swims for beach triathlons) take precedence during this time of the year, but resistance training should continue to be a staple of your weekly regime. Hitting the gym when you are already covering dozens or hundreds of miles per week is not easy. There will absolutely be times when your body is screaming to call it a day and rest/recover instead of continuing to push itself. Yet as we've already stressed, strength training during these heavy training periods will keep the body strong, injury resistant and functioning optimally until it crosses the finish line.

The keys to maintaining a strength training program when these distances are being covered are having a "big picture" view of the training calendar, knowing what aspects of training are most valuable and listening to your body. So, while strength training can be put on the back burner during these weeks in favour of event preparation, it should not be pushed totally off the stove, because that only leaves us with a big mess.

THE BIG PICTURE

Marathoner seeing the small picture: "I ran 15 miles/ 24km yesterday and I'm super sore today. I should have done some recovery stuff like foam roll or gone in the cold tub after my run, but I was too tired and then last night I went out for wings and beers with my friends and got to bed late. My program says I should lift weights today, but my body is too exhausted. I'm going to take the day off so I'm ready for my speed workout tomorrow." To be totally honest, both of us are guilty of seeing the small picture at times. It's fine, just don't make a habit of it!

Marathoner seeing the medium-sized picture: "I ran 15 miles/ 24km yesterday and feel pretty decent considering where I am in my training plan. The mileage was tough, but I took care of my body and I should be ready for my speed workout tomorrow. I'm supposed to go to the gym today, but I want to crush my speed work this week and be ready for the race in two weeks. I'm going to shut down the gym for now, but I'll go back as soon as this marathon is over."

Marathoner seeing the big picture: "I ran 15 miles /24km yesterday and normally I would be pretty sore today, but the foam rolling, stretch, great dinner and good night's sleep really helped me recover quickly. I definitely don't feel 100 percent (did you hear me say I just ran 15 miles /24km?!), but I want to compete in endurance events for a long time and make this kind of training a lifestyle, so I'm going to make sure I get my weight training done today so my body keeps improving and I have a good career, not just one good event."

Resistance training is by no means a quick fix. While the long-term benefits of developing muscular size, strength and endurance are almost inarguable, the work required to reap those rewards can be difficult, uncomfortable and sometimes grueling. This is made even harder when the athlete in question is covering dozens or hundreds of miles worth of endurance work. The key during this phase is to think about that big picture. Sure, taking a day off or cutting resistance training out of your training program might feel great in the short term, but this is not good for your long-term athletic development or your overall health.

Keep in mind that a stronger body in the gym is also a stronger body at the finish line. If you plan on having a long and successful career in endurance events, being stronger will help your body endure the training, competition and lifestyle associated with these sports. Also, as the body ages there is a normal decline in the overall amount of muscle mass and bone density, so establishing higher baseline levels and maintaining these as you age will make your body healthier, more resistant to injury and more durable throughout your lifespan, as well as translating to more success on the road, track or pool.

So, while there is no magic pill for a healthier body, resistance training is something like a daily multivitamin that can sometimes be a pain in the neck to take but will deliver on the promise of better overall health and better race performance when taken regularly.

WHAT'S IMPORTANT?

When covering peak mileage, the main focus of training should be expanding the body's aerobic base and covering a progressively higher number of quality miles (pace, running form, breath control, etc.). Resistance training is still important to overall athletic development but should be scheduled around long runs/rides/swims to allow for peak performance during those sessions. Proper changes to strength training workouts should be made to allow for the body to maintain the strength built during previous stages while not negatively affecting endurance workouts.

The best way to do this is to look well in advance at the entire peak mileage phase and pick days where it looks like you should be able to have good training sessions. In general, the day after the longest or most intense endurance session is good for light resistance training. This will help the body recover from the previous day's workload and give sufficient recovery time before the next session. A few days later is generally a good time for a more intense session because the body has recovered from the long run but still has a few days to prepare for the next one. The day immediately following the long session should be comprised mainly of recovery techniques, bodyweight exercises, light resistance like dumbbells or kettlebells, and mobility exercises that move your body through complete ranges of motion. The other day should be the more intense day with barbell exercises, heavier loads and total body training.

There are multiple ways to put together training during this stage (see Chapter 16), but the important thing is to plan all workouts around the long runs/rides/swims that will be the cornerstone of event preparation as the race gets closer.

LISTENING TO YOUR BODY

Yes,"listening to your body" is a cliché. But it became a cliché because it contains some element of truth. Being in tune with your body and how it reacts to different training factors is invaluable in this type of training. This will improve with age and experience, but having a general idea of what your body can handle and how it will feel is a crucial step in becoming a lifelong endurance athlete.

When an athlete is covering a ton of miles there are multiple factors that can be manipulated to determine how efficiently they will recover. Training factors such as distance, pace, elevation and terrain as well as lifestyle factors like sleep, nutrition and recovery tactics will all play a role. Knowing how to adjust these will make a huge difference in the overall success of the athlete. When utilized correctly, resistance training should be a positive factor that builds the body instead of further tearing it down.

With this in mind, there should be a clearly designed plan in place of when to strength train and exactly what to do during each session. However, because we are human beings and not robots or computer programs, there must be some flexibility in the training schedule to allow for human factors such as extreme soreness, extended fatigue, poor nutrition, lack of sleep, scheduling conflicts, injury and if you're female, where you are in your menstrual cycle. The key to training effectively while listening to your body is knowing how to modify workouts to fit your current physical state. Changing sets, reps, loads and exercises is instrumental in performing quality training when the body is fatigued. Let's look at some ways to alter workouts to accommodate the body during this phase.
(*Note:* These are listed in order from most desirable to least desirable.)

1. Decreased intensity: This entails doing the prescribed exercises for the prescribed number of sets/reps, but with less weight. This will still provide the balance, range of motion and muscular activation of doing the entire training session with less stress on the exercising musculature and none of the prolonged soreness of handling heavy loads. However, while decreasing intensity is a good way to deal with short-term fatigue, athletes and coaches should be cautious not to allow these new weights to lower the bar for future training. Nobody wants to be in the "I used to be able to do XX but I'm not that strong any more" club.

2. Decreased volume: This modification involves reducing the total number of sets/reps performed during the session. Cutting out the last set or dropping the volume on each set (for example, performing 3 sets of 8 reps instead of 3 sets of 12 reps of an exercise) is a good way to make sure all exercises are done at a reasonable intensity level to stimulate muscle growth without the lasting effects of grueling longer sets. Again, it's important to make this modification with the idea of moving back to previous volume levels as soon as possible.

3. Exercise modifications: We've provided a table of exercise progressions and regressions (see Table 2.1 on p.20), but keep in mind that tweaking range of motion, the placement of the load or type of resistance can make a huge difference to how the body responds to certain

exercises. If the program calls for Barbell Back Squats, but you are still feeling the effects of yesterday's hill repeat workout on the bike, then Kettlebell Goblet Squats, Overhead Squats with a light training bar or even going on a Leg Press machine might be a better option. Similarly, if your upper body is really tight and sore after a few days of intense training, Push-ups and self-massage with a foam roller or massage ball might be a better option than heavy Bench Presses. Modifying exercises is not an excuse to "take the easy way out", since any exercise can be challenging under the right conditions. The aim is to stimulate the body differently and aid in both recovery and strength maintenance.

4. Taking a day off: Let's face it, there are days when going to the gym will be almost impossible. Even with recovery techniques, good nutrition, proper hydration and enough sleep, the mileage during this phase will occasionally make your body feel like it needs a time-out. By no means is this an ideal scenario, but it is a real scenario. Skipped sessions should be the exception and not the rule and whenever possible taking a "day off" should mean taking a break from heavier resistance training and not a day off from preparing your body.[3] Massage, foam rolling, light core work, flexibility development, hydrotherapy and various other modalities are all good options to help the body feel better before the next speed/endurance session. If all else fails and you absolutely need a day without physical activity, enjoy the day, eat/drink/rest and get back on schedule as soon as possible.

TRAINING EMPHASIS

Resistance training during this phase should focus on maintaining as much of the muscle mass and strength gained during the previous stages as possible while still performing at optimum levels during long endurance sessions. This is something of a balancing act, whereby the body must be stimulated enough to retain strength, but not so taxed that it is sore or unprepared for the longer and more intense swimming/biking/running sessions. There will be some level of experimentation necessary during this phase to gauge how the body will react to various levels of strength training, but if a good baseline was set during the base & build phase, it will be easier to determine how to continue training when mileage is greatly increased.

EXERCISE SELECTION

Until this point, we have talked extensively about progression or how to make exercises more challenging in order to elicit a desired response from the body. This is the first stage of training that may actually demand *regression* or a simplification of movements to allow the body to perform well during brutal endurance sessions.

There are days when we have heavy lifting sessions planned that must be altered due to fatigue and soreness. Selecting and modifying exercises that will provide enough stress that strength is developed or maintained without affecting other aspects of training (i.e. being too sore from lifting that you have a bad run/bike/swim the next day) is one of the keys to consistently adding resistance training to your weekly routine.

This is particularly true of lower body exercises, such as Squats and Lunges, which are still valuable during this period but may have to be modified so that they can be done correctly in the context of the overall training program. For example, Barbell Back Squats are a great exercise that will be beneficial to almost all athletes (barring a few extenuating circumstances) when done during weeks that contain a "reasonable" amount of other types of training. However, if heavy Barbell Back Squats are added to a training load that already includes running 75 miles (120km), cycling 150 miles (240km), swimming 10 miles (16km) and a few speed/plyometric sessions, the Squats may become the "straw that breaks the camel's back" and result in overtraining or acute injury. During weeks like this, dumbbells, medicine balls, kettlebells or even bodyweight might be a better option than loading up a bar with 45lb (20kg) plates and getting after it in the squat rack. These types of modifications will allow the body to maintain range of motion and flexibility while the central nervous system reinforces important motor patterns without overstressing the exercising musculature or the axial skeleton.

While having a plan is undeniably important for any kind of success and everybody knows the cliché "failing to plan is planning to fail", there needs to be some flexibility with exercise selection when we are asking so much of the body. See Table 2.1 on p.20 for some exercise regression examples that will make doing basic or Foundation Exercises possible when the body is too fatigued to do the "real" versions.

PROGRAM INTEGRATION

As indicated previously, integrating resistance training during the peak mileage phase of training can be a bit tricky. The goal is to find a balance between doing enough strength training that muscular strength and endurance are maintained or even improved without having a negative effect on actual endurance training. Like most things, this is easier said than done.

When it comes to incorporating resistance training into an already strenuous endurance training schedule, factors like intensity, volume, total load and exercise selection must be carefully manipulated to ensure the body stays as strong as possible while traversing so much total mileage.

Using the NSCA definition for "intensity" – basically how much weight is being lifted[1] – we will look at the amount of weight on the bar (or dumbbells or kettlebells or machines or ... well, you get the point) in relation to a 1-rep max. While there is almost no need for most endurance athletes to ever truly test their 1-rep max (beyond bragging rights), there is a definite value in estimating a rep max for a few of the basic or Foundation Exercises. A rep max is the number of quality repetitions that can be performed at a specified weight or the maximum weight that can be lifted for a specified number of repetitions. For example, if an athlete loads 100lb (45kg) on a barbell to attempt as many good reps as possible and successfully performs 10 reps, but can't do the 11th rep, then their 10-rep max is 100lb (45kg) for that exercise. Moving forward, every time the athlete bench presses they can use 100lb (45kg) as a guideline for their maximum and adjust their training sets accordingly. To make life easier for you, in the Appendix we've provided a 1-rep max calculator. Since there's no reason for an endurance athlete to be maxing out, simply perform the maximal number of repetitions of a manageable weight and then use the chart to figure out what your 1-rep max is. This can then be used to guide your resistance choices for the Foundation Exercises.

Using this model, we can adjust intensity based on factors such as what we hope to attain from the training session (size, strength, power, etc.) and other training factors (mileage, speed development, proximity to events, etc.). During the peak mileage phase of training, a goal of roughly 80 percent intensity is a good benchmark for most exercises. There will most likely be days where 80 percent will feel like 100-plus percent because of the level of fatigue from endurance sessions and 65–75 percent will be more realistic, but deviating too much from this guideline will not stimulate the body enough to have any real effect on strength. You will literally be going through the motions. Training much higher than 80 percent, even on days when you feel great, may overly fatigue the body and result in poor performance over the next few days.

'Volume' is defined as the total amount of reps being performed.[1] During this phase of training, 80 percent volume is a good general rule as well. If a strength training session during the base & build phase consisted of 200 total reps, dropping that to around 160 total reps is a good goal. There are multiple ways to make this adjustment, such as eliminating one set of each exercise, dropping 20 percent of the reps from each set (for example, sets of 8 instead of 10 reps) or reducing the number of training days per week. The optimal choice for most people is dropping roughly 20 percent of the reps from each set. This allows the body (which is already dealing with fatigue from the increased mileage) to move some weight around during each set with a decreased risk of injury and soreness since those are both largely the product of more volume per set.

A NOTE ON NUTRITION

During the peak mileage stage of training, the body will be burning a lot of calories. In all likelihood this is the most active time of the year for most athletes and the body will need increased caloric intake (aka food) to have enough energy for extended endurance sessions, strength training and recovery. Also, if this is your first time adding resistance training to your program, keep in mind that your body will be burning even more calories because of the increased workload and require more calories to recover properly and stay healthy.

When we train, we break the body down – it's through the recovery process that our muscles repair themselves and come back bigger and stronger. If the raw materials for these repairs (protein, carbohydrates, fats, vitamins and minerals) are not sufficient, this repair process will suffer. Endurance athletes face a bigger risk of caloric deficit than most people because of the massive number of calories being burned during their endurance training. During this phase, therefore, total caloric or food intake should be increased to deal with these demands. The exact amounts of this increase differ greatly between athletes; factors such as age, gender, size, body composition, metabolism and digestive differences will determine the exact amount of macro and micronutrients necessary to keep up with the elevated training level.

TAPER

Most endurance training programs include a taper phase during the days/weeks leading up to important competitions. This is a period of reduced overall training volume to allow the body to recover before strenuous events while maintaining elevated levels of cardiovascular functioning.

Ideally, this will allow the athlete to step to the starting line with a well-trained, highly efficient cardiovascular system and energy metabolism along with a body that feels good from a period of decreased activity. When this training–taper–race transition is done properly, it puts the athlete in the best position for success because of the combination of a healthy, rested body and efficient internal functioning.

Too often, however, this taper period is accompanied by a complete cessation of all resistance training. This is commonly seen in collegiate swimming programs where the taper is started a few weeks prior to conference championship meets and total distance in the pool is steadily decreased over two to three weeks. A lot of coaches will stop sending swimmers to the weight room when they are tapering in an effort to reduce their overall workload and aid the recovery process. The thinking here is solid; the problem is the execution. If athletes have been training for several months in a particular way that included regular resistance training and suddenly that component is completely removed, there will most likely be some negative effects. These may range from generally not "feeling strong" (this isn't going to become a sports psych discussion, but we're not sure anybody would put "feeling weak" at the top of the list of things necessary for peak performance) to actual muscular weakness and atrophy if the taper period is extended long enough.

TRAINING EMPHASIS

The best way to address tapering in the weight room is to make the overall volume and intensity of resistance training mirror the taper on the roads/track/bike/water. If the overall mileage is decreased by 20 percent per week, the strength training volume should also be reduced by about 20 percent. There are multiple ways to address this reduction of workload, and personal preference will play a large role in what method each individual should choose. In general, maintaining a regular schedule (i.e. not skipping days), slightly reducing intensity (weight lifted) and significantly decreasing volume per session (number of sets/reps) is the best approach.

Individualized nutrition

Endurance athletes are highly individualized when it comes to what they consume prior to training and racing. There are people who can eat a three-course meal and immediately run a 10K at race pace; then there are other people who eat a granola bar at 7 a.m. and still feel sluggish at noon. Eating prior to resistance training sessions is no different. The nutrient breakdown and timing of your pre-training meal is largely based on your body and metabolism, but avoiding training on an empty stomach and sticking to the plan that you know works for you are two rules of thumb that apply to just about all situations.

Also, while resistance training can be reduced significantly in the days or weeks immediately before a big event, there is no reason to spend that time binge-watching television shows and becoming a doughnut aficionado. The extra time in your schedule is a great opportunity to take advantage of recovery techniques that may have been pushed to the back burner due to lack of time during other training phases. Instead, get a massage, use intermittent compression boots or cryotherapy facilities, spend extra time foam rolling or using other self-massage tools, and work on mobility. These activities are valuable to overall athletic development and health without being as physically demanding as resistance training. This will be time well spent as the body will feel more refreshed, recovered and ready as the big event gets closer.

While tapering training for big events is almost a necessity for most athletes, it should be noted that not all events are created equal and not all events deserve the same amount of tapering. The biggest events of the training year, such as marathons, multi-day cycling stage races, IRONMAN triathlons and races where your time or finish will determine the rest of your season (i.e. a local marathon that is also a major marathon qualifier), all demand a reduction in training in the preceding weeks. Smaller or less important events that are often used as "training races", such as charity 5Ks, organized century rides and sprint triathlons, however, can mostly be prepared for without a lot of tapering.

The most important factor when planning a training schedule around several events is picking out which ones are the most important to you and putting your body in the best position to succeed at those events. For example, if you are running a local marathon in May and a major city marathon in November, your training year would break down into basically two training cycles to prepare for the big races with the summer months in between them as your off-season. This means that the months leading up to May and November will follow the base & build–peak mileage–taper model and the summer would function as the off-season, during which you can focus more on resistance training and getting stronger. There may be some shorter races over the summer, but these can be treated like intense training sessions with little to no disruption to the overall training schedule. Sure, there may be some exceptions to this model. If your whole family has been running a particular 5K for years and you want bragging rights at the BBQ later that day, you might want to take it easy for a few days leading up to the race so you can beat your cousins. If your employer is sponsoring an event and you want to make a good showing in front of your coworkers, a few days of lighter training loads and recovery work might make you look like a star to your department. However, there is no need to disrupt training for these smaller events for any significant length of time.

To put this in perspective, collegiate swimming and track teams only taper for big events such as conference meets and national qualifiers. If they really reduced their training load to prepare for every dual meet, local event and regular competition, there would literally be no time left to train. Similarly, in a sport like baseball that is predominantly anaerobic, but for which the number of games, practices, skill development sessions, bus trips, flights, hotel stays and late nights make the season a figurative marathon, most teams only alter training for the playoffs, rivalry series or individual player needs. Similar to training for endurance events, the season is just too long to allow for resting/tapering before every game and still expect to really accomplish any long-term development.

Planning a race/training calendar several months or a year in advance will allow you to get a "big picture" view of your season and make the proper adjustments to both endurance and resistance workouts for peak performance on race day.

EXERCISE SELECTION

The goal during the taper phase should be performing the Foundation Exercises you have been doing throughout training and altering volume/intensity in a similar way that endurance work is being reduced. Depending on how the body is reacting, this may not be possible and exercise regressions may be necessary. If Barbell Front Squats are going to impede your recovery process, Overhead Squats with a dowel or Kettlebell Goblet Squats might be a better option to reinforce that motor pattern, maintain flexibility/range of motion and stimulate the lower extremity musculature while aiding the recovery process.

Picking exercises while tapering should be done with the idea of continuing the training program with as little soreness and fatigue as possible. There will be an element of trial and error the first few times this is attempted, so it's better to be overly cautious than too aggressive. If you select an exercise regression that is "too easy" and you don't feel like you got anything out of it, you can always do additional sets or pick another exercise the next time you train. However, if you pick an exercise that is too challenging and you wake up sore, stiff or fatigued, it is almost impossible to go back and undo that damage.

PROGRAM INTEGRATION

Integrating resistance training during a taper is not that difficult if a few key principles are kept in mind. The overall goal of this integration is keeping the body as strong as possible while not being too sore or fatigued to properly recover in time for the event. Ideally, weight training will take place the same number of days per week as during the peak mileage phase of training but with modifications to volume, intensity and exercise selection to aid in the recovery process. Through the years, we've experimented a bit with adjustments to volume and intensity during the taper phase and have come up with an 80 percent "rule". Using 80 percent of the volume and intensity from the peak mileage phase will help you maintain muscle strength and, most importantly, reinforce the proper motor pattern.

A few general guidelines to follow:
- Frequency (sessions per week): 2–4
- Volume (total number of reps): 80 percent of the peak mileage phase
- Intensity (total weight lifted): 80 percent of the peak mileage phase
- Exercise selection: lean toward the more basic regressions when applicable

If your basic schedule during the peak mileage phase was something like this:
Sunday: recovery
Monday: resistance training (upper body emphasis)
Tuesday: speed work
Wednesday: resistance training (lower body emphasis)
Thursday: low mileage/tempo
Friday: light total body resistance training and long run prep
Saturday: long run

then your schedule while tapering should look roughly the same, with a few notable changes to individual sessions.

One thing to remember during the taper phase, which experienced competitors already know, is that this is not the time to try anything new. In the same way that you wouldn't wear a brand new pair of shoes from a new company on race day or eat unfamiliar foods the night before a race, resistance training should be kept familiar in the week or two before the event. There is a time and place to try new things. This is *not* it. Stick to the script, make smart modifications and be ready to bring it on race day!

We've mentioned before that coaching is both art and science. While this is obviously true during all phases of training, it leans more toward "art" during the final few days before a big event. Other phases of training demand rigid adherence to the physiological principles that govern human development. Successfully tapering, though, is dependent on knowing your body (or the bodies of the people you are training) as well as their mental and emotional state and putting them in the best overall position to succeed.

To enable this, it is therefore also important to dedicate time and energy to mental preparation, visualization, race strategy and event-specific preparation (terrain, climate, equipment, etc.) and to fine-tune the fitness base established during earlier training phases.

For novice competitors, there will be a few times when they get it wrong. At the finish area of most events, variations of "I shouldn't have..." or "Next time I will..." or "I ate more fettuccine alfredo and drank less water than I have in my entire life..." (Michael Scott after running a charity 5K on *The Office US*) can be easily overheard. However, with experience, things should improve. Nevertheless, by putting thought into proper planning and adhering to a few basic principles, there is a better chance that the event will be a positive experience.

PLANNING TO SUCCEED

Implementing proper periodization into a training program gives the athlete the best chance for improved performance and minimizes the risk of injury. It also ensures the appropriate amount of work is being done during any given time of the year. Breaking the year down into four main phases and planning all training appropriately within each phase allows for the correct amount of work to be performed and enough rest/recovery to happen that real gains can be made.

As stated previously, clearly delineating the four phases of the year based around your biggest events creates the roadmap for your training. This map will provide guidance as to when to add new exercises, when to put more weight on the bar, when to take it a little easier in the gym and when to push yourself. Once this general framework is in place there is some room for variation (sets/reps, rest intervals, exercise progressions/regressions, etc.) but the overall purpose of each phase is clear and the decisions made during that phase should contribute to that purpose.

As you become more experienced with resistance training, making changes and modifications on the fly will become second nature. Replacing Barbell Back Squats with Dumbbell Goblet Squats when your legs are brutally sore from a hill workout will be an easy decision. Hopefully, adding a few extra kilograms to a set of Barbell Back Squats when you are feeling good in the off-season will be just as easy a decision. With experience will come mastery of training modalities and a knowledge of your body that will let you adjust your training appropriately during any time of the year or training phase.

Everybody knows that "failing to plan is planning to fail" is a cliché, but it really applies here. Putting time and thought into how and when to add resistance training to your training plan is the key to getting stronger, more injury resistant and on pace to … Finish Strong!

1. Earle R., *Essentials of Strength Training and Conditioning,* 4th ed. (Human Kinetics, 2016)
2. *ACSM's Guidelines for Exercise Testing and Prescription,* 10th ed. (Wolters Kluwer, 2018)
3. Starrett, K., *Becoming a Supple Leopard,* 2nd ed. (Victory Belt, 2015)

9

MOVEMENT IS MEDICINE – THE IMPORTANCE OF MOBILITY EXERCISE

The areas around the starting line of a race or the transition area of a triathlon can be interesting places. There is a lot of nervous energy and excitement in the air as athletes prep for the big event. We always find it fascinating to watch athletes go through their pre-race warm-up rituals. There is always some combination of mental and physical preparation that occurs. Physically, athletes warm up to improve blood flow to the muscles and joints so they can move more freely. Some have very basic or quick routines while others have very deliberate, involved regimes. Part of moving more freely is performing stretching and joint mobility work. As endurance athletes, we don't need to perform splits like a gymnast (although you might psych out the competition if you could) but we also can't have the inability to reach our arms completely over our heads, like some bodybuilders. These rituals that we see at the start line are carried over from what endurance athletes are doing in their daily training, since in order to achieve the ability to move more freely, we need to be incorporating mobility exercises as part of our regularly planned resistance training.

Allowing the muscles to actively move through a greater range of motion will help improve your performance and will aid in keeping you injury free. In this chapter, we will explain the benefits of including mobility exercises in your regular resistance training program and provide you with our favorite go-tos that are useful at targeting common problem areas for swimmers, cyclists and runners.

FLEXIBILITY VS. MOBILITY

Let's clear up an important question: "What's the difference between flexibility and mobility?" Flexibility is quite simply the ability of a muscle to lengthen. Mobility is the ability of a joint to move through its natural full range of motion. Quite simply, flexibility is useless during *active* endurance events, while mobility is of the utmost importance. The main culprit for limits to mobility is restriction in the myofascial tissue. Myofascia is the combination of muscles and fascia and they play a role in how we move actively and passively. Most people understand that muscles shorten and lengthen by way of contractions to allow for human movement. Unfortunately, most people don't understand what the fascia is and how it plays a role in movement. Deep fascia can influence how freely muscles slide over one another, while the superficial fascia is like a net that covers the outer portion of the muscles, thus connecting them in the kinetic chains. Restrictions in the myofascia are a major cause for restricted mobility. Mobility may also be limited by nerve tension, capsular tightness and a lack of smooth bony surface articulations (i.e. arthritis).

Sticking with the idea of myofascial tissue providing the restriction in mobility, it is important to understand that it isn't the same as having a tight muscle on one side of a joint. There are many instances where there is proper flexibility in one muscle but the prime mover (muscle on the other side) doesn't function properly to take the joint through its full range of motion. Let's take, for instance, the hamstrings and hip flexors. Everyone is always concerned about hamstring flexibility limiting hip flexion. We've worked with numerous athletes who could *passively* stretch their hamstrings well past 90 degrees of hip flexion when lying on their back, but when asked to *actively* do the same motion, couldn't reach the same position. This is because the hip flexors have a level of dysfunction that restricts them. Happily, all restrictions that are myofascial, nerve or capsular in nature can be treated effectively through mobility exercises.

Now that you have a better understanding of what mobility is, it should come as no surprise to you that performing mobility exercises as part of our regular resistance training will help to improve the performance of your muscles. Since muscles generate torque (rotary force) around joints, imagine what that means if we can actively produce force through a larger range of motion. Cyclists always make sure to pump up tires to decrease rolling resistance and improve mechanical efficiency, and the same should apply to joints. Failing to add mobility exercises into your training is the equivalent of going out for a ride on soft tires – you're seriously limiting your performance.

MOBILITY AND AGING

A quick word about aging. At this point, it has been well documented that as we age, our soft tissue makeup undergoes changes that lead to increased stiffening that reduces mobility in joints.[1] If you've been at your sport for a while, like we've been, then you've probably noticed that you can't simply get by with the same routine you were using to loosen up 10 years ago. All connective tissues (skin, cartilage, fascia, ligaments, tendons, and yes, even muscles) are made up of a combination of collagen (think stiffness), elastin (think elastic, like a rubber band) and extracellular matrix (think water content). Over time, the proportions of these compounds change and the tissues take on a stiffer, less hydrated form, which becomes less mobile. This is why it is especially important as we age to really focus on hydration and continue to perform mobility exercises to help resist the effects of these cellular changes. If we want to have enough longevity in our sport to eventually reach the podium (that's always our goal), then including mobility exercises in our training program will be crucial.

MOBILITY AND CRAMPING

Along the lines of what we've mentioned above regarding aging, let's discuss how this affects cramping during your extended training bouts or competitions. Any of us who get to participate in hot and humid conditions at some point have likely dealt with muscular cramping while exercising. Certainly, your ability to keep muscle cramps at bay has a lot to do with managing your water, sodium and potassium intake during exercise. What's more, while there isn't any scientific evidence stating that having optimal mobility decreases muscle cramps (frankly, it would be near impossible to study), we do have some anecdotal evidence that suggests that it will in fact help.

We dealt with a male marathon runner client who experienced calf cramps any time he was training or racing in hot and humid conditions. He was a coached athlete and did know how to manage the cramps using salt tablets and sports drinks, but while he was the type of guy who did some strength training, he never committed to stretching post exercise and never engaged in any mobility exercise. One year, he decided to take yoga classes twice a week. In consequence, he reported that he experienced cramps at a much lower rate than he had prior to taking the classes, and that he hadn't changed anything else.

This anecdotal story is supported by science: the 'National Athletic Trainers' Association Position Statement on Fluid Replacement' states that stretching after having muscle cramping does aid with recovery,[2] so it's possible that mobility exercise can have a bit of a prophylactic effect.

MITIGATING INJURIES WITH MOBILITY EXERCISES

Mobility exercises are also super important for reducing the risk of overuse/chronic injuries by helping to keep our bodies balanced. In Section 1, we introduced you to the joint-by-joint concept, which described which areas of the body require stability through resistance exercise and which require the ability to move more freely through mobility exercise. We have worked with numerous individuals who were strong as an ox because they were religious about performing a regular resistance training program, but still fell victim to overuse/chronic injuries.

One client in particular was a successful collegiate cross-country runner who fits this description. He was diligent in strength training, had his body strong and balanced – and didn't *appear* to have any postural syndromes. Nevertheless, two strong seasons were derailed with injuries. Once we screened him with some movement assessments, we discovered that a lack of mobility was the root cause of his problems. He had restrictions in his great toe extension, ankle dorsiflexion and muscle tightness throughout his lower extremity. Using a number of mobility exercises and introducing him to yoga flows (including a lot of Down Dogs) helped him have a strong, injury-free senior campaign.

Our point here is this: strength and mobility are equally as important, yet mobility often gets overlooked – other than some simple static stretching post workout (if at all). This is a mistake, since failure to include proper mobility exercises in your resistance training program may leave you vulnerable to injuries as well as missing potential performance gains.

In our years of performing movement assessments on clients, we've further narrowed down the common problem areas where endurance athletes lack mobility. When performing your discipline for extended periods of time, the body tends to assume certain postures, which then lead to these common restrictions. Eventually, restrictions in our muscles, fascia and joint capsules ultimately limit our ability to move freely. In the rehabilitation community we have a simple saying: 'movement is medicine'. By including mobility exercises in our strength training sessions we can help

Strength and mobility

Getting your body primed for success in endurance sports requires attention to *both* resistance and mobility exercises. Most people realize that stronger muscles will lead to improved performance, but don't recognize that moving a stronger muscle through a larger functional range of motion is really what will lead to the performance gains they are looking for. Without mobility exercises, our body will end up unbalanced and fail to reach its full potential.

the body resist the likelihood of experiencing these common restrictions. In the following pages, we've identified the most important areas for each sport to mobilize, the rationale behind it and descriptions of a few exercises that will help.

MOBILITY EXERCISES FOR SWIMMERS

What's your pre-swim ritual on the pool deck? Are you the person making big arm circles, flying your arms open and closed, hugging your shoulder across your body or stretching your arms way over your head while moving your trunk from side to side? We both do something similar to this but no matter how hard we try, we don't look as intimidating as Michael Phelps. Nevertheless, all of these things help to improve our shoulder mobility, which is important for performance.

In freestyle swimming, stroke power is produced by the arms and is further enhanced by rotation in the trunk (thoracic spine). At your swim practice, you've likely done single arm drills as part of your warm-up with the goal of increasing your ability to rotate your neck and trunk. If you're doing this as part of your swim training, wouldn't it make sense to add it to your dry land routine via mobility exercises?

Another key area that can hinder your performance is a lack of shoulder internal rotation caused by tightness of the posterior capsule and shoulder musculature. If we fail to address that lack of motion, we might miss out on finishing the last 20 percent of our stroke, which will make us less efficient (and we all know the key to being a good swimmer is efficiency).

Taking a *targeted* approach to including the mobility exercises commonly needed for swimmers will allow us to properly use muscles to generate force and keep our bodies in optimal position to reach peak performance.

Targets:
- thoracic spine mobility (rotation)
- shoulder mobility (internal rotation)

THE LOWDOWN

The thoracic spine consists of 12 vertebrae that make up the upper and mid back. These vertebrae all have attachments for ribs. The ribs from vertebrae 1–10 all connect together via the ribcage while the ribs on vertebrae 11 and 12 are floating. Additionally, the thoracic spine vertebrae have spinous processes that point downward off the back, which limit extension. All of this winds up making extension and rotation at the thoracic spine difficult. It is quite important to have mobility in the thoracic spine since it represents the trunk, and having good trunk rotation on the pelvis during freestyle will help with proper stroke mechanics. Further, having mobility in the thoracic spine is critical since the shoulder moves over the ribs via the scapulothoracic joint (this isn't a true joint, rather it's a functional region). A limit in the motion at the thoracic spine can then in turn affect the position of the scapula, which can affect what happens at the glenohumeral joint (the true shoulder joint), which may leave it vulnerable to injury.

Shoulder impingement is a condition at the shoulder whereby the soft tissues of the shoulder grind against the superior bony structures, causing pain and discomfort with overhead activities. In a study of shoulder impingement by Yamamoto,[3] individuals who had a normal posture in the thoracic spine experienced impingement at a rate of less than 3 percent, while for those with a thoracic spine kyphosis (rounded forward), more than 65 percent had impingement. Clearly, there is a connection between the thoracic spine and shoulder injuries such as impingement. Tate[4] reported that competitive swimmers had a prevalence rate between 41 percent and 91 percent for shoulder pain. Therefore, one key to keeping the shoulders pain- and injury free is maintaining the mobility in the thoracic spine.

Coaches will agree that shoulder mobility is important for initiating the catch phase to achieve early vertical forearm (EVF) and the pull phase. It is well known that overhead throwing athletes and swimmers often lack shoulder mobility, specifically shoulder internal rotation due to the repetitive nature of their sports. During the pull, the internal rotators of the shoulder produce force to propel the swimmer. As this motion is repeated, the capsule and posterior rotator cuff muscles may become tight and therefore limit the amount of internal rotation motion that the shoulder has. Torres[5] found an internal rotation deficit of up to 12 degrees in swimmers compared to 4.9 degrees in a control group. This restriction can adversely affect the catch and pull phases of the freestyle motion.

As endurance racing swimmers, our typical workouts are between 2,750 yards (2,500m) and 5,500 yards (5,000m) so it should come as no surprise that the repetitive stroke motion creates some restrictions at the posterior shoulder. It is therefore critical to stretch the structures of the posterior capsule and posterior rotator cuff so that we can optimize performance (finish our strokes) as well as reduce the risk of shoulder injuries. A study by McClure[6] found the Cross-body Stretch to produce greater shoulder internal rotation compared to the Sleeper Stretch, and it is therefore our recommended intervention of choice.

BOOK OPENERS (STANDING THORACIC SPINE ROTATION)

Figure 9.1
Book Openers start/
finish (A) and
midpoint (B)

Thoracic spine mobility, specifically, rotation is critical in the freestyle swimming motion. This exercise will target stretching the erector spinae, latissimus dorsi and other large back muscles and surrounding fascia that may have become restricted over time. There are only small amounts of rotation between each thoracic spine segment so it is critical to preserve every bit of the range of motion.

START

Stand in a staggered stance facing closely to a wall. The toes of the forward foot are in contact with the wall, the shoulders are raised to 90 degrees and the elbows are bent to 90 degrees so that both forearms are touching the wall. The knee of the forward leg must also be in contact with the wall (this is critical as it locks the pelvis in once the movement starts).

MOVEMENT

Rotate the trunk toward the side with the leg that is staggered back. The arm on this side leaves the wall and rotates as far as it can. The eyes should follow the hand as this allows for a greater range of motion. It is critical that the toes, knee and forearm of the wall side of the body remain in contact with the wall to lock the pelvis in place.

MIDPOINT

Depending on how much rotation you have in your trunk, you will be looking back over your hips.

END

Slowly return to the starting position until the traveling arm makes contact with the wall once more and you are facing front. Repeat on the other side and for the required number of reps.

DOING IT RIGHT

- Keep your core tight.
- Keep your front foot toes, knee and forearm in contact with the wall.
- Follow your hand with your eyes.

TIPS

- With each repetition, try to go a little further.
- Keeping the core engaged for this exercise activates the oblique muscles, which is important.

VARIATIONS

- **Side-lying Thoracic Spine Rotation**
  Lie on your side with the bottom leg fully extended and the knee of the top leg bent to 90 degrees with the knee making firm contact with the floor. Rotate the trunk so that the top shoulder and arm make contact with the ground.
- **Thread the Needle**
  Assume a hands and knees position and engage the core. Place a foam roller to the outside of the arm that you will rotate toward. Reach under your body with the opposite arm and engage the forearm with the foam roller as you rotate the trunk.

BRETZEL

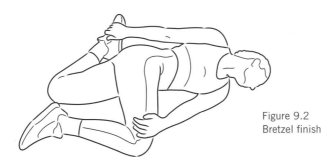

Figure 9.2
Bretzel finish

This exercise will target stretching the quads and hip flexors of one leg, the glutes and piriformis of the other leg, the lower back and, most importantly, will help create rotation in the thoracic spine. Tight myofasicia can be the cause of the restricted motion and moving to end ranges will help to stretch it.

START

Lie on your side with your neck supported. Take the top leg, bend it up and twist it over to the 90/90 hip/knee position, then push the inside of the knee to the floor. Use the arm on the side where the knee is to reach over and lock the knee down to the ground by placing the hand on the outside of the thigh just above the knee. Kick the bottom leg back, reach down and back to grab the top of the foot with the other hand.

MOVEMENT

Pull back on the bottom leg so that you feel a stretch in the hip flexors. Roll your trunk over and attempt to lie on your back, trying to get the back of the top shoulder to meet the ground. You will feel a twisting sensation through your thoracic spine as you rotate. Hold the end position for 30 seconds and perform 3 sets. Repeat on the other side.

CROSS-BODY STRETCH

Backed by research evidence, this stretch is important for swimmers as it will help to stretch the posterior capsule of the shoulder and muscles of the posterior rotator cuff, which often tighten and restrict shoulder internal rotation.

START

While standing, place your buttocks and back against a wall. Bring the shoulder to be stretched up to a 90-degrees angle and pull it across your chest. Use the hand from the other arm to create force slightly higher than the elbow so that you feel a stretch in the back of the shoulder. It is important to keep the core tight to prevent compensatory movement in the trunk and only stretch at the shoulder. Hold this for a full 30 seconds. We recommend 3 repetitions. Repeat on the other side.

DOING IT RIGHT

- The stretch might feel uncomfortable but should not hurt.
- Keep the core tight and limit the rotation of the trunk.

TIPS

- We prefer to do this with our backs against a wall to limit the compensatory movements. Sometimes people will rotate the spine rather than getting a full stretch at the shoulder.
- Avoid doing this if you have acute shoulder impingement as it will irritate the structures involved.

Figure 9.3
Cross-body Stretch start

VARIATION

There is also evidence to support the Sleeper Stretch as being effective, so that is a perfectly good option as well.

Sleeper Stretch – lie on your side with your hips in line with your shoulders. The knee from the top leg should bend to 90 degrees and slide forward to make contact with the ground for stability. The shoulder you wish to mobilize on the ground, flexed to 90 degrees with the elbow is flexed to 90 degrees. Move the palm toward the ground until you feel a stretch on the posterior shoulder and apply over-pressure from the other hand for a minimum of 30 seconds and perform 3 sets. Repeat on the other side.

DOORWAY STRETCH

Due to the repetitive nature of the swim stroke, the pecs (specifically pectoralis minor) tend to get tight and then cause forward shoulder and kyphotic thoracic spine postures, which are linked to shoulder injuries. Therefore, we use this stretch to help rebalance the muscle lengths to achieve optimal posture.

START
Stand centrally in a standard-sized doorway with the door open. Raise your arms up so that your forearms make contact with the door jambs (they should be raised high so that your elbows are at the level of your ears). Your feet should be staggered and you can lean in as if entering the door so that you feel a stretch in the front of the shoulders. It is critical that the core is tight and there is no arching of the lower back; this is a major compensation that often occurs. Hold the stretch for a full 30 seconds. We recommend 3 repetitions.

DOING IT RIGHT
- Keep your elbows high – at the level of your ears.
- Keep your core tight and the lower back flat.

SAFETY
The reason for holding the shoulders high (elbows by ears) is so that you stretch the pectoralis minor rather than the anterior shoulder capsule (which is undesirable).

VARIATION
If its more convenient, you can easily use a corner for this.

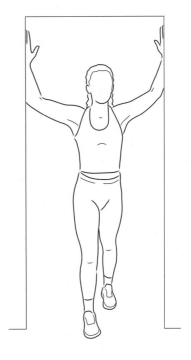

Figure 9.4
Doorway Stretch start

MOBILITY EXERCISES FOR CYCLISTS

Ask any cyclist what is the correct number of bicycles you should own and they will proudly tell you N+1 (where N is the number you currently own). RJ thinks that a similar formula (N+2) should apply to the number of thoracic spine mobility exercises cyclists should be doing judging by the postures he sees in most of the cyclists while out on his weekend long rides.

There really is nothing better than the camaraderie of a long group ride and feeling the wind through your hair (through the helmet, of course). As fun as it is to be out there riding, the hunched-over nature of road, MTB and time trialing can take a toll on our trunk (thoracic spine) posture. Over time, this could limit our rib mobility, which in turn could limit our lung expansion, thus affecting our performance. Last time we checked, most cyclists like to brag about their functional threshold power (FTP), and we don't need to give any of them an excuse for having a decline. Our major power production out on the bike comes from our hips, so keeping them strong and mobile is critical to keeping those FTPs high!

Tightness at the hip can also affect the overall alignment of the lower extremity through a pedal stroke. When looking from behind a rider, things are optimal when the hip, knee and foot are stacked in a line. When the knee is running outward or inward, this is typically an indication of imbalanced hip muscles that need strength and mobility work. No matter what the alignment, focusing on the mobility of a rider's hips and thoracic spine through their resistance training program will certainly help boost their power and help them brag about their FTP even more.

Targets:
- hip mobility (all directions)
- thoracic spine mobility (extension)

THE LOWDOWN

Whether we are riding the hoods, drops or down in aero, our bodies end up in a posture where the thoracic spine tends to bend forward (kyphosis). As we assume any posture for a long period of time, eventually creep sets into the tissues and it is then hard to return to that beautiful normal upright posture. Couple that with the fact that many of us work desk jobs for a living, typing on our computers, and the "forward hunch" becomes an even bigger issue. In a study of elite and masters male cyclists, a large percentage were found to have hyper-kyphotic posture of their thoracic spine.[7]

Another area of vulnerability for cyclists is lack of hip mobility. Our position on the bike features the trunk leaning over the legs so we are in perpetual hip flexion. Continually doing the same motion will build up small contractures at the joint capsule as well as limiting the range of motion of muscles (especially the hip flexors).

THE WORLD'S GREATEST STRETCH

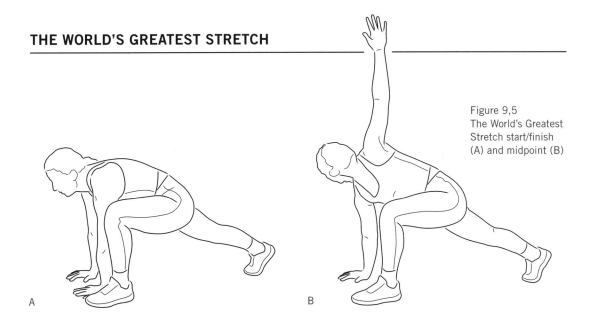

Figure 9,5
The World's Greatest
Stretch start/finish
(A) and midpoint (B)

A

B

It's not called the World's Greatest Stretch for nothing. This mobility exercise will help mobilize the myofascia of the hip, shoulder and thoracic spine (to name a few areas). Mobility exercises that hit all the "problem" areas like this are a great choice, especially if you are time crunched.

START
Get down in a position similar to a track starting position. Both arms should be firmly extended and planted on the ground, the back leg extended at the hip and knee and toes making firm contact with the ground (the knee should not be resting on the ground). The front leg will be at the 90/90 hip and knee flexion position and should be positioned just outside the arm, with the foot planted firmly on the ground at the same level as the hands. The trunk is close to parallel to the ground.

MOVEMENT
Slowly begin to rotate the trunk toward the forward leg side and take that arm up into the air. The elbow should be fully extended, the shoulder blades should be engaged and the eyes and head should follow the motion of the hand up toward the ceiling.

MIDPOINT
If you have good mobility of your hips, thoracic spine and shoulder, your top shoulder should be in a stacked position over the shoulder of the arm that is planted firmly on the ground. The head and eyes are looking at the hand of the arm pointed to the sky. The back leg is extended as much as possible so that the knee isn't contacting the ground and the toes are actively gripping the floor. The front knee and hip continue to maintain the 90/90 position and the foot is firmly planted on the floor at the level of the hand that is on the floor.

END
Slowly bring the arm back down to the start position. Some people will also reach this arm across the body underneath the arm that is planted to increase the stretch at the back of the shoulder and the hip. Repeat on the other side.

FOAM ROLLER BACK EXTENSION

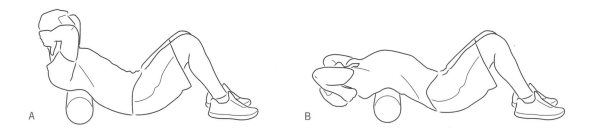

Figure 9.6
Foam Roller Back Extension start/finish (A) and midpoint (B)

The best way to avoid the kyphotic posture in the thoracic spine (which is essentially flexion) is to move in the opposite direction – extension. A foam roller is a great piece of equipment to help perform this important mobilization.

START

Lie on the ground on your back with your knees bent to 90 degrees and your feet and buttocks firmly planted on the ground. Lean the trunk upward enough to place the foam roller on the ground perpendicular to your body at the level of your shoulder blades. Hold the arms in front of your face by bringing both shoulders up just past a 90-degree position, then bend the elbows to 90 degrees to allow your hands to cradle the back of your head. The arms provide support to the cervical spine, which is crucial for injury prevention. Additionally, this position moves the scapulae away from the thoracic spine, allowing it to be exposed and move more freely.

MOVEMENT

While keeping the head and neck supported by the arms, slowly arch back over the foam roller until you reach the end of the extension. Continue to maintain contact of the feet and buttocks with the ground and avoid lifting the hips. Take a few deep exhales to sink further back and get an improved stretch. It is not uncommon to hear a pop, which is a simple cavitation of the facet joints of the spine and is perfectly normal in most cases.

END

Use the core muscles to sit back up while continuing to support the head and neck. Adjust the foam roller to hit another segment of the thoracic spine between the shoulder blades and repeat. We recommend working on at least three spots.

TIPS

When you reach the end of the range of motion, exhale to sag into the movement.

SAFETY

Always keep the head and neck supported to avoid injury.

DOWN DOG

Figure 9.7
Down Dog midpoint

If you haven't stepped out of your comfort zone and tried yoga, you are missing out on its physical benefits. Not only is yoga a wonderful way to provide mobility to the joints through the various poses, but it also helps build tension throughout the muscles. One pose that is commonly performed in yoga flows is the Down Dog. This exercise will help stretch the entire superficial back line (posterior kinetic chain). That alone will add mobility to the ankles and hips, which are needed in cycling. Additionally, planting the hands strongly into the ground depresses the scapulae and extends the thoracic spine. Once again, this exercise is a bit of a time-saver since it helps mobilize two of the common problem areas for cyclists – the hips and the thoracic spine.

START
Start in a good High Plank or Push-up position. The feet should be placed shoulder-width apart and hands placed slightly to the outside of the shoulders. The trunk, pelvis and legs are strong in a neutral alignment.

MOVEMENT
Lift the back of the hips high to the sky while pushing away from the hands. The heels will move closer to contacting the ground (depending on your flexibility) and the knees will remain extended. The core is held tight, and the scapulae are retracted.

MIDPOINT
Your body will make two sides of a triangle with the ground making the third side. The trunk and arms (one side of the triangle) should be in line and rigid and the whole lower extremity (the other side of the triangle) should be in line and rigid as well.

END
Slowly lower the body back to the Push-up position. Repeat for the required number of reps.

MOBILITY EXERCISES FOR RUNNERS

At the beginning of every weekly track workout, RJ's triathlon team takes time to perform a dynamic warm-up that focuses on loosening up the muscles of the trunk and the lower extremity. While it's a nice ritual that allows athletes to chit-chat with teammates and watch the sunrise over the NYC skyline, some important work is also being performed. Moving our muscles through end ranges of motion will help us to open up our stride, allowing us to be faster. By contrast, tight hip flexors or hamstrings will limit our stride, which will inhibit our performance.

However, while dynamic warm-ups are great at loosening up our muscles and fascia before we do a run workout, including targeted mobility exercises in our planned resistance training programs will further improve our mobility at our hips and ankles, which will help improve run performance and mitigate the risk of overuse/chronic injuries.

Aside from attempting to improve muscle flexibility at our hips, mobility exercises can help release some of the small capsular adhesions that can build up as a result of repeated motion and cause restriction. A lack of ankle dorsiflexion can also disrupt our running mechanics. This restriction could be a result of a tight gastrocnemius, tight soleus or tightness in the joint capsule. Regardless, failure to address this will not allow us to keep our body's center of mass over our foot during terminal stance, which can lead to issues up the kinetic chain. Unfortunately, the knee is usually the area affected by this restriction in ankle mobility.

Whether you are the runner who just laces 'em up, heads out of the door and takes off on their training run, or the one who plots a thorough dynamic warm-up, adding mobility exercises to your regular strength and mobility program will help you achieve peak performance, stay injury free and keep on running.

Targets:
• hip mobility (all directions)
• ankle mobility (dorsiflexion)

THE LOWDOWN

The repetitive nature of running creates maladaptive behaviours of the body in the form of shortened muscles and capsular contractures. RJ has worked in the medical tent for the NYC marathon for a number of years and his secret for moving people along who were there with general muscle soreness and tightness was to apply long axis distraction to their leg (pulling on their legs to free up the hip) and massaging and stretching the piriformis muscles (deep hip muscles that help with external rotation) that were so overworked. He would then perform a series of internal and external rotations of their hips without really spending too much time toward the end ranges as that can be uncomfortable. The next most important thing he would do for those finishers was to stretch their calves (both the gastrocnemius and, most importantly, the soleus muscle). In a nutshell, resetting the hips and ankles after long bouts of running is critical to restoring normal joint mechanics. Here are some exercises to help you do just that.

90/90 HIP ROTATIONS

Actively engaging the muscles to create rotation at the hip helps to mobilize the myofascia. For years, clinicians have used techniques where recruiting musculature on one side of a joint causes a relaxation at the other side, which aids with stretching of those muscles (PNF stretching). This mobilization technique is great since it doesn't require any equipment and will help to loosen up the restrictions you may feel from the tight muscles.

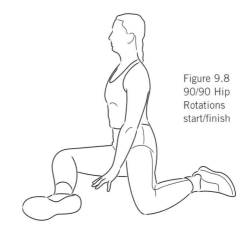

Figure 9.8
90/90 Hip
Rotations
start/finish

START

Get on the floor and place one thigh forward with the knee bent to 90 degrees and the lower leg coming across the body. The outside of the ankle and the side of the knee should be actively in contact with the ground. Place the other leg out to the side from the trunk, bend the knee to 90 degrees and face the lower leg backward. The inside of the ankle and knee should be actively in contact with the ground (or close to it). Both sit bones from the pelvis will be in contact with the floor. The trunk posture should be held upright so that the lower back isn't rounded, hyperextended or leaning to the side. Hands can be folded in front of your heart or on the ground.

MOVEMENT

Actively push from the lateral ankle of the front leg and pull from the medial ankle of the back leg to move the body into a mirror image of what it previously was. The hip that was externally rotated in the front will become internally rotated and will now be in the back, and vice versa. The sit bones will move on the floor to assume this new position. Continue to focus on the upright posture of the trunk. Focus on really trying to make good contact with the knee and ankle of the front leg. Perform 10 slow repetitions.

DOING IT RIGHT

- Keep the trunk upright.
- Drive through the ankles to initiate the movement.

SAFETY

If you've been diagnosed with hip impingement, this may be painful and could be contraindicated.

VARIATION

Many people will use this same setup but just perform it as a static stretch. To improve the stretch of the glutes in the forward leg, the trunk often hinges forward a bit. If you choose to do this, we recommend 3 sets of 30-second holds on each side.

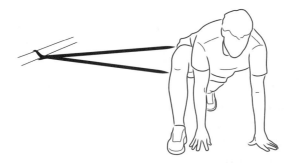

Figure 9.9
Band Distraction Hip
Lateral midpoint

Joint mobilizations have been used by clinicians for years to assist with improving joint mobility due to tightness in the joint capsule. Pulling laterally and posteriorly on the hip will allow the hip to produce greater amounts of motion in all directions. There are numerous variations that can be performed, but we have found the following two to be safe and achieve the mobility you are looking for. Using a heavy resistance band in place of the clinician's hands can be a good way to produce similar results.

START

Take a heavy resistance band and anchor it to a very solid object at an attachment point about level with your hips when in a half-kneeling stance. Position yourself so that you are facing perpendicular to the band. Place the band around the leg that will be forward, as close to the hip as possible, and ensure there is strong tension. Bring the front knee and hip to approximately a 90/90 position and plant the foot firmly. Move the other leg back so it is extended at the hip and knee with the toes firmly engaged with the ground. Flex the trunk forward to the outside of the front leg so it is low and parallel with the ground. Extend both arms and plant them into the ground to the side of the forward foot.

MOVEMENT

Perform small oscillations forward and in the direction away from the band attachment point to help "open up" space in the hip. It is important to maintain full body tension throughout and let the band pull the hip laterally. Repeat on the other side.

DOING IT RIGHT

- Engage enough tension through the heavy resistance band.
- Plant the feet and hands firmly into the ground for support.
- Engage the core for added stability.

SAFETY

If this creates discomfort that's OK, but if it's painful, abandon this technique.

BAND DISTRACTION HIP POSTERIOR

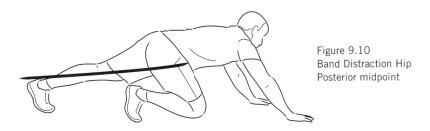

Figure 9.10
Band Distraction Hip
Posterior midpoint

Similar to the lateral band distraction, the goal of the posterior distraction force is to create space at the hip joint by stretching the joint capsule, thus adding mobility to the hip. When you don't have rehabilitation clinicians available to assist you, the heavy resistance bands are a fantastic way to accomplish the same goal. Maintaining "clean," full hip movement is a key for runners to avoid overuse injuries.

START
Take a heavy resistance band and anchor it to a very solid object at an attachment point about level with your hips when in a kneeling stance. Position yourself so that you are facing directly opposite to the band in a quadruped position. Place the band around the leg that you wish to mobilize as close to the hip as possible, and ensure there is strong tension. Move the knee and hip of the leg being mobilized to approximately a 90/90 position, then kneel on the knee with the toes firmly engaged with the ground. Take the other leg back and extend it at the hip and knee with the toes firmly engaged with the ground. Flex the trunk forward so it is low and parallel with the ground. Extend both arms and plant them into the ground.

MOVEMENT
Perform small oscillations forward, away from the band, to help open up space in the hip. Push the trunk forward while maintaining full body tension throughout and let the band pull the hip posteriorly. Consider changing the angle of the hip being mobilized (by changing where the toes are contacting the ground). Repeat on the other side.

DOING IT RIGHT
- Engage enough tension through the heavy resistance band.
- Plant the feet and hands firmly into the ground for support.
- Engage the core for added stability.

SAFETY
If this creates discomfort that's OK, but if it's painful, abandon this technique.

BAND DISTRACTION DORSIFLEXION

This is a self-applied mobilization with movement. The goal is to improve dorsiflexion range of motion at the ankle, which may have been restricted due to tightness in the joint capsule. The band drives the talus bone into the mortise to help create space in the posterior aspect of the joint capsule that was restricting the motion.

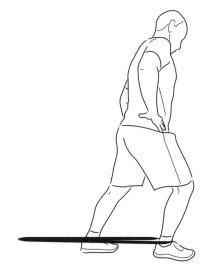

Figure 9.11
Band Distraction Dorsiflexion midpoint

START

Take a heavy resistance band and anchor it to a very solid object at a low attachment point. Stand facing the opposite direction of the attachment point and place the band over the front of the ankle joint (aim to get this between the two bony protuberances at the sides of the ankle). Step forward until there is a good amount of resistance felt pulling your leg back and firmly plant your foot (your knee should be stacked over your ankle). Move into a staggered stance, with the leg that has the band placed forward and the other leg a half step back. Drop down into an athletic stance with the knees bent. Place your hands on your hips and keep an upright trunk posture.

MOVEMENT

Slowly lean your weight into the forward leg. You will dorsiflex at your ankle and your knee will start to move past your toes. Continue to keep the foot firmly planted on the ground and maintain a tight upright posture through the trunk.

MIDPOINT

Once you can't move the knee over the toes any further, you have reached the end point and should hold this position for 10 seconds.

END

Slowly resist, coming back to the start position. Repeat on the other side and for the required number of reps.

VARIATION

Some people will perform this in a half-kneeling position with the knee of the back leg on the ground and the front leg bent to 90 degrees.

SLANT BOARD DORSIFLEXION

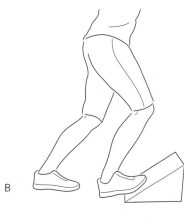

Figure 9.12
Slant Board Dorsiflexion stretching the gastrocnemius (A) and the soleus (B)

The slant board is without a doubt one of the most important pieces of equipment in any home gym. The ankle can reach about 30 degrees of dorsiflexion in weight bearing. Most slant boards have multiple positions, but we recommend going as aggressively toward 30 degrees as possible. This will benefit both the flat-arched and pronated groups of people as well as the high-arched and supinated groups, as both often have tightness in the calves (gastrocnemius and soleus), predisposing them to a number of overuse/chronic injuries. The muscles/tissues of the plantar fascia, Achilles tendon, gastrocnemius, hamstrings, sacrotuberous ligament and erector spinae make up what is described as the 'superficial back line' in Anatomy Trains *(sorry, we are academics so we have to nerd out every once in a while). The superficial back line is essentially the posterior kinetic chain. Remember, a faulty muscle in the chain could lead to injuries elsewhere along the chain. If you don't have a slant board, they are often available at the gym.*

START

Place the slant board in front of a wall. Place one foot on the slant board with the heel making contact on the bottom and the forefoot making contact toward the top. If you are unable to make solid contact with the heel, you will need to adjust the board to a less aggressive angle. The weight initially should be on the back foot, which is not making contact with the board, so you can adjust the placement of the foot. The trunk should be in an upright posture and hands can reach out against the wall for support.

Part 1 (gastrocnemius stretch): The knee on the front leg should be fully extended and the body's center of gravity should be over the heel of this foot.

Part 2 (soleus stretch): The knee on the front leg should be bent approximately 20 degrees and the body's center of gravity should be placed over the heel.

MOVEMENT

Gradually shift your weight forward on the leg contacting the board and lean in so that the center of gravity moves toward the toes. The trunk should continue to be held tight and will move closer to the wall. This should be performed for both the gastrocnemius and the soleus muscles separately. Each should be done in 3 repetitions of 30-second holds. Repeat on the other side.

VARIATION
If you don't have a slant board, an ankle rocker is another great device to help stretch the gastrocnemius and soleus muscles.

SOFT TISSUE MOBILITY WORK

Some of you may have gone to a rehabilitation clinician for some help with soft tissue mobility and received either Active Release Therapy (ART), strain-counterstrain technique, cupping, pin and stretch, or instrument assisted soft tissue mobilization (IASTM) – also known as Graston technique. These treatments work by improving the mobility of the muscle and fascia. Remember, all the muscles are surrounded by fascia and the interaction of the two will result in your available range of motion. It is greatly important for muscles to remain at their optimal resting length so they can create optimal tension. Postural syndromes result in the muscles on one side of the body being long and weak while the muscles on the other side of the body are short and facilitated. Often, trigger points will develop within the muscles, which then makes them short – rendering them suboptimal. Trigger points will often also give off referred pain patterns. While explaining the specific referred pain patterns falls beyond the purview of this book, you should understand that simply fixing a problematic trigger point may eliminate some of the pain that you have in an adjacent area of the body. Many of the treatments that rehabilitation clinicians use are therefore focused on reducing trigger points in the muscle and making the fascia around the muscles more supple, to allow for smooth, unrestricted, optimal motion.

However, you don't need to spend additional time and money seeking out the assistance of a rehabilitation clinician to mobilize your myofascia. Self-myofascial release can be performed easily and effectively to help maintain mobility. A 2015 systematic review[8] (a research paper that summarizes all the research on a topic) on the effects of self-myofascial release shows that it is useful for making short-term improvements to muscle flexibility and reducing muscle soreness without having negative effects on performance. The paper went on to recommend performing 3 sets of 30-second holds for each muscle.

To do this, every athlete should as a minimum have a foam roller and a hard rubber ball for their home gym so that they can perform self-myofascial release. Many people use the foam roller in a rolling pin or back-and-forth manner, spanning the entire muscle. Our recommendation is to find the tight area where the trigger points exist and simply let the weight of the body press against the trigger point, allowing it to "reset", thus making the muscle pliable again. Clinicians commonly do this technique with their hands and will hold for a minimum of about 30 seconds. It may feel uncomfortable at first, but you should feel a mushing sensation under that once taut area.

MYOFASCIAL TISSUES TO FOAM ROLL

As endurance athletes, we put our muscles and joints through the same repetitive motions for many miles and, over time, restrictions occur. Different sports place different demands on our muscles based on the movement patterns. Below, we've identified key muscles on which athletes should perform self-myofascial release. Running and cycling are lower extremity-dominant sports so targeting the muscles that surround the hip, knee, foot and ankle is recommended. By contrast, swimming is much more of an upper extremity-dominant sport, with the exception of the kick, which should be initiated from the glutes. Swimmers should therefore target the muscles of the trunk and shoulder. The smaller muscles of the shoulder will require a hard ball to target the correct location.

- Runners and cyclists: iliotibial band, quadriceps, hamstrings, adductors (groin), calves (gastrocnemius and soleus), gluteus maximus and gluteus medius, plantar fascia
- Swimmers: gluteus maximus, gluteus medius, iliotibial band, latissimus dorsi, triceps, pectoralis minor, infraspinatus

If the concept of performing mobility exercise is something new for you, there's no reason to be fearful. Remember, one of our goals is to pull you out of your comfort zone, teach you something you were unfamiliar with and get you faster. You can't build a better you without an open mind. If all we had you do was perform strength exercises, then sure, you'd have stronger, more powerful muscles, but you'd lack *functional movement*. Being able to move your joints through large functional ranges is what will make you an improved endurance athlete. Recognize that using mobility exercises that target areas that are prone to being restricted in athletes who participate in a particular sport is important for reaching new personal bests and keeping yourself healthy and training.

You triathletes out there may be wondering: "Do I have to do all of these?" The answer to that is … yes, but not each exercise on every day you train, we'll take it easy on you. Or perhaps you are a runner and don't have the "common problem areas" of a runner, but know you have a restriction in thoracic spine mobility like a cyclist. If this is the case, simply swap out some of these mobility exercises in your plan for the one that is more applicable to you. We recognize that people's restrictions can be individualized and using the right exercise to target those restrictions is important.

All of our training plans include mobility exercises done in conjunction with the strength exercises. When performed regularly, the mobility exercises will allow your muscles and joints to move through a larger, more desirable range of motion and ditch that poor, restricted movement that limits you from achieving your goals. Performing one without the other would be like Sonny without Cher. Mobility exercises allow our joints to move more freely, through greater ranges of motion and help keep our bodies balanced and primed for success.

1. Daley, M. J. and Spinks, W. L., 'Exercise, Mobility and Aging', *Sports Medicine*, 29(1) (2000), pp. 1–12
2. McDermott, B. P., Anderson, S. A., Armstrong, L. E., et al., 'National Athletic Trainers' Association Position Statement: Fluid Replacement for the Physically Active', *Journal of Athletic Training*, 52(9) (2017), pp. 877–895
3. Yamamoto, A., Takagishi, K., Kobayashi, T., Shitara, H. and Osawa, T., 'Factors involved in the presence of symptoms associated with rotator cuff tears: a comparison of asymptomatic and symptomatic rotator cuff tears in the general population', *Journal of Shoulder and Elbow Surgery*, 20(7) (2011), pp. 1133–1137
4. Tate, A., Turner, G. N., Knab, S. E., Jorgensen, C., Strittmatter, A. and Michener, L. A., 'Risk factors associated with shoulder pain and disability across the lifespan of competitive swimmers', *Journal of Athletic Training*, 47(2) (2012), pp. 149–158
5. Torres, R. R. and Gomes, J. L., 'Measurement of glenohumeral internal rotation in asymptomatic tennis players and swimmers', *The American Journal of Sports Medicine*, 37(5) (2009), pp. 1017–1023
6. McClure, P., Balaicuis, J., Heiland, D., Broersma, M. E., Thorndike, C. K. and Wood, A., 'A randomized controlled comparison of stretching procedures for posterior shoulder tightness', *The Journal of Orthopaedic and Sports Physical Therapy*, 37(3) (2007), pp. 108–114
7. Muyor, J. M., López-Miñarro, P. A. and Alacid, F., 'Spinal posture of thoracic and lumbar spine and pelvic tilt in highly trained cyclists', *Journal of Sports Science and Medicine*, 10(2) (2011), pp. 355–361
8. Beardsley, C. and Skarabot, J., 'Effects of self-myofascial release: A systematic review', *Journal of Bodywork and Movement Therapies*, 19(4) (2015), pp. 747–758.

10

UNLOCKING THE SECRET TO A STRONGER CORE WITH ANTI-ROTATION EXERCISES

Hopefully by now we have you convinced that incorporating regular resistance and mobility training into your overall endurance training program is going to make you a faster and more powerful athlete. When resistance training programs are properly periodized around your race season, there will be slightly different focuses based on where you are in the schedule. One area that will *always* benefit by being a focus is the strength of your core musculature. In all of our combined years working with athletes, we've never met one who couldn't benefit from a bit more core strengthening.

You've probably heard it a hundred times by now that your core is the most important area to strengthen for both injury prevention and peak performance. The reason some of you haven't fully embraced this concept is that nobody ever explains *why* the core is such a critical area to strengthen. Or, perhaps you have bought in, but your core strengthening program lacks direction and creativity. Once you understand how the body works, you'll understand why certain core exercises are superior to others.

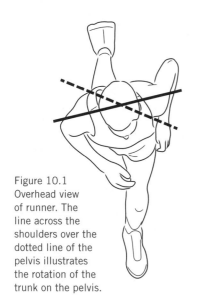

Figure 10.1 Overhead view of runner. The line across the shoulders over the dotted line of the pelvis illustrates the rotation of the trunk on the pelvis.

THE FUNCTION OF THE CORE IN ENDURANCE SPORTS

In a nutshell, the core is the pivot point for all functional movement. During running, the trunk continually rotates back and forth on the pelvis. In Figure 10.1, you can see an overhead view of a runner. As the right arm moves forward, the left leg moves forward and vice versa. If this didn't happen, we wouldn't propel ourselves, we'd just spin. There is a strong connection of the front of the right shoulder with the front of the left hip and vice versa. Because of this constant rotating back and forth of the trunk on the pelvis, it's quite common for runners who have a weak core to start having lower back pain after long training sessions. As a runner, having a strong core is crucial to improving power transfer and staying healthy.

During cycling, the ability to stabilize the pelvis while making a downstroke produces more power to the pedal. When you are out on your group rides, start taking notice of the hip and spine movements of your fellow riders out there (be sure you still have your eyes on the road for obstacles – you can't appreciate these movements when you're flying over your handlebars). It's likely you will see some riders who constantly have an S shape up their spine and hips and who rock excessively back and forth. Triathletes listen up! The S shape is even further exposed when we are riding in an aero position on a TT bike. This is an indication of one of two things: 1) poor core stability, or 2) quite possibly a seat height that's a bit too tall for the rider. If it is poor core stability, the rider is "leaking" valuable watts through that wimpy core. Additionally, for road racers coming out of the saddle for a sprint or MTB riders taking on a steep climb, it's critical to lock the core down to eliminate power "leaks." No matter the type of riding, we need to engage core muscles to minimize the hip hike/hip drop motion, which is really motion at the pelvis and trunk. The leg can produce greater force when it is coming from a steady, solid pelvis, so don't lose out on the ability to throw down some extra watts. In addition to the hip hiking issue, there is also a natural forward/backward rotation of the pelvis and trunk where they meet (although it is much smaller than that which occurs during running).

Riders who do not have a strong core (or have a poor bike fit) will often complain of lower back pain during longer rides. Having superior core strength is therefore especially critical for an IRONMAN triathlete since he/she will be spending a long time in the saddle followed by a long time on the run. Unfortunately, we've seen many triathletes struggling through back pain that could affect their ability to finish the race. Once again, having stability at the pivot point between the pelvis and the trunk becomes critical. Figure 10.2 shows the hip hike that you would see in a rider with a weak core.

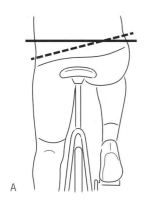
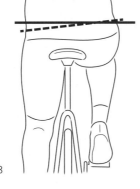

Figure 10.2
Excessive pelvic drop (A) and minimal pelvic drop (B). The solid line illustrates the connection of the trunk and pelvis. The dotted line illustrates how much movement occurs between the trunk and pelvis.

Freestyle swimming also makes use of this critical pivot point at the core. During swimming, we need to stabilize the core while kicking and rotating our trunk to breathe without allowing the pelvis to over-rotate. There is a strong connection with the posterior of the shoulder and the contralateral glute (as well as the anterior shoulder and contralateral hip). Have you ever seen someone who stops kicking when they turn to breathe? That's an indication that their glute muscle isn't connecting well with the shoulder by way of their core.

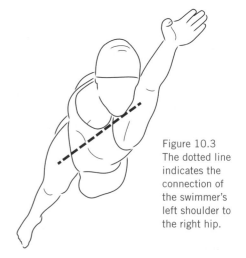

Figure 10.3
The dotted line indicates the connection of the swimmer's left shoulder to the right hip.

Figure 10.3 shows one side of the "X" pattern making the kinetic chain that links the shoulder to the contralateral hip. If the muscles of the kinetic chain are not functioning properly it will be detrimental to force production during the stroke, and could potentially become more of a problem if it causes asymmetrical movement that may put the shoulder in a vulnerable position for an overuse injury. We discuss this idea of kinetic chains further below.

UNDERSTANDING THE "X" KINETIC CHAINS

Pardon us while we nerd out a bit. We are academics at heart so we get excited about sharing information that we find interesting. We promise to put this in terms that you will understand and we hope that you'll then have an even better appreciation for the information. Put simply, we have a couple of "X" patterns by which muscles transmit forces through our bodies. Many rehabilitation specialists, such as physical therapists, physios and athletic trainers like RJ, are familiar with the book and the teachings in *Anatomy Trains* by Dr. Thomas Myers.[1] The reason we have to include this information for you is that it was game changing for RJ as a clinician when he read it some years ago. We think it will be just as game changing for you as an athlete and will help you unlock some hidden power as well as keeping your body balanced and healthy.

In his book, Myers describes seven distinct myofascial lines (kinetic chains), which help contribute to human posture and movement. It's important to understand that muscles don't work individually – they work together in kinetic chains. For example, to do a simple Biceps Curl, the muscles of the chest and back must contract to create a stable end point and the position of the wrist as dictated by the forearm musculature also has a role. If there is a weakness anywhere in this kinetic chain, it will ultimately affect the ability of the bicep muscle to generate force. Remember that myofascia is the combination of muscle and fascia. In Section 1, we discussed the importance of keeping the myofascia in the body well balanced. When balanced, the force vector produced by the muscles of the kinetic chain has a robust magnitude and is placed in the optimal direction. When we let any muscle become tight or weak or allow any fascia to become restricted, we will get out of balance and become susceptible to chronic/overuse injuries. Additionally, our performance will be limited since our force production through the kinetic chain will be affected. The magnitude of the force vector is smaller and the direction of forces is suboptimal.

It's quite common for a clinician to educate an athlete on the importance of the kinetic chain by stating 'your kinetic chain is only as strong as its "weakest link".' While this helps to make a point, one thing we've noticed from years of experience is that the area where the 'X' patterns cross (the core) happens to be the most crucial link! When this link fails, we lose the ability to generate power through the chain, which negatively affects our performance and leaves the muscles through the rest of the chain weakened. This may affect our joints, leading to overuse/chronic injury. Hopefully at this point you're saying 'Oh man, these kinetic chains sound important, can you please tell me more about the muscles that make up each of these chains and how they transmit forces?' Ask and you shall receive...

In his book, Myers details two kinetic chains that have the most impact on the rotations that occur during sports movements: 1) the spiral line and 2) the functional line. One pivot point we constantly have motion at whether we swim, bike or run is between the pelvis and the trunk. The muscles that make up the functional line and spiral line cross the pelvis and the trunk and help to create stabilization between the two segments. In Figure 10.4, you can see the functional and spiral lines with the "X" superimposed over them so you understand which muscles connect together to produce force.

The linkage of the muscles that make up the functional line (kinetic chain) is important to the movements in running, cycling and swimming. Earlier in this chapter, we discussed the pivot points of the trunk and pelvis that occur during each sport. While *some* movement is natural and is needed, this area does best if it has a good deal of stability, to limit excessive movement. A well-balanced functional line will help create this stability.

This kinetic chain has both an anterior (front) and posterior (back) portion to be aware of.

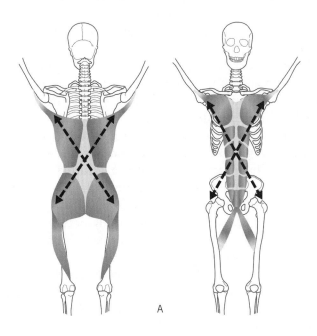

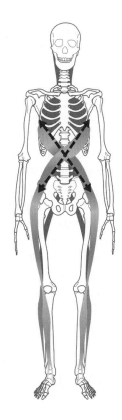

Figure 10.4
The functional lines (A) and spiral lines (B)
(from *Anatomy Trains*).[1]

The muscles/structures that make up the front functional line are the pectoralis major (chest), rectus abdominis (core) and the adductor (groin). In the front, to perform rotations, the right pectoralis generates tension through the rectus abdominis and the *opposite* hip adductor, resulting in trunk forward bend and rotation to that side. It can be thought of as half of an 'X'. The muscles/structures that make up the back functional line are the latissimus dorsi (upper back), thoracolumbar fascia (connection of mid and lower back), gluteus maximus (buttocks) and vastus lateralis (outside quad muscle). Similar to the way the front works, to perform rotations, the right latissimus dorsi will generate tension through the *opposite* gluteus maximus, resulting in trunk back bend with rotation to that side. When the front kinetic chain is balanced with the back kinetic chain and the right side is balanced with the left, we are able to effectively stabilize the pivot point of the trunk and pelvis.

Another kinetic chain – the spiral line – literally wraps around the body where you can visibly see the 'X' pattern that crosses the core. The most important link is in the middle (the muscles that highlight this important section are the serratus anterior and the obliques). Interestingly, the muscles that make up this kinetic chain run down the leg and also up to the neck. For those of you who crave an extra anatomy lesson, the muscles/structures that make up this line are the splenius capitis (the muscle at the base of the skull) > rhomboids on the opposite side (the muscle between the shoulder blades) > serratus anterior (the rib muscle) > external/internal oblique (the muscles that connect the ribs to the abdominal region) > tensor fascia latae (the hip muscle) on the opposite side > IT band > anterior tibialis (the front shin muscle) > peroneus longus (the lateral shin muscle) > biceps femoris (the hamstring) >sacrotuberous ligament > sacral fascia > erector spinae (the deep back muscles up the central back). Similar to the functional line, these work best at creating stability when they are balanced (the right side of the 'X' is similar to the left side of the 'X'). When the muscles that provide connection of the trunk and pelvis are strong, we can effectively generate tension and produce stability at this crucial point.

RJ remembers that when he was a student, the instructors were always telling him that "everything in the body is connected" but he couldn't conceptualize it because he was a visual learner. Once he had read *Anatomy Trains* and had seen the pictures of the myofascial lines, he had that "aha moment" that helped him to understand the kinetic chain concept. This allowed him to become a better sports medicine professional. Hopefully, now that we've shared this information, you too have gained a greater appreciation for how muscles and kinetic chains work, especially which kinetic chains are responsible for creating a strong, stable core. As endurance athletes who are completing training sessions with high volume/time spent in our sport, the sheer number of rotations that occur between the trunk and the pelvis is massive! If we ignore the importance of the stability of this most important link in the kinetic chain, we will most certainly struggle. Properly planned and executed resistance training is the best way to eliminate weak links in these kinetic chains.

Previously, we've described how rotation occurs in all of our endurance sports. Therefore, it should make sense that we will tell you to train with some rotational movements (often termed "anti-rotation"). The key to anti-rotation exercises is a slow, controlled eccentric movement along with a slow, controlled concentric movement.

One thing we've seen over the years working with numerous athletes is that they are performing core work either statically (Planks) or with movement only in the sagittal plane (Crunches). The mistake here is that this simply isn't how we move. It doesn't take into account the force production of the important kinetic chains – functional lines and spiral lines. Therefore, we suggest performing some anti-rotation exercises, along with the core exercises that you've been doing all along. This is because we've found weak, neglected oblique muscles to be the cause of a number of overuse/chronic injuries as well as being the "leak" in the kinetic chain when it comes to performance.

UPPING THE "ANTI"

So what is an anti-rotation exercise? Anti-rotation exercises involve resisting twisting to one side and maintaining a stable core position. Placing unbalanced or asymmetrical forces through the core helps to create stability by recruiting the muscles and ultimately strengthening them. As mentioned earlier, if the body *rotates* at the core (as in the pivot points discussed above regarding the runner, cyclist and swimmer), then it makes sense to do some rotational core exercises – however, the key to these will be that they are slow, controlled movements. We're sure you've seen exercises like a Rotational Medicine Ball Toss, which is plyometric in nature and helps to build power, but remember, we want to train with sport specificity, and in endurance sports, power at our core isn't what we need; rather, we need endurance. One of our favorite pieces of equipment to help with anti-rotation exercise is the TRX® Rip Trainer, though no special equipment is actually needed. Simply use uneven loads, and use your core to resist the twisting motion that the load is trying to create. The sport-specific exercises that will be introduced later in this section will include some of our favorite anti-rotation exercises.

Perhaps you now understand the concept of anti-rotation exercises, but you are still skeptical of their true value for providing core stability. Here are a couple of examples of athletes who had successful outcomes after incorporating these exercises.

We worked with a 30-year-old male age group triathlete who specialized in IRONMAN and IRONMAN 70.3 distances. He actually had a lot of experience doing resistance and mobility training and was getting his workouts in at least four times per week on top of his triathlon training. He was having recurrent SI joint dysfunction (lower back pain) that was affecting his performance, especially on the run. He admitted that he was a unilateral breather when swimming and was in the process of learning to become a bilateral breather. In thinking about his problems, we realized he had a side dominance issue (one side of his spiral line was working while the other was not), which brought him out of balance. The fix for him was quite easy – we simply added 2 sets of two anti-rotation exercises (we mixed it up so he didn't get bored) to his training days. His SI joint dysfunction went away in a month. Since then, he has become a proficient bilateral breather when swimming and continues to incorporate anti-rotation exercises in his training. He hasn't dealt with SI joint dysfunction since.

Another interesting client we worked with was a 25-year-old female elite age group triathlete. After qualifying for age-group Nationals for the Olympic distance, she starting preparing for two more IRONMAN 70.3 races on her schedule. Once her aerobic sport training sessions started to get longer, she started to get recurrent right knee pain when running and sometimes was dealing with tendinitis in her left shoulder when swimming. Like many triathletes we know, she used the "I don't have time to go to the gym" excuse and only went once per week. When we asked what she did at the gym, she said she used most of the machines and did a full body workout. She made two critical errors here: 1) unplanned workouts that lacked purpose and 2) failure to stress her muscles frequently enough to build strength. A movement assessment uncovered that her glute on the side of the knee pain was underperforming and dysfunctional.

If only one side of the "X" is functioning properly, the dysfunction in the other one is likely to lead to an injury. When considering how to manage her problems, we realized it would be best to take a kinetic chain approach and possibly "clean up" the dysfunction by assigning some anti-rotation exercises, on top of a full body biweekly strength training program. We therefore included 2 sets of two anti-rotation exercises, similar to what we used with our other client. Her overuse/chronic injuries quickly went away and she had a super year performing at a very high level.

THE COMMON CORE

The question we get all the time is "Can I still do some of the Crunches and Planks that I used to do?" Of course! All athletes can use a stronger core – therefore we support any repetitions performed that target core musculature (as long as your form is good). Just understand that some of these common core exercises *isolate* that particular muscle, which will help to improve the strength of just that muscle. It doesn't mean that it will improve the overall *functional strength* of your core. Whether we are swimming, biking or running, we constantly have rotation occurring between the trunk and pelvis, and there's no single muscle responsible for that – it's the product of kinetic chains. The only way to strengthen the muscles of the kinetic chains is through exercises that mimic those rotations – aka anti-rotation exercises! However, if you are able to isolate and improve the strength of one of the muscles involved in a kinetic chain, that should also help to improve the function of that chain, so feel free to continue those common core exercises you are so familiar with alongside the anti-rotation ones.

For those of you who aren't familiar with these few common core exercise gym staples, we've described them below.

Plank – Lie prone, prop up on your elbows and engage your toes to the ground. Elevate your body above the floor and hold the shoulders, hips, knees and ankles in a straight line. Engage your core muscles to keep the body rigid. Hold the position for at least 30 seconds. Remember to breathe.

Variations:
Side Plank – Lie on your side and prop up on the elbow of your bottom arm and your bottom foot. Engage the core muscles to hold the shoulders, hips, knees and ankles in a straight line.

High Side Plank - Perform the side plank but use a straight arm with the hand making contact with the ground rather than the forearm.

Crunch – Lie on your back and bend your knees to a 90-degree position while maintaining contact of your feet with the ground. Clasp your fingers behind your head, or cross your arms across your chest. Engage your core to lift your trunk off the ground enough so your scapulas come off the ground as well. Perform 10–15 repetitions.

Variations:
Crossover crunch – Use the same set-up for the crunch. When raising your trunk, move the shoulder toward the opposite knee and alternate through repetitions.

Butterfly crunch – Bend the legs so that the soles of the feet touch and the heels are brought closely to the buttocks. Lift the trunk in the same motion as the crunch.

Bird Dog – Assume a quadruped (hands and knees) position. Ensure that the knees are below the hips and the hands are below the shoulders. Keep the core muscles active to hold the low back in a neutral position. Simultaneously raise the arm and contralateral leg so that they become in line with the trunk and pelvis and then return to quadruped. Perform this movement slowly to limit motion between your low back and pelvis.

Variations:
If you are unable to hold the spine in neutral while performing the bird dog well, start by simply raising a single arm or a single leg to make the exercise easier.

Rowing Bird Dog – Perform the exercise as described above, but instead of raising your arm, perform a rowing motion with the arm while extending the contralateral leg back.

We hope you have just had that 'aha' moment like RJ did after reading *Anatomy Trains*. It made him a better sports medicine professional ... and we sincerely hope this new information makes you into a stronger endurance sports athlete. Just like you, we're all about seeing new personal bests, and purposeful core strengthening will let us achieve those goals.

As a recap, most purposeful core strengthening has to be performed in a way similar to how the trunk moves on the pelvis during our sport movement – and that's through anti-rotation exercises. Our programs therefore all feature these to optimally strengthen and balance the functional line and spiral line to keep the pivot point of the trunk and pelvis stable. If you've struggled with some lower back pain in the past, we're confident adding these exercises to your regular resistance training program will help correct some of the pain that was likely caused by dysfunction. This should unlock some hidden potential you have, so get ready and primed to make some key changes to your core strengthening routine and go out and crush the competition.

1. Myers, T., *Anatomy Trains: Myofascial meridians for manual and movement therapists,* 2nd ed. (Churchill Livingstone, 2009)

11

THE EXERCISES THAT EVERY ENDURANCE ATHLETE NEEDS TO KNOW

Building a resistance training program is like building a house and the Foundation Exercises in any program function in the same way as a foundation to a house. If it's rock solid, structurally sound and put together with expert craftsmanship, it puts the entire house in a good position to remain standing regardless of what may come its way. Establishing this solid foundation doesn't guarantee a great program will be constructed around it, but without a good foundation it's almost certain any training program will fail.

Mastering these six exercises and knowing how to manipulate sets, reps, rest intervals, volume, intensity and total workload will allow you to make the transition from being the new person in the gym to a seasoned vet. Also, learning variations of each of the six Foundation Exercises and knowing how/when to implement them will give you the tools you need to train at an appropriate intensity level throughout the year. For example, Barbell Back Squats are a great exercise, but don't necessarily need to be performed a few days before a race. Can we alter the load and use a Squat variation that will allow us to get similar muscular activation and mobility without the associated soreness to the lower extremity and loading of the torso? Yes, we absolutely can, and knowing when to make those changes is crucial to your long-term success in the gym and at the finish line.

There are countless exercises, variations of those exercises and modifications to those variations that will stress the musculature of the human body in a way that will develop strength and hypertrophy. Some of these exercises are great and will absolutely make the body bigger, stronger and more durable. Some are not so great because of issues like angle of pull, putting the body in a less than optimal position and an unfavourable risk vs. reward equation. For example, doing a heavy Barbell Front Squat while standing on a physioball might be great in theory, but in reality there are too many things that can go wrong to make it a realistic option for most people.

Angelo is a busy guy. He has a full-time job in college athletics, adjunct teaches several classes a semester, competes in several races every year and has a family. He loves to train, but sometime life gets in the way, so when he's pressed for time he makes it a priority to get in some of these Foundation Exercises. On good days, he has the time to actually get in the squat rack and do multiple sets of fairly heavy Back Squats. On days when he's fatigued from a long weekend run or has to hurry to pick up his daughter from school, he might do Medicine Ball or Band-resisted Squats. These are not exactly the same exercise, but both develop the Squat motor pattern, put the body through a good range of motion and develop the musculature of the lower extremity.

Similarly, there is a seemingly never-ending stream of specialized training equipment released into the marketplace. Some of these innovations are game changers that will become staples in strength training (padded plyo boxes, resistance bands, rubberized medicine balls, etc.), while some are clearly gimmicks that seem like jokes only a few years after release (the Shake Weight™). Access to the newest and most advanced training equipment is nice and may aid in some aspects of physical development, but is absolutely more luxury than necessity. Some of the best exercises and movements can be done with minimal equipment and in some cases no equipment at all. A testament to this is the fact that most "innovations" in the resistance training market are attempts to improve on these basic movements (the "perfect" Push-up, etc.) instead of introducing new movements.

Establishing a baseline level of proficiency in the Foundation Exercises is necessary before you attempt the more complicated movements that will allow for more variety and proper periodization throughout the year. While there are obviously things that make certain exercises painful or impossible for some people – due to previous injury, genetic factors, muscle imbalances, lack of mobility or the wear and tear of thousands of miles over the course of an endurance sport career – the goal should be to get as close to perfect technique as possible on these Foundation Exercises before more complicated variations are attempted.

In some cases, this may require people with experience to scale back and reduce the weight being lifted in order to perform movements properly. This is fine and a natural state of affairs when teaching the body to perform the movements correctly. For example, if you can squat 100lb (45kg) to about a 45-degree angle of knee flexion (commonly called a Quarter Squat), the weight on the bar may need to be reduced to 75lb (35kg) or less in order to do a "full" or 90-degree Squat (knee bent to 90 degrees with the upper leg parallel to the ground). The weight may be less, but the body will be getting a much better training stimulus and respond with improved strength.

Now that we understand the importance of a solid foundation, let's take a look at some of the building blocks we will use to make it strong, durable and able to withstand the test of time.

FOUNDATION EXERCISES

These six exercises are the foundation of your program. They are the exercises that only get cut out or skipped in extreme circumstances (the gym is on fire, you are in a body cast, etc.). If your training plan were an album, these are the big hits. If your training were a restaurant menu, these are the signature dishes. If your training plan were a house, these are the foundation.

Squats are arguably the best exercise for total body strength development available to the endurance athlete. More complicated movements like the Deadlift and Olympic weightlifting exercises may be better at developing peak power and strength, but when it comes to simplicity, safety, muscle fiber recruitment, enforcement of proper biomechanics (when done properly) and efficiency, the basic Bodyweight Squat is simply unmatched.

Traditionally, Squats are tough on the body and central nervous system. They require almost every muscle in the body to fire in a synchronized pattern that may feel unnatural to novice lifters. The interesting thing about this unnatural feeling is that in some ways the Squat is one of the most natural motor patterns for human beings. If a toddler drops a toy on the floor, their instinct is to squat down to pick it up. Most of the time, their Squat technique is textbook perfect with their weight shifted back toward their heels, their feet flat on the ground, hips moving backward before they start their descent, back flat, shoulder blades retracted and head neutral. Somehow, sometime between being a toddler and a teenager, this basic movement becomes incredibly challenging for most people. Whether we should blame our sedentary lifestyle, footwear choices, decreased mobility of the body as we mature or any combination of factors can be debated. What cannot be debated is that most endurance athletes would benefit from squatting in some capacity.

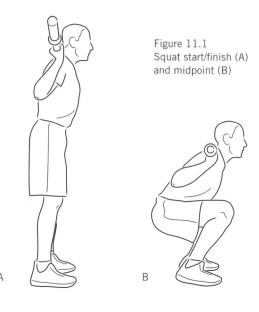

Figure 11.1
Squat start/finish (A) and midpoint (B)

A   B

START

Stand with feet shoulder-width apart or slightly wider with the toes pointed outward. The knees should be aligned with the toes and should remain that way throughout the movement. The hips are directly under the shoulders with the core held tight and the shoulder blades retracted. The head is neutral with the eyes looking slightly upward. Placement of resistance will vary based on type of Squat being performed.

MOVEMENT

Begin by pushing the hips backward to shift the weight toward the heels; this will keep the feet flat and properly align the body for the later stages of the descent. Once the weight is shifted posteriorly, lower the hips until the upper leg is parallel to the ground and the knee is at a 90-degree angle. The upper body should be almost totally upright with a "flat back" (no flexion of the lumbar vertebrae) and retracted shoulder blades.

MIDPOINT

Feet should be flat on the ground, knees bent to 90 degrees and behind the toes, the upper leg parallel to the floor and the upper body upright.

END

Return to the standing position by driving up from the bottom position with feet remaining flat on the ground and the majority of the force being exerted through the heels. The back should remain flat and shoulder blades should remain retracted. Repeat for the required number of reps.

DOING IT RIGHT

- Keep your feet flat with weight on the heels.
- Keep the knees behind the toes throughout the movement.
- The goal of every rep is getting the upper leg parallel to the floor and the knee to 90 degrees before coming out of the bottom position.
- Maintain a flat back with shoulder blades retracted.
- The pace should be slow and controlled on the down phase, but stand up "Like you mean it!"

SAFETY

- Master Bodyweight Squats before using any kind of resistance.
- Use spotters when necessary. *Note:* Make sure spotters know how to safely spot this lift.
- Even though the Squat is a "leg exercise", be cautious of total body positioning because back pain or injury can occur if it's done improperly.

VARIATIONS

- Barbell Back Squat – hold a barbell across the shoulders behind the head.
- Barbell Front Squat – a barbell is held across the shoulders in front of the head with shoulders flexed to 90 degrees.
- Barbell Overhead Squat – a barbell is held directly overhead with a wide grip, elbows fully extended and biceps in line with the ears. Start with very light weights as a barbell or even a wooden dowel might be enough resistance until this advanced movement is mastered.
- Dumbbell Goblet Squat – hold a dumbbell just under the chin.
- Medicine Ball Squat – hold a medicine ball in front of the chest.
- Squat and Press or Thrusters – dumbbells are held at the shoulders during the descent of the Squat and then pressed upward on the way up. Elbows should be fully extended when the standing position is reached.
- Box Squats – A box is placed just behind the lifter and the squat is performed until the glutes and hamstrings touch the box. Box height should be set to just below the kneecap to allow the lifter to reach a 90-degree angle at the knee.
- Bodyweight Squats – Perform the squat using only bodyweight for resistance. Hands can be placed behind the head or the arms can be extended to counterbalance the movement.

Squat variations

There are more Squat variations than IRONMAN races. Most of these are valuable and have a place in a training program. Picking the right variation for your body at any particular time in training is a skill that you will develop with more experience in the gym. If it's the day after a light run in the off-season, now's the time to load up some plates and put the bar on your back. If it's the day after a hilly 10-mile (16km) run at race pace, Bodyweight Squats or light Medicine Ball Squats are a better option.

LUNGE

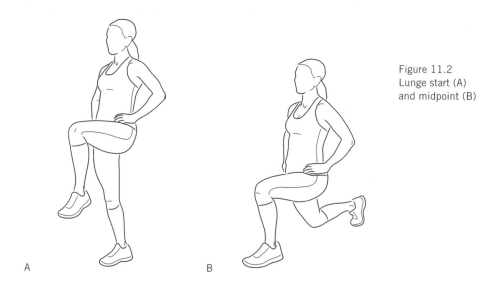

Figure 11.2
Lunge start (A)
and midpoint (B)

A   B

If the Squat is the best way to develop total body strength on two legs then the Lunge is the best way to develop strength in the legs while they are moving independently, which is how most endurance activities are performed. To put it another way, if Squats are the Avengers *movies, Lunges are like* Iron Man *and* Captain America *films: they don't necessarily bring together all the key players at the same time, but they are absolutely necessary to building the complete franchise. Start with Bodyweight Lunges before adding resistance.*

START

Stand with feet shoulder-width apart or slightly wider, with the toes slightly pointed outward. The knees should be aligned with the toes and remain that way throughout the movement. The hips are directly under the shoulders with the core held tight and shoulder blades retracted. The head is neutral with the eyes looking slightly upward. Placement of resistance will vary based on the type of Lunge being performed.

MOVEMENT

Raise the left leg until the upper leg is parallel to the ground with the ankle dorsiflexed (toe pulled up toward the knee). The toe should be slightly behind the knee and pulled upward toward the knee. Keep the right foot anchored in position and extend the left knee as the body moves forward until the left foot is placed firmly on the ground far enough from the starting point that the Lunge can be completed with the lower limb remaining perpendicular to the floor. Once this position has been firmly established, lower the body until the right knee is about 1 inch (2.5cm) from the floor and then forcefully push off the left foot to return the body to the starting position.

MIDPOINT

The upper body and the front shin should be parallel to each other and perpendicular to the floor. The front knee should be bent to 90 degrees with the upper leg parallel to the ground and the back knee should also be bent to 90 degrees with the knee about 1 inch (2.5cm) from the floor. The upper body should be upright and centered over the back knee. The front foot is flat while the back foot is on the ball/toes.

END

Return to the starting position, ready to perform the movement on the opposite leg. Repeat for the required number of reps.

DOING IT RIGHT

- If the front shin is not perpendicular, the athlete has not stepped the correct distance away from the starting point. One way to help this is to put tape or some other marker on the ground to visually show how far to step forward for each rep.
- If the upper body does not remain upright (in most cases, the back will round and force the upper body to lurch forward), it most likely indicates a weakness in the core. Until core strength is improved, resistance should be reduced or even eliminated until this can be done properly.

SAFETY

- Master Bodyweight Lunges before adding resistance.
- Incorporate Lunges into daily warm-ups and use plenty of variations of this basic movement a few days per week to master technique and develop proper motor patterns.

VARIATIONS

- Dumbbell Lunge – dumbbells are held in each hand with the arms hanging at the sides of the body.
- Barbell Lunge – barbell is placed across the shoulders behind the head.
- Barbell Front Position Lunge – place the barbell across the shoulders in front of the head with the hands on the barbell, elbows flexed and the upper arms parallel to the ground.
- Barbell Overhead Lunge – take a wide grip on a barbell and extend the bar directly overhead. Perform the specified number of lunges while keeping the elbows fully extended, biceps in line with the ears and shoulder blades pulled tight against the rib cage.
- Walking Lunge – after each Lunge is performed, the back leg steps forward to become the front leg for the next rep and the body moves forward throughout the set. This is a great variation for endurance athletes because it adds a forward propulsion component. You can also add resistance to the Walking Lunge in the form of dumbbells, barbells, kettlebells, a medicine ball or a weighted vest.
- Reverse Lunge – this employs the same technique as a regular Lunge except the initial step is taken backward and the foot is placed behind the body before the downward motion is initiated.

HIP HINGE (AKA POSTERIOR CHAIN DEVELOPMENT)

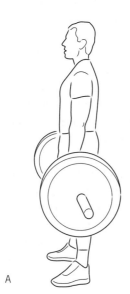

Figure 11.3
Hip Hinge (Romanian
Deadlift) start/finish
(A) and midpoint (B)

A

B

The Hip Hinge is one of the hardest movements to teach and master thanks to a range of factors, including lack of hamstring flexibility, poor hip mobility, poor posture, lack of lower back strength, inability to keep the scapulae retracted with resistance, and poor kinesthetic awareness. This can be due to spending too much time in the seated position (cars, desks, computers, etc.) or hunched over video game controllers and cell phones. There is also a natural inclination to overtrain the quads (aka the muscles you can see) and undertrain the hamstrings. These factors, combined with the natural strength deficit of the hamstrings compared to the quads, puts many endurance athletes in a weak position when they train and also at possible risk for injury.

If we view the lower extremity as a car, Squats and Lunges would be the engine and their strength could be measured in horsepower. Hip Hinge exercises like Romanian Deadlifts (aka RDLs), Good Mornings and Kettlebell Swings can be viewed as the braking system. If the strength/power of these systems are not equal (or fairly close) then the athlete is most likely on course for injury or poor performance in the same way a car with an incredibly powerful engine but weak brakes is on course for disaster.

Mastering the Hip Hinge is essential to balancing the strength of the knee extensors (the "kick" phase of running or swimming and the push phase of cycling) and the knee flexors (the recovery phase of running or the pull phase of cycling). The posterior chain can be trained with other methods, such as Machine Leg Curls, Glute Ham Raises or partner-assisted Leg Curls, and while these movements all address knee flexion and are valuable components to a comprehensive resistance training program, most athletes cannot handle enough resistance to actually address the natural imbalance between extensors and flexors using these exercises.

To prove this idea, think of a person who is a "good squatter" and can handle a hefty weight on a Barbell Back Squat with quality technique. This same person cannot leg curl anywhere near that amount of weight. In our experience in the field, about 30–50 percent of what an athlete can successfully squat can be leg curled and sometimes this number is significantly lower. If we aim to balance anterior to posterior strength ratio, we need to become proficient at the Hip Hinge in order to add resistance to exercises like Romanian Deadlifts and volume to exercises like Kettlebell Swings and thereby stimulate the musculature of the posterior chain enough to make significant strength gains.

There are multiple exercises that address this Hip Hinge motion, but we will take an in-depth look at the Barbell Romanian Deadlift or RDL as the baseline version of this movement. If necessary, there are multiple regressions (see Table 2.1 on p.20) if Barbell Romanian Deadlifts are not possible at the present time, and various progressions that can be implemented when you are ready. However, a Barbell Romanian Deadlift (even with minimal resistance at first) is a reasonable goal for most healthy adult endurance athletes.

Hamstrung

Hamstring injuries are incredibly common in all sports. Hamstring tightness and weakness is also incredibly common in athletes. These facts are not unrelated! Whether you have strained your own hamstring or had a professional player's hamstring pull ruin your fantasy season, chances are you have been affected by a hamstring injury in some capacity. Developing hamstring strength and mobility is the equivalent of doing preventative maintenance on your car. Regular oil changes don't guarantee you won't ever have car trouble, but they improve your chances of avoiding issues.

START

Stand with feet hip-width apart with the majority of the weight shifted toward the heels. Knees are slightly bent and aligned with the toes and should not move from this position throughout the movement. The upper body is erect with the shoulder blades retracted and the entire torso is leaning slightly in front of the hips from the waist. Arms are relaxed with a shoulder-width grip on the bar that is in contact with the quads.

MOVEMENT

Begin easing the bar down the legs while maintaining contact during the entire motion. This will give the body a mechanical advantage by keeping the body's center of gravity and the bar's center of gravity close to each other and thereby allowing more resistance to be handled and decreasing the chance of injury. During the descent, the back should remain flat, the hips should remain high and there should be very little movement at the knee or ankle while the hip is "hinging" to lower the bar toward the ground.

MIDPOINT

"The midpoint goal of a Romanian Deadlift is a 90-degree angle at the hip with the torso parallel to the ground." This may not be possible for beginners or people with abnormally inflexible or weak posterior chains. The initial goal should be to get as close to this position as possible with the lower back flat and the shoulders pulled back. As soon as the lower back starts to flex or round or the shoulder girdle starts to pull forward, the descent should stop, the body should be repositioned and the movement should be performed within that range of motion until strength and flexibility are improved to complete the movement to the goal position safely.

END

Once the upper body is parallel to the ground, the athlete should return to the standing position while maintaining proper posture, keeping the bar in contact with the legs and the movement occurring at the hip. This movement should be felt in the glutes/hamstrings. If you feel back pain/discomfort then the movement is most likely being performed incorrectly or through too big a range of motion for your current strength/mobility level. Repeat for the required number of reps.

DOING IT RIGHT

- Flat lower back – the movement should be initiated at the hips with minimal movement of the vertebral column. If rounding of the lumbar spine (lower back) occurs, the bulk of the work moves from the glutes and hamstrings to the lower back and the movement can become dangerous.
- Big chest or shoulders pulled back – shoulder blades should be retracted to be tight against the back of the ribcage and chest muscles should be protruding forward.
- Weight on heels – weight should be balanced near the back of the foot and the toes should be able to move with minimal disruption to balance and posture.
- Move at the hip instead of the knee – the knees should be slightly bent when each rep is started and there should be almost no movement at the knee joint after this initial positioning.
- The bar stays in constant contact with the legs – maintaining good posture and keeping the center of gravity of the bar as close as possible to the body's center of gravity are both crucial to safely and effectively performing this exercise. The best way to do this is to keep the bar as close to the legs as possible throughout each rep.

- Aim to get the upper body parallel to the floor without posture breakdown – if the upper body is parallel to the ground, the hip is most likely at a 90-degree angle and this is a good indicator that you are moving through the proper range of motion.

TIPS

- Start with very little resistance (just the barbell or possibly a PVC pipe or dowel).
- Incorporate some kind of Hip Hinging in all training sessions to ingrain the proper motor pattern. This can even be part of the warm-up if done with no resistance.
- Once good technique has been established, don't be scared to put some weight on the bar.

SAFETY

- Only move through a range of motion that can be performed safely without any rounding of the lower back or shoulder girdle.
- Keep the weight shifted toward the heels and the bar in contact with the legs to align the centers of gravity.
- If discomfort or strain is felt in the lower back, the exercise is being performed incorrectly and technique needs to be changed or improved.

VARIATIONS

- Bodyweight Good Morning – perform the Romanian Deadlift with your hands behind your head. This is great during warm-ups or stretching.
- Kettlebell Swings – reach down using Romanian Deadlift form to grab a kettlebell from between your legs. Hold the kettlebell with two hands and swing it forward as you extend the back.
- Dumbbell Romanian Deadlifts – use dumbbells rather than a barbell and perform the same motion.
- Single Leg Dumbbell Romanian Deadlifts – stand on one leg and hold a dumbbell in the hand on the opposite side of the

planted leg. As you hinge at the hip, the back leg goes back for a counterbalance.

- Deficit Romanian Deadlifts on elevated platform – stand on an elevated platform to allow the plates to go further than the bottoms of the feet and provide a greater range of motion.

Other posterior chain exercises

- Machine Leg Curls – Supine or Seated Leg Curls on a machine designed for knee flexion are a great way to isolate the hamstrings.
- Physioball Leg Curls – while lying on your back with your heels resting on a physioball and hips bridged off the ground to put the body in a straight line from ear to ankle, slowly flex the knees to roll the physioball toward the hips while keeping the hips elevated. Slowly roll the ball back to the starting position.
- Slide Board or Towel Leg Curls – lie on the ground with the hips elevated and the heels on a towel that is placed on either a slide board or hardwood floor. Flex the knees to drag the towel across the surface until further flexion is not possible. Slowly extend the knees to return to the starting position.
- Glute-ham Raises – use a glute-ham or hyperextension bench to lock the ankles in a fixed position where the knees are situated on the front pads of the bench. Forcefully flex the knees and drive the knees into the pads so the body is pulled to an upright position. Slowly extend the knees to return to the starting position.
- Partner Leg Curls – kneel on a pad/mat and have a partner brace the lower legs on the surface. Slowly lower your upper body (knees to head) to the ground with your hands in a "ready" position to catch yourself at the bottom of the movement. When your body is parallel to the floor and your hands touch the ground, push yourself back to the starting position.

Note: These are all good ways to develop the musculature of the posterior chain, but when it comes to total body strengthening and mastering a motor pattern that will aid in quality movement, incorporating some kind of Hip Hinge is the best option. As training progresses and the athlete gains experience and strength it is optimal to view the Romanian Deadlift (and variations) as the "big exercise" of the workout and the other movements as the "auxiliary exercises" of the session.

HIP BRIDGE

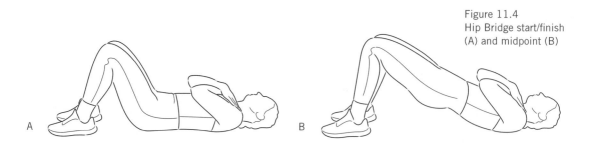

Figure 11.4
Hip Bridge start/finish
(A) and midpoint (B)

The ability to forcefully extend the hip is fundamental to forward propulsion in running, swimming and cycling, and doing so while maintaining a stable core and proper posture can be the difference between dragging yourself across the finish line and celebrating a new personal best.

There are various types of specialized machines to make resisted hip extension possible, most of which are expensive, somewhat difficult to find in a commercial health club and don't demand the upper body and core work in a way that will functionally transfer to the track or pool. While a few of these machines have a place in a comprehensive training program, some of the best ways to train hip extension in a way that will impact most endurance sports don't require any special equipment or resistance beyond the body's own weight.

Working Hip Extension or Hip Bridges into a training program is a bit of a tricky proposition. The movement clearly works the core muscles to keep the upper body in a good position while the hip is extending, but it can also be viewed as a hamstring-dominant movement based on the amount of stress placed on the posterior chain to perform the exercise properly. In most cases, it's best to view this movement as a Foundation Exercise and plan sets, reps and resistance accordingly while acknowledging that it's very taxing on the core muscles and that lower training loads for the abdominals, lower back and obliques can be used on days with a moderate or higher number of Hip Bridges.

START

Lie on the ground in Sit-up position with the feet flat on the floor, knees flexed and the heels as close to the body as possible. Relax the upper body and cross the arms in front of the chest. If this position is too difficult, the arms can be extended away from the body and the palms can be placed flat on the floor. This will provide a bigger base of support until enough strength and balance is developed to cross the arms on the chest.

MOVEMENT

Forcefully drive the heels into the floor and extend the knees and hips so that the pelvis moves up toward the ceiling with the heels and shoulders firmly planted on the ground.

MIDPOINT

The heels, shoulders and back of the head maintain contact with the ground while the hips are extended as high as possible with the core held tight. Ideally, the knee, hip, shoulder and ear should all be aligned and there should be no bend in the waist or "dip" in the hip/pelvis area.

END

Slowly lower the hips back to the ground while keeping the arms crossed and the core tight. Repeat for the required number of reps.

DOING IT RIGHT

- Drive the heels into the floor as you press your hips to the ceiling.
- Continue driving the hips straight up until the ear, shoulder, hip and knee are aligned.
- Keep the head and both shoulder blades in contact with the ground for the entire number of desired reps.

TIPS

- Start with a slow tempo and work on holding/squeezing the top position properly before progressing to heavier resistance.
- If performing the movement with arms crossed is too difficult due to a lack of balance, begin with the arms extended and palms flat on the floor. This will establish a wider base and allow the proper muscles to fire with less resistance. As this version is mastered, move the hands in closer to the body to reduce the width of the base and make the exercise more demanding, until the arms can eventually be taken off the ground and crossed on the chest.

SAFETY

- This movement is fairly taxing to the core and posterior chain. Plan for soreness the first few times it is performed.
- Work toward a full range of motion so that the knee, hip, shoulder and ear are all aligned when the hip is fully extended.
- Keep the core tight and pull the belly button toward the back during the entire movement while working on proper breathing.

VARIATIONS

- Resisted Hip Bridge – do the exercise with a weight plate, medicine ball, barbell or kettlebell across the hips.
- Elevated Hip Bridge – raise the shoulders on to a bench to make the exercise more difficult.
- Single Leg Hip Bridge – take one leg off the ground and extend that knee straight out away from the body and perform the same movement with one leg at a time.
- Banded Hip Bridge – perform the exercise with a resistance band just below the knees to ensure there is no knee valgus.

Figure 11.5
Push-up start/finish (A) and midpoint (B)

The ability to both push and pull with the musculature of the upper body is severely lacking in some endurance athletes. Whether this is the result of genetic predisposition, lack of training, range of motion issues or a combination of factors can be debated. What cannot be debated is that proper functioning and an adequate level of strength in the upper body will aid in both endurance performance and normal activities of daily living.

There is a generally accepted principle that the upper body has five angles of push and five angles of pull. For now, let's focus on the angles of push and worry about the angles of pull when we look at Pull-ups. If the upper body anatomy is functioning properly, the body should be able to push in roughly 180 degrees of motion, ranging from pressing straight overhead to straight down from the shoulder. Since training in all 180 degrees would take forever, require a mind-numbing amount of equipment and there is a large amount of crossover with the musculature that is used in many of the positions, most training programs focus on five main positions from which to push.

Table 11.1 opposite lists the five possible angles of push, the prime movers or main muscle activated during that movement and the popular exercises that stress those muscles and that angle. It is important to train all five angles on a regular basis to develop strength throughout the entire range of motion.

For this reason, an angle should only be avoided if there is an injury preventing that movement from being done properly and without pain. Please keep in mind that these degrees can be altered slightly to allow for individual anatomical differences

ANGLE	PRIME MOVERS	POPULAR EXERCISES
Overhead press	Deltoids	Shoulder Press with Dumbbells or Barbell
45-degree incline press	Deltoids and pectoralis major	Incline Bench Press or Decline Push-up
Horizontal press	Pectoralis major	Bench Press or Push-ups
45-degree decline press	Pectoralis major and triceps	Decline Bench Press or Hands Elevated Push-ups
Vertical downward press	Triceps	Triceps Press or Dips

Table 11.1

and modified for injuries if they are incredibly uncomfortable or prevent you from performing the exercise safely. Also, not all exercises or angles are for all people. For example, overhead presses are a great way to build the musculature of the shoulder girdle, but if they cause pain due to impingement or immobility then they should be replaced by a more comfortable option until the issue has been addressed and the body has returned to proper functioning.

Also, some of the angles may not be ideal for some endurance athletes due to the nature of their sport. Swimmers deal with incredible amounts of stress on their shoulders by moving their bodies through the steady resistance of water for potentially hundreds or even thousands of miles over the course of a year. For this reason, we have found that the reward of overhead pressing (stronger shoulders and related musculature) is usually not worth the risk (overuse injuries, pain, inflammation, etc.) for most swimmers.

So, not all pushing exercises are right for all bodies. That said, the horizontal push, which engages the musculature of the chest, shoulders, back and arms to move the hands straight away from the chest, is the safest and most effective way to build upper body strength. Also, it is the simplest or most foundational of the ways our body can push and should be established and perfected before other angles are attempted. The most basic way the body can push horizontally that requires no equipment and a very low level of strength and coordination is the basic Push-up. It is for this reason this exercise is one of the most popular exercises in history and has stood the test of time, being used from the earliest records of physical training right through to the most current trends in the modern fitness industry. Other options, which require equipment, are the Dumbbell or Barbell Bench Press.

And yet despite the basic Push-up being one of the most rudimentary ways the human body can push and the foundation of all other pushing exercises, a shocking number of people cannot perform even a few reps correctly. Keep in mind that these are not just overweight, sedentary people who haven't done anything physical since their gym teachers forced them to exercise in high school. A lot of competitive endurance athletes with low bodyweights, a healthy BMI (Body Mass Index) and who run hundreds of miles a month cannot do a proper Push-up.

It may be unclear how doing a Push-up will help with most endurance sports, but to keep it simple and not rehash what has been stated in other sections, a stronger upper body will result in better posture, improved breathing, more efficient running mechanics and a decreased risk of injury and premature fatigue. One of the clearest ways to reap these rewards that requires nothing besides your body is the exercise that has been around longer than almost any other.

START

Lie prone (aka on your stomach) on the ground with your toes curled to the floor and your hands flat on the ground directly under your shoulders. Your elbows should be pinched in and roughly 45 degrees away from the ribcage and the head should be neutral or looking directly at the floor.

MOVEMENT

Push both hands into the ground with equal force to raise the body until your elbows are fully extended. The core should be engaged with a focus on pulling the belly button into the back and keeping the shoulders, hips, knees and ankles in a straight line.

MIDPOINT

Arms are fully extended and the body is in a straight line from the ear to the ankle. Shoulder blades are retracted and the body looks "flat like a table".

END

Arms are bent with the elbows around 45 degrees off the ribcage and the chest is back on the ground with the hands directly under the shoulders. Ideally, the entire body should touch the ground at the same time. If a single body part hits the ground way ahead of the others it is an indication that there is a weakness in the kinetic chain and that weakness must be identified and addressed if good Push-up technique is going to be achieved. Repeat for the required number of reps.

DOING IT RIGHT

- Place your hands directly under your shoulders so that the arms are perpendicular to the ground when they're fully extended.

- Keep the core (abdominals, obliques and lower back musculature) tight for the duration of every set.
- The body should rise and lower as one unit or like a "table" or "board."
- Keep the elbows in or the upper arms about 45 degrees off the ribcage. This will eliminate unnecessary stress on the shoulders.

TIPS

- If you are not yet strong enough to do "real" Push-ups, try one of the variations listed below, but focus on the quality of each rep over the quantity of reps.
- Continue to use Push-ups to supplement training even after more complex movements have been implemented. (For example, a few sets of Push-ups are a great way to end a predominantly upper body day in the weight room.)
- Push-ups are a fantastic way to get some upper body training in if you can't make it to the gym, so try knocking out some sets after your run or as soon as you get out of the pool or off your bike.

SAFETY

- Limit "chicken winging" or having the elbows very far away from the body during the range of motion. This places an undue amount of stress on the shoulders and can make the exercise painful or dangerous for people who are already stressing their upper bodies, such as swimmers.
- Limit the body moving up or down in disjointed phases or "doing the worm" (if you remember old-school breakdancing moves). This normally indicates a lack of core strength and will cause pain if done repeatedly over time.

VARIATIONS

- Hands Elevated Push-ups – the hands are elevated on a bench while the feet stay on the floor. This puts the body at a roughly 45-degree angle, which makes performing a Push-up easier than being parallel to the floor.
- Eccentric/negative Push-ups – these involve going slowly during the down phase of the Push-up to fire the muscles eccentrically. They can be done for short durations (3–5 seconds per rep) for beginners who are struggling with Push-ups or for longer durations (8–15 seconds per rep) for experienced lifters who want more of a challenge.
- Barbell Bench Press – lie on a horizontal bench with feet flat on the floor and buttocks and upper back in contact with the pad. Grip the barbell with hands shoulder-width apart and slowly lower the bar until it touches the chest. Keep the elbows at a roughly 45-degree angle away from the ribcage and forcefully return the bar to the starting position.
- Barbell Incline Bench Press – perform the Barbell Bench Press with the bench set to a 45-degree incline.
- Dumbbell Chest Press – lie flat on a horizontal bench while holding one dumbbell in each hand with the elbows fully extended. Slowly lower both dumbbells to chest level and then forcefully extend both arms to return to the starting position.
- Alternating Dumbbell Chest Press – perform the dumbbell bench press with one side of the body while stabilizing the other side with the arm fully extended and the dumbbell over the shoulder/chest. Alternate which side is working and which side is stabilizing for the desired number of reps.
- Alternating Dumbbell Incline Chest Press – perform the Alternating Dumbbell Chest Press on a 45-degree inclined bench.
- Unstable Surface Chest Press – perform the chest press on an unstable surface such as the physioball. BOSU ball or balance board.
- Knees Down Push-ups – these are Push-ups with the knees on the floor instead of the feet. This creates a smaller mass to elevate from the floor and is good for people who are new to resistance training.
- Resisted Push-ups – using rubber bands, weighted vests or any additional resistance to make Push-ups more challenging.
- Suspension Trainer Push-ups – perform push-ups grasping the handles of the suspension trainer.
- Bench Dips – support the body with the hands placed at the edge of a bench, the knees bent to 90 degrees and the feet flat on the floor. Slowly flex the elbows so the hips move toward the ground. When the hips reach about 1 inch (2.5cm) from the ground, use the triceps to forcefully extend the elbows until they are fully extended and the body returns to the starting position.

Figure 11.6
Pull-up start/finish
(A) and midpoint (B)

Much like in the lower body, if the posterior muscles of the upper body (mainly the lats, rhomboids and rear deltoids – aka "The Back" in bodybuilding terms) are weak or significantly weaker than the anterior muscles (mainly the pectoralis major and minor and the anterior deltoid), range of motion issues, poor movement patterns and injury will often result.

This issue is compounded by two main factors that place many people in a poor position (pun intended) regarding back strength. The first is the genetic predisposition that many people are naturally stronger at pushing than pulling. To prove this, ask an untrained group of people to do Push-ups and Pull-ups and the majority will be able to perform more quality Push-ups than Pull-ups. The second is an issue that can be blamed on a combination of society, culture and natural human vanity. If endurance athletes have weight trained at all, they have normally performed pushing exercises like Push-ups, Bench Presses and Dumbbell Presses. If you disagree, go into any health club and see what piece of equipment gets more use, the bench press or the Lat Pull-down machine. Furthermore, if you put most inexperienced people in a gym they will flock to the bench or dumbbells (to do some kind of pressing movement) like runners to the water station at the 22nd mile (35th kilometre) of a marathon on a hot race day. This may be a product of not being properly educated about the importance of the back musculature, feeling a sense of comfort with exercises they know how to perform or the natural human inclination to train the parts of the body that are visible every time they look in the mirror. While the actual causes for this situation can be debated for days, it's clear that the majority of people perform way too many pushing exercises at the expense of the equally (if not more so) important pulling exercises.

Also, let's be clear that there is nothing wrong with pushing exercises and they have a place in any comprehensive strength training program. If the upper body is going to be strong and durable, exercises such as Push-ups, Bench Presses and Shoulder Presses and their various progressions and regressions are valuable movements during all phases of training. However, these exercises should be balanced with an equal amount* of pulling exercises for the upper back.

(*Many strength training programs advocate doing two or three times as much pulling for the upper body as pushing to balance out the effects of a lifetime of doing excessive push work. While this philosophy has a place when working with people who have trained incorrectly for years and whose push/pull ratio is very unbalanced, it is not usually necessary when dealing with endurance athletes who have very little experience with resistance training. However, the exact ratio of push to pull exercises can be modified based on the individual, their training history and their anatomical differences.)

Much like the push muscles, there are five main angles for the pull muscles. These should all be addressed in order to build a strong back and develop a balanced body, but the most basic of these exercises, which will be the foundation of almost all back training, is the Pull-up and the associated progressive and regressive versions.

Table 11.2 below lists the five angles of pull that are possible for the human body, the prime movers or main muscles activated during that movement and the popular exercises that stress those muscles and that angle. Pulling exercises are incredibly important for endurance athletes because they allow the body to maintain good posture, have good running mechanics and efficient breathing techniques during long sessions/events.

ANGLE	PRIME MOVERS	POPULAR EXERCISES
Overhead pull	Latissimus dorsi	Pull-ups or Lat Pull-down
45-degree incline pull	Latissimus dorsi	Leaning Back Lat Pull-down
Horizontal pull	Latissimus dorsi and rhomboids	Inverted Row, Dumbbell Row or Seated Machine Row
45-degree decline pull	Latissimus dorsi, rhomboids and trapezius	Low Row
Vertical pull	Trapezius	Shrugs

Table 11.2

START

Place your hands shoulder-width apart on a horizontal bar with your thumbs wrapped around the bar to develop grip strength, with your body hanging straight down. The knees can be flexed to slightly lessen the resistance and legs can be crossed at the ankle to aid in body control, but neither of these is mandatory and their use is largely based on personal preference.

MOVEMENT

Using the back musculature (instead of the momentum generated by swinging the body), pull the body to the bar until the chin is above it and the upper chest is in contact with the bar.

MIDPOINT

The chin is above the bar, the upper chest is touching the bar and the body is hanging vertically and relatively still.

END

Slowly lower the body to the hanging position while eccentrically controlling the back muscles and not "falling" or "flopping" back to the starting position. Lowering slowly and under control will avoid injury caused by undue stress to the shoulders and elbows, and controlling for tempo during the downward phase is a good way to ramp up the intensity of a very basic exercise. Repeat for the required number of reps.

DOING IT RIGHT

- Aim for full arm extension or getting all the way down to start each set and between every rep.
- Make sure the chin is rising over the bar at the highest point of every rep performed.
- Maintain a slow and controlled pace on the way down of every rep.

TIPS

- Pull-ups will be very difficult or impossible for many novice lifters. Have a plan for progression and goals to keep moving in the right direction.
- Use a spotter or assistance bands when first attempting Pull-ups.
- Keep track of how many good reps can be performed and build it into your programming to attempt a personal best reasonably often.

SAFETY

- Limit swinging or "kipping" at all costs. This is not at all a shot at CrossFit; if you are an elite CrossFitter and competing at a high level, then kipping absolutely produces a mechanical advantage over traditional or strict Pull-ups, but there's really no need for this for the overwhelming majority of the population.
- If regular Pull-ups produce pain or discomfort, experiment with different grips and grip widths to attain a comfortable position. Often, turning the grip inward (in which case the exercise is often called Chin-ups) or using a bar that will allow for a neutral grip will alter the training effect slightly, but may make a world of difference.
- Communicate with spotters and make sure everybody is on the same page before any set is started. Also, spotting should be done with both hands at the lower back and not the buttocks or ankles.

VARIATIONS

- Pull-down – this is a machine that uses a pulley system to allow weight to be pulled down toward the torso. It's great for novices who struggle with Pull-ups because they can lift less than their bodyweight.
- Inverted Row – using a bar that is at about waist height, grip the bar with the heels on the ground and keep your hips in line with

the shoulders and ankles. Pull the chest to the bar and slowly lower your body to the starting position.

- Inverted Row on Suspension Trainer – perform the inverted row on a suspension trainer such as the TRX, Blast Straps or other similar apparatus.
- Pull-Ups vs. Chin-Ups – commonly, the term "Pull-Up" refers to doing this movement with a pronated grip or the palms facing away from the body and "Chin-Up" refers to doing the movement with a supinated grip or the palms facing toward the body. Chin-Ups allow more musculature to be used and therefore are easier than Pull-Ups. Both exercises are valuable, but in most cases beginners should master "Chin-Ups" before attempting "Pull-Ups".
- Band-assisted Pull-ups – hang a large rubber band over a Pull-up bar and bend one knee to place it into the loop of the band. The band will help you on the way up by pulling your body toward the bar.
- Partner Spotted Pull-ups – have a spotter use both hands at the lower back to help you complete the desired number of reps.
- Resisted Pull-ups (bands, vests, dumbbells, etc.) – use resistance to make the body "heavier" and Pull-ups harder to perform.
- Shrugs – hold a barbell with a shoulder-width grip, core tight and knees slightly bent. Shrug the trapezius muscles to raise the bar as high as possible while keeping the arms fully extended.

WHAT'S MY MOTIVATION?

The six Foundation Exercises are the bedrock of the Finish Strong training method. Once a baseline level of strength has been established by mastering these exercises and performing them consistently, you will start to see notable improvement in how you feel and perform. When you are proficient with these exercises and committed to doing them regularly, you can start adding more advanced variations, sport-specific auxiliary exercises (see Top 10 lists) and more demanding mobility work. These progressions are great and should be the goal of anybody working hard in the gym, but none of them is possible without establishing the base of strength, mobility and coordination necessary to perform these six Foundation Exercises correctly on a regular basis.

12

ALL THE RIGHT MOVES – AN INTRODUCTION TO SPORT-SPECIFIC EXERCISES

At this point, you understand the six exercises that make up the foundation of your resistance training program. All of our training programs include a heavy dose of these, which will make your body stronger and more powerful and ready to reach performance levels you haven't yet met, but it is the specialized exercises that target the muscle groups important for your endurance sport (whether it is swimming, cycling, running or all three) that will really allow you to flourish in your sport and start gunning for podium finishes. The sport-specific exercises in the following chapters are meant to improve the strength and endurance of key muscles, reinforce a proper motor program and provide stability to improve body alignment in areas that are vulnerable to overuse injuries. Each individual sport has individual demands and failure to recognize and address this would be downright neglectful.

Just like your aerobic sport training, resistance training requires *specificity*. When you've signed up for a race with a hilly bike course, you wouldn't do all of your training rides on the flats, would you? No, because you'd just find yourself underprepared. Well, similar to having specificity in your discipline-specific training, it's important to have specificity in your resistance training. Our sport-specific exercises are meant to make sure that your body will be fully prepared for the demands of your sport and will help you make some big jumps in your performances as well as aiding with injury prevention.

You'll notice most of these targeted sport-specific exercises are a bit more complex in nature and are usually multi-joint and multi-planar – which mimics the demands of your sport. For our fellow multisport athletes, our programs will incorporate some of the targeted exercises from each of the three sports, so that your body can meet the demands of each.

Mastering the Foundation Exercises and then moving on to the specific exercises for your sport is the weight room version of building a general aerobic base of conditioning before moving on to preparing for the specific distance, terrain and conditions of your actual race.

The term "sport specificity" means many things to many people and the exact definition can be argued endlessly by training professionals. That said, there are two main schools of thought when it comes to the idea of sport specificity in the weight room, and then there's our approach:

1. Sport-specific approach: all athletes are different and all sports place different demands on the body so all methods of training should be radically different for each type of athlete.
2. General development approach: all human bodies are identical in form and function and a basic, generalized training program that makes the body stronger will benefit the athlete in not only sport but also activities of daily living.
3. Finish Strong approach (aka "somewhere in the middle"): except in cases of injury or dysfunction, human bodies are incredibly similar and will respond to generalized and basic resistance training programming in much the same way with increased size and strength. These physiologic changes are advantageous in most sports. However, because there are obvious differences in the demands each sport places on the body, there are specialized movements and exercises that would be more beneficial to individuals preparing their body for a unique competition.

For example, by this point in the book you should already know that we are fans of the Squat, and while we believe all athletes can benefit from the Squat motor pattern, there is a world of difference between how a marathoner implements it into his/her training and a powerlifter puts it into theirs.

This individual difference based on the activity or sport for which we are preparing the body can be looked at as a "¾ Rule" or "75 Percent Rule". This means that about 75 percent of what happens in a gym can be the same or very similar across all athletic situations. These are the basic or Foundation Exercises found earlier in this book. As a college strength and conditioning coach, Angelo has worked with athletes ranging from extreme power (baseball) to extreme endurance (cross country) and everything in between. Even at the extreme ends of that spectrum, all athletes can benefit from having better control of their bodies, stronger prime mover muscles and being better at movements like squatting, lunging, pushing and pulling. This makes up the 75 percent or the majority of the training we do across the board with all athletes.

The remaining 25 percent is made up of the specialized exercises that will really benefit one population. Things like Calf Raises and Dorsiflexion to aid in the battle against shin splints or Step-ups to develop single leg driving power are much more valuable to a runner than a swimmer because those exercises either stress the body in a way somewhat like the sport itself, directly address the musculature that is used in the sport or aid in injury prevention by allowing proper movement around joints or tissues that are often injured or overused in training or competition.

Now that we have established some ground rules and the rationale for why some exercises are better for certain types of athletes than others, we can look at the Top 10 exercises for swimmers, for cyclists and for runners. Keep in mind these are the 25 percent that should be added to programming *after* Foundation Exercises have been mastered and the athlete has a strong enough strength base to try some new movements. Also, they should not take the place of the Foundation Exercises but rather be added to the program when the athlete is ready for an increased volume of resistance training. These are the icing on the cake or the sauce on the pre-race pasta dinner. We will then tell you how to correctly implement them in the training templates in Section 3. Let's do this!

13

TOP 10 EXERCISES FOR SWIMMERS

The initial jump from following the "little black line" while swimming laps in a pool to swimming in open water and not seeing the bottom can be unnerving for some athletes. Our hope is that adding some targeted swim-specific strength and mobility exercises to your regular training routine doesn't fall into that category! Open water swimming can be incredibly challenging as you have to navigate waves, currents, body contact with other swimmers and restricted shoulder movement from full-body wetsuits – all while maintaining a proper swim stroke. On top of all of these factors, the little black line to follow is gone (unless you are swimming the IRONMAN Lake Placid course with the underwater cable) and you are sighting buoys every fourth stroke, which is an added movement that requires muscular endurance.

Whether you're in the lead pack or somewhere behind, swimming a distance of a mile or more can create fatigue and ultimately creates a breakdown in proper mechanics. As your mechanics begin to fall apart, you are less efficient in the water and lose some of your speed. The goal of resistance and mobility training in swimming is to keep the target muscles strong, and keep the body in the optimal position to continue to be both powerful and efficient in the water, thus making you faster.

As you've grown older and wiser, you've busted the myth that you can't go swimming until 30 minutes after eating, so now it's time to bust the myth that endurance athletes don't need to do resistance training. While form will always be king as the body attempts to efficiently deal with the hardships of fluid dynamics presented by water, adding some power to an already refined swim stroke will most definitely make you faster in the water. IRONMAN-branded races have adapted to a time-trial start, but there are many other races that still continue to do age-group wave starts. If you're the person who has been struggling to stay with the lead pack of your wave then you need a performance edge to get up there and not lose valuable time through being unable to take advantage of drafting the pack. No, that edge will not come from a more expensive wetsuit or speedsuit, rather it will come from being able to maintain a stronger, more powerful stroke throughout the course of the race. Adding in regular resistance and mobility training to your swim training will help you go from a guppy to a shark.

Whether you are getting ready for the Alcatraz Challenge, the Manhattan Island Swim or the 2.4-mile (3.9km) swim for your next IRONMAN, these specialized exercises in conjunction with a heavy dose of the Foundation Exercises will keep your muscles primed for success. Swimming fast is much more form dependent than simply powering through the water with a forceful stroke. The focus of the strength training is therefore to maintain the balance of the myofascial kinetic chains to keep the overuse injuries at bay and also aid performance.

While the pull is generated largely by two massive muscles (pectoralis major and latissimus dorsi), the muscles of the rotator cuff and scapular stabilizers are also important. These are much smaller in nature but must manage to counteract the pull forces in order to avoid having the forward shoulder posture (as discussed in Chapter 5).[1] In addition, the core is essential, especially the obliques, since the trunk rotates on the pelvis with each stroke. Having a good hip core to join the abdominal core is also key.

With this in mind, it shouldn't shock you that our focus will be on the scapular stabilizing muscles, rotator cuff and the core (including the hip core). Remember, in all of our programs, the sport-specific resistance and mobility exercises will make up about 25 percent of exercises. This targeted approach will help you shave off valuable time in your OWS events or triathlons by having you maintain a powerful stroke throughout.

We really want your core to resist fatigue while training and racing and to help with this we have Shoulder Taps, Dead Bug Paloff Press and Dumbbell Windshield Wipers. To help you produce a more powerful kick, we've included Clam Shells, Hip Thrust March and Physioball Flutter Kicks. To make for an improved powerful stroke, you'll be doing Dumbbell Standing Reverse Fly, Cable Push/pull, Cable Cross-pull – Low to High and Dumbbell Alternating Chest Press. With regularly planned resistance and mobility training, you'll be the shark in your next race rather than the prey.

1. Dumbbell Standing Reverse Fly
2. Cable Push/pull
3. Dumbbell Windshield Wipers
4. Clam Shells
5. Hip Thrust March
6. Dumbbell Alternating Chest Press
7. Cable Cross-pull – Low to High
8. Physioball Flutter Kicks
9. Dead Bug Paloff Press
10. Shoulder Taps

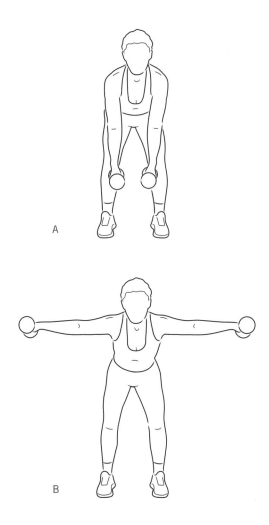

Figure 13.1 Dumbbell Standing Reverse Fly start/finish (A) and midpoint (B)

It is crucial for swimmers to have strong upper backs and shoulders. In Chapter 9, you learned that having a stable scapula holds the shoulder in the correct alignment and keeps it free from injury. This exercise will help work the scapular stabilizers as well as the posterior deltoid, which is critical for the recovery in the freestyle stroke.

Reverse Fly can be performed on a machine and also on a bench with dumbbells, but when performed in standing, it also provides good core activation as well as working the posterior kinetic chain, both of which are important for swimming.

START

The starting point is essentially the Deadlift position. Standing with your feet shoulder-width apart, with a slight bend in the knees, push your hips back and bend from the hips so that the trunk is parallel with the floor. Look forward while keeping your neck, shoulders and hips in proper alignment. The back should not be rounded or hyperextended – keep it neutral. Hold the dumbbells downward in front of the knees with a neutral grip.

MOVEMENT

Keeping the hamstrings and glutes active without moving, and the core tight, holding the trunk stiff, fly your shoulders outward by trying to pinch the scapulae together. The elbows should remain as straight as possible.

MIDPOINT

Continue to maintain the stable bent-over position. Once the shoulders can't move out to the side any further, slowly lower them back to the starting position. Resist the movement with the scapular muscles and continue to keep the legs and core tight.

END

Return to the start position and continue to keep the core and leg muscles engaged for all of the repetitions.

DOING IT RIGHT

- Push your butt back, similar to how you would for a Romanian Deadlift.
- Bend at the hips, not at the low back.
- Pinch the shoulder blades together.

TIPS

- If you struggle with the Romanian Deadlift, you might opt for a machine or to perform this on a bench, since it is supported.
- We often see people use too much resistance and then have a lot of movement compensations, which reinforce a poor motor pattern.

SAFETY

- Make sure your surroundings are clear and safe since your arms will come out wide while you perform the exercise.
- Come up slowly from the bent-over position – fast positional changes can cause a sudden drop in your blood pressure, which could make you light-headed.

VARIATIONS

- Single Arm Dumbbell Reverse Fly – perform the movement as described above, but only raise one arm at a time. This increases the need for the trunk muscles to stabilize the body and prevent it from moving.
- Reverse Fly on Physioball – place your chest on a physioball and your feet shoulder-width apart and perform the arm movement described above. The unstable surface makes it harder.
- Reverse Fly on Incline Bench – place your chest on a bench angled at 30–45 degrees, with your feet resting on the ground, and perform the exercise described above.
- Reverse Fly using Cable Column – stand upright, facing the two cable columns, grab the handles with opposite hands and perform the movement described above.

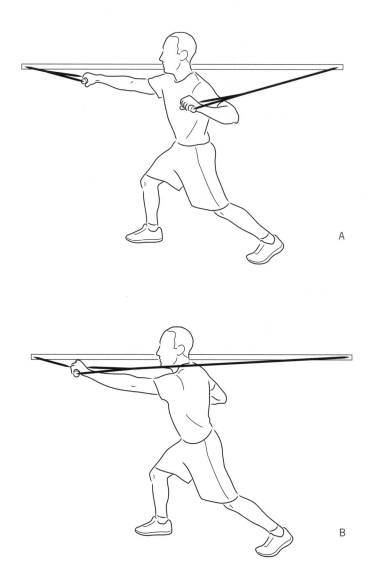

Figure 13.2 Cable Push/pull start/finish (A) and midpoint (B)

This is a great exercise to incorporate in order to create some thoracic spine rotation as well as working the functional myofascial chains.

START

Set up the cables at your shoulder height. Position yourself so that you are in the middle of the cable columns and adopt a staggered athletic stance (knees slightly bent) with your feet firmly planted on the floor. Grasp the cable handle with the arm that's on the same side as the foot that is staggered forward; the arm will reach back on the side with the leg that is staggered back to grab the other cable handle (the legs and arms on the same side are either forward or backward). Hold the chest high and the core tight so that there is no hyperextension or rounding of the lower back.

MOVEMENT

Perform a rowing motion with the forward arm, keeping the elbow tight to the body and ending the movement when the hand is just in front of the armpit, and simultaneously swing forward the arm that's reaching backward, using a punching motion. The rowing arm has a retracted stable scapula and the punching arm uses a forceful contraction of the triceps and pecs. There will be a slight turn felt between the trunk and the pelvis, but both should still remain facing forward.

MIDPOINT

This should look like a running motion (the arms and legs of the same side are doing the opposite movement – forward or backward). The trunk is still upright and steady and the core is still contracted so the spine doesn't hyperextend.

ENDPOINT

Slowly resist the weights from pulling the arms back to the starting position. Resist the turn of the trunk and pelvis. Continue to keep the feet planted firmly on the ground. Repeat for the required number of reps.

TIPS

- By performing the eccentric action of this exercise more slowly, it serves as an anti-rotation exercise.
- It is best to use the same weight for both the pull and push.

SAFETY

Don't start with too much weight as there will be a great deal of compensations made and they will likely come at the core.

VARIATION

Prone on a bench – set up the bench between the two cable columns so that when you lie on the bench your head will be toward one column and your feet toward the other. Grab the cables and perform the alternating movement described above.

A

B

Figure 13.3 Dumbbell Windshield Wipers start/finish (A) and left side (B)

The trunk twisting on the pelvis is a motion that continually occurs during the freestyle swim stroke, therefore it's essential that we train for it. This exercise really activates the internal and external oblique muscles of your core, which make up part of your spiral line (kinetic chain). This exercise can be performed as a rotation exercise, but our preference is to make it anti-rotation. When you do this, the focus is on resisting the eccentric phase in a very slow and controlled manner.

START

Lie on the floor on your back. Bend both your hips and knees to a 90-degree position. Hold the dumbbell straight upward with a locked-out elbow. The dumbbell will serve as a counterweight for your legs. Your scapulae should be retracted, feet and knees held together, and keep a tight core.

MOVEMENT

Begin by slowly rotating the legs from the hips to one side with the goal of positioning the side of the foot and the side of the knee level with the ground (you may not be able to go that far). The trunk remains in a neutral position and the dumbbell should remain overhead (try not to move it to the opposite direction of the legs – this is natural as it is a counterbalance). This lowering of the legs action should be very slow so that it acts as an anti-rotation exercise.

MIDPOINT

When the sides of the knee and the foot make contact with the ground.

END

Move the legs slowly to the starting position by recruiting the oblique muscles and other core accessory muscles. Repeat on the other side and for the required number of reps.

DOING IT RIGHT

- Keep the scapulae retracted and elbows locked for the duration of the exercise.
- Slowly rotate the lower extremity and resist the urge to lower the legs to the ground.

TIPS

As you get stronger, you will be able to progress from having bent knees to straight knees (this increases the lever arm and makes the exercise harder).

SAFETY

Do this on the ground rather than on a bench. We've seen people do this on a bench but with the smaller base of support, there is a risk of falling.

VARIATIONS

- Barbell or Medicine Ball Windshield Wipers – simply substitute the barbell or the medicine ball for the dumbbell and perform the movement described above.
- Straight Leg Dumbbell Windshield Wipers – perform the movement described above but with the knees straight.
- Physioball Dumbbell Windshield Wipers – assume the bent knee and hip position described above and place them on a physioball. Control the slow rolling movement of the ball under the legs.

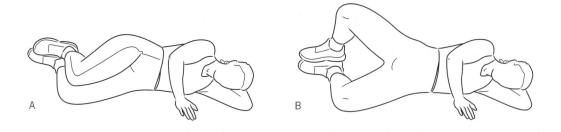

Figure 13.4 Clam Shells start/finish (A) and midpoint (B)

This exercise is a favorite among rehabilitation clinicians for helping to fix clients struggling with knee pain and other overuse/chronic conditions in the lower extremity. Having the strength in the hip external rotator group will aid in holding the leg in an appropriate alignment – this will be especially important for those of you who are triathletes. This exercise will produce strength in the glutes and the smaller external rotator muscles such as the piriformis. As an added bonus, it's another one you can easily perform from home when you can't make it to the gym.

START

Lie on your side, bend the elbow of the arm on the floor and cradle your head in your hand. Place the other hand comfortably on the floor at about chest level. Bend the hips to a 45-degree angle and the knees to 90 degrees. The shoulders should be in line with the hips and the feet (the knees are forward). The top shoulder isn't rolled forward or back (the trunk assumes a stiff posture).

MOVEMENT

Create a tight core – this will assist the movement of the hip core muscles. Begin by externally rotating the hip, then bring the top knee away from the bottom knee, while maintaining contact of the heels. Resist the urge to have a really large range of motion by rolling the trunk (this is an undesirable compensation).

MIDPOINT

The knees are away from each other and the heels are touching. The shoulders, hips and feet are still in a straight line on the same plane.

END

Slowly lower the knee of the top leg back to meet the knee of the bottom leg. This should be a slow and controlled eccentric contraction of the hip external rotators. Repeat for the required number of reps.

DOING IT RIGHT

- Resist the urge to roll the trunk forward or backward.
- Keep the core tight to create a more forceful contraction at the hips.

TIPS

- Sometimes we set up someone who's new to this exercise with their back against a wall (this helps make them aware of the urge to roll the trunk to assist the motion).

- You can work many different angles from the hip (many clinicians advise clients perform this at 0 degrees, 45 degrees and 90 degrees of hip flexion).
- Start with bodyweight rather than using the resistance band around the thighs.

VARIATIONS

- Vary the angle of the hip flexion position (0 degrees, 45 degrees, 90 degrees) – simply change the hip flexion angle to work different muscle fibers while doing the movement described above.
- Perform with heels elevated – hold both heels 6 inches (15cm) above the ground while you open and close the Clam Shell.
- Perform with heels elevated and holding a ball between the heels – hold both heels 6 inches (15cm) above the ground while holding a ball between the heels and opening and closing the Clam Shell.

HIP THRUST MARCH

Figure 13.5 Hip Thrust March start/finish (A) and midpoint(B)

Whether you favour a two-beat or four-beat kick, you'll want to have strong glutes to help you produce power from your lower extremity in the water. As we outlined in the Foundation Exercises chapter, the Hip Bridge is an essential movement in strength training, and the Hip Thrust March is just one of the many variations available. We like this exercise for swimming since it requires full core engagement while keeping the glutes active. The alternating action also mimics the kicking motion, similar to the Flutter Kick but at a much slower tempo.

START

You will need a standard flat bench on which to perform this exercise (it can also be done from the floor if you don't have a bench – in which case it will be more of a Glute Bridge March rather than a Hip Thrust March). Set up so your body will be at right angles to the bench, with your feet on the ground. Place your shoulder blades flat on the middle of the bench and cross your arms across your chest. Pinch your buttocks to create a tabletop position so that your knees, hips and shoulders are aligned. You will have a 90-degree bend in the knee and the feet will be placed firmly on the ground slightly more than shoulder-width apart. Drive the weight through your heels to recruit the glutes to produce this position.

MOVEMENT

Slowly lift one leg off the ground by contracting the hip flexor, keeping the 90-degree bend in the knee. Continue to bring that leg up until the hip reaches a 90-degree position. The trunk should not rotate, the buttocks should not drop and there should be no valgus collapse in the knee of the leg that is still planted on the ground.

MIDPOINT

The shoulders are in contact with the bench. The knee of the planted leg is in line with the hips and shoulders. The leg that moved is in the 90/90 hip/knee position. The core remains tight and the glutes are very active to keep the hips from dropping.

END

Slowly lower the leg while preventing the hips from dropping and any trunk-twisting compensations. Keep the shoulder blades retracted and the body in a straight-line position until the body returns to the starting position. Repeat on the other side and for the required number of reps.

DOING IT RIGHT

- Focus on keeping the hips high.
- Keep the core tight while pinching the glutes.
- Drive through your heels.

TIPS

- You need to have done Single Leg Glute Bridges successfully on the floor before you move on to this exercise.
- Use this relatively "easy" exercise when your body feels too fatigued for more strenuous back work.

SAFETY

- Make sure the bench is secure.
- Be sure to breathe as you perform the exercise (many people hold their breath).
- Try to keep your neck relaxed and not strain.

VARIATIONS

- Resisted Hip Thrust March – add a barbell or other weight at the hips while performing the motion described above. This will make it harder.
- Glute Bridge March – perform the movement described above with the upper body supported by the floor.

DUMBBELL ALTERNATING CHEST PRESS

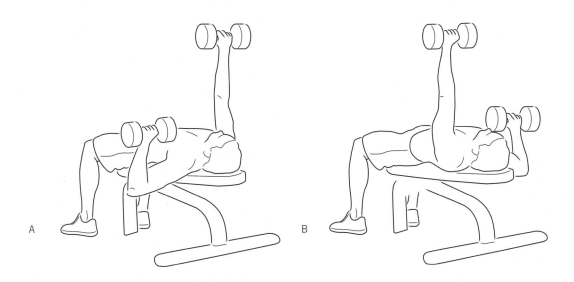

Figure 13.6 Dumbbell Alternating Chest Press right side (A) and left side (B)

Although a conventional Chest Press is fine, we feel this one fits the bill for specificity for swimmers. Dumbbell exercises like these are isolateral, which means you will build stability throughout the shoulder while creating the strength of the pectoralis major (that ever-important giant muscle used during the pull phase of the freestyle stroke). Single arm moves like these also create an unbalanced situation, so they actually also serve as an anti-rotation exercise. The absence of a strong active core during this exercise will limit how much resistance you can push.

START

Lie on your back on a flat bench. Your head, shoulders and back should be firm against the bench and the feet should be placed firmly on the ground slightly more than shoulder-width apart. Grip the dumbbells and hold them slightly above the level of the chest over the armpits (the elbows will be a little bit more flexed than 90 degrees). The core is tight, the lower back is flat against the bench and the upper extremity is tight and active.

MOVEMENT

Forcefully drive the dumbbell of one arm upward and slightly medial over the body until the elbow is close to being fully extended (but do not fully extend it). Resist the pelvis from rolling and the feet from having uneven pressure on the ground (if this occurs, you do not have enough core strength to manage that load yet). The opposite arm's dumbbell remains in the start position just over the armpit, waiting for its turn to move, once the active arm has been lowered again.

MIDPOINT

The feet remain flat on the floor and the hips, shoulders and head remain firmly against the bench. The arm with the moving dumbbell is extended upward (elbow not quite locked out). The large pectoral muscle is contracted, pulling that arm toward the midline of the body. The opposite hand remains clutching the dumbbell over the armpit.

END
Slowly resist the lowering of the dumbbell down to the start position with the hand slightly higher than the armpit. Repeat for the required number of reps.

DOING IT RIGHT
- Keep the feet firmly planted on the floor.
- Keep the core tight, to resist the hyperextension of the lower back.

TIPS
- You will require a strong core in order to manage a heavier load.
- If you are going heavy, make sure the spotter grabs your wrists instead of trying to push up at your elbows.

SAFETY
- Don't bring the dumbbell down quite as low as the armpit and never wider than the armpit as this is a vulnerable position for the anterior shoulder capsule.
- Don't drop the dumbbell when you've finished as it could smash your toes, or someone else's.

VARIATION
- Incline Dumbbell Alternating Chest Press – do the exercise described above on a bench that is inclined to a 30–45-degree position.
- Physioball Alternating Chest Press – do the exercise described above but with the back supported on a physioball. Keep in mind this will require a very strong contraction from the glutes to hold the hips at the level of the shoulder.

CABLE CROSS-PULL – LOW TO HIGH

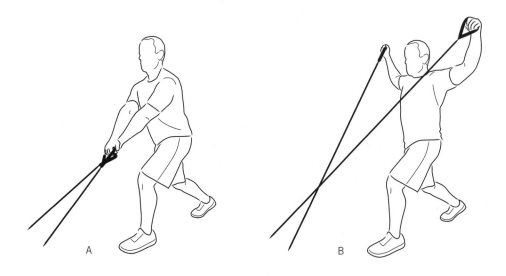

Figure 13.7 Cable Cross-pull low to high start/finish (A) and midpoint (B)

This is a fantastic exercise for building strength in the scapular stabilizing muscles, which are critical for proper shoulder alignment. This will yield improved performance and decrease the risk of overuse/chronic injuries. Since this exercise is done in standing, full kinetic chains need to be active in order to create a stable base.

START

Set up the cable pulley at its lowest anchor point. Stand facing the pulleys in a centered position a couple feet from where they are in line together. Grab the left handle with the right hand and the right handle with the left hand (one arm will be over the other – be sure to switch which is the top hand between sets). Place the feet in a staggered athletic stance with a slight bend in the hips and knees (be sure to switch which foot is staggered forward between sets). Build tension through the legs and tighten the core. Your scapulae will be protracted at this point since your arms are crossing one another.

MOVEMENT

Forcefully pull across and up with both arms at the same time so that the hands are high and the cables make an "x" pattern. The scapulae will retract to cause this position. If the core is not held tight or the weight resistance is too great, it's common to see hyperextension compensation in the lower back, which you don't want.

MIDPOINT

The body is in a staggered athletic stance with the arm high and the cables making an "x" pattern.

END

Slowly resist the down phase by not allowing the scapulae to be pulled into protraction. Continue to maintain the posture in the lower extremity and control the lower back to avoid hyperextending or rounding. The arms will cross over one another at the finish. Repeat for the required number of reps.

DOING IT RIGHT

- Keep your core tight.
- Pull up and out.

TIPS

- You will need to use very low weight for this initially.
- Control the cables during the down phase so the weights don't crash.
- If you don't have cables, you could use tubing anchored low, and use the crossing pattern.

SAFETY

There should be no hyperextension or rounding of the lower back.

VARIATIONS

- Cable Crossover Pull – High to Low – switch the pulley to a high setting so that you pull downward with both arms instead up upward.
- Using resistance tubing – in the absence of a cable column, use resistance bands that are anchored low and perform the movement described above.
- From a half-kneeling stance – instead of standing on both feet, drop into a half-kneeling stance to make it harder by being less stable.

PHYSIOBALL FLUTTER KICKS

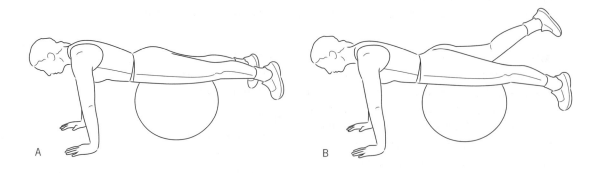

Figure 13.8 Physioball Flutter Kicks start/finish (A) and midpoint (B)

This exercise mimics freestyle kicking on dry land and helps build core strength and good glute activation for a powerful kick. The instability of the ball really challenges the muscles of the core to engage to hold the body in proper streamlined alignment.

START
Carefully roll out on your stomach on a mid-sized physioball. Position your pelvis directly over the ball and steady yourself with stable arms. The arms should be fully extended with the scapulae retracted and the fingers grabbing the ground. Raise your legs so that the knees, hips and shoulders are in a straight line balancing over the ball at the pelvis. The core should be fully engaged to ensure that the lower back doesn't round or hyperextend.

MOVEMENT
Start to kick to a two-beat, four-beat or six-beat rhythm while maintaining good body position. Perform sets of 1-minute duration. Assume a normal steady breathing pattern while kicking and holding the core tight.

END
Carefully roll back to the start position and avoid falling off the ball. Repeat for the required number of reps.

DOING IT RIGHT
- Keep the core tight.
- Keep the scapulae retracted and depressed.

TIP
Kicks don't have to be large. Try to keep them similar to what you'd do in the pool.

SAFETY
Physioballs are highly unstable pieces of equipment, so go slow as you place your trunk over the ball.

VARIATION
BOSU Ball Flutter Kick – rather than a physioball, use a BOSU ball, which will be slightly easier since it is more stable.

Floor Flutter Kick – when there is no gym equipment available, lie prone with the arms extended over your head and perform the flutter kick.

DEAD BUG PALOFF PRESS

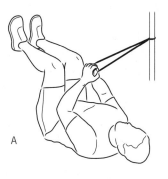

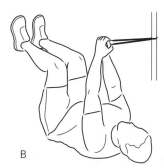

Figure 13.9
Dead Bug Paloff Press start/
finish (A) and midpoint (B)

The Standing Paloff Press is one of the most commonly used anti-rotation exercises. When done even with a sturdy band, it is relatively easy to resist the trunk rotation that the band tries to create. The Dead Bug Paloff Press is much more advanced and won't require a very thick resistance band as it is extremely challenging thanks to it being performed lying on your back with your legs and arms elevated.

START

Assume the Dead Bug position – head, trunk and pelvis in a straight line supported by the ground, both hips bent to 90 degrees and both knees also bent to 90 degrees. The shoulders rest at the side of the body and the hands grasp the resistance band in the middle of the belly. The knees and ankles should never be touching – they should be approximately 3–4 inches (7.5–10cm) from each other (this is a key to the difficulty of the exercise). Tie the resistance band to a solid object, such as a bench or weight rack, at the height of the stomach, and hold it taut. The core is extremely active.

MOVEMENT

Maintain the body in its current position and simply press upward away from the belly with both hands on the resistance band. The goal is to hold the trunk and the pelvis in a neutral position and not rotate toward the attachment of the resistance band. The only thing moving should be the arms in an upward movement. Contract the trunk and core muscles to resist the compensatory movements.

MIDPOINT

The body is held in a Dead Bug position with the arms fully extended.

END

Return the arms to the starting position with the hands resting on the belly. Resist all rotary motion at the trunk and pelvis. Repeat for the required number of reps.

DOING IT RIGHT

- Fully engage the core musculature from start to finish.
- Hold the legs in the same position throughout the exercise.
- Keep the lower back flat against the ground.
- Remember to breathe!

TIPS

- Perform this with a spotter so they can explain what compensations you are making (you will feel quite a bit of movement at your legs).
- Do not use a heavy resistance band – you are already in a very unstable position and it will be challenging regardless of the resistance.

SAFETY

- Don't attach the resistance band to anything that isn't stable.
- Don't hold your breath.

VARIATIONS

- Standing Paloff Press – assume an athletic stance next to an object with a resistance band attached to it. Grasp the band with both hands holding it to the chest until the band is taught. Slowing extend the arms straight out but resist the body from rotating.
- Alternating Limb Dead Bug – assume the position described in the exercise above minus the resistance band. While keeping the core tight, slowly extend the opposite arm and leg and then return them to the starting position. Alternate sides each repetition.

SHOULDER TAPS

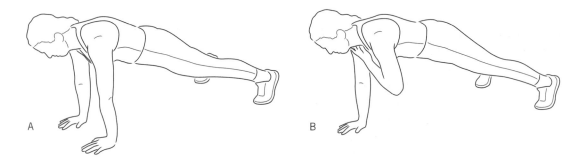

Figure 13.10 Shoulder Taps start/finish (A) and left side (B)

Here's another easy anti-rotation exercise that doesn't require any equipment, so it's ideal for those of you who can't get to the gym and need to settle for a quick workout at home. This exercise will build shoulder stability as well as providing the activation of the obliques that is so critical.

START

Assume the "up" position of a Push-up but with a wide base of support at the feet rather than the usual "feet together". Lock out your elbows and place your hands just outside the shoulders. The wider the feet, the bigger the base of support (which you will want initially). The shoulders, hips, knees and ankles should be in a line.

MOVEMENT

Pick up one hand and slowly cross it over to touch the opposite shoulder. This will move you from a stable four-point stance to a much less stable three-point stance. The goal is to only move the hand to touch the shoulder while resisting movement elsewhere in the body. It is common to see the hips pike up or rotate as a compensation. The shoulder of the moving hand also will want to dip down. Resist all of the compensatory movements.

MIDPOINT

The hand of one arm is gently touching the top of the shoulder. The body remains in perfect alignment, as it was when both hands were on the ground

END

Move back to the starting position with both hands on the ground just outside the shoulders. Repeat for the required number of reps.

DOING IT RIGHT

- Widen your legs for a bigger base of support.
- Move slowly and in a controlled manner through the movement.
- Resist the compensations – this is an anti-rotation exercise.
- Don't pike at your hips.

TIPS

- Perform over a line on the floor so you can see your movement compensations.
- People who are new to this go relatively quickly, which is somewhat counterproductive since the slow and controlled resistance of the compensation is the important part of the movement.

SAFETY

You will need to have good wrist, elbow and shoulder stability for each of the plant hands to do this properly.

VARIATIONS

- Hip Taps – instead of tapping your opposite shoulder, slowly reach down and tap the hip on the same side.
- Arm Overhead – instead of tapping your opposite shoulder, slowly reach the arm outward overhead.
- Push-up Shoulder Tap – after tapping the opposite shoulder, perform a Push-up, then follow that by tapping the other shoulder.

EXERCISES TO AVOID

As a general rule, avoid overhead shoulder exercises (i.e. Military Press) as they may place a great deal of stress on the shoulders. Additionally, the focus should not be on strengthening the chest (although the pectoralis major is a powerful internal rotator for the pull). If you paid close attention to the earlier chapter on injury prevention, you'll understand that having two sides balanced is the key. If you were to focus on the chest, you may end up with forward shoulder posture, which may predispose you to shoulder injuries. Therefore, we make a general rule that you should perform two back strength exercises for every chest exercise.

Incorporating regularly planned resistance training with your swim training doesn't have to be time-consuming and complex. We understand that with all the hours you are spending in the pool (or preferably in the lake or ocean) training for your next event, you often think there's no time to get to strength training. Those of you who are triathletes are especially crunched for time as you are swimming, running and cycling along with trying to fit in your work, your family and other obligations. Our programs never feature long workouts, to make training more realistic. Also, we've provided exercises to target all the right muscle groups to make you more powerful in the water while helping to keep you free from overuse and chronic injuries. By providing you with these go-to exercises, you'll be able to strengthen the muscles most important to your swim performance each time you head to the gym. If you are lacking time, keep things simple and just perform these targeted exercises so you can get the most bang for your buck.

We know that becoming a faster swimmer takes commitment. We also know that working with a coach to improve the efficiency of your swim stroke is critical for making big gains. After that, if you are looking for that final edge on your competition, increasing the power output from your stroke is your main option. Stronger muscles will help reduce fatigue in the water and help you maintain the proper mechanics of your swim stroke, and most importantly, help you Finish Strong!

---

1. Rouard, A. H. and Billat, R. P., 'Influences of sex and level of performance on freestyle stroke: an electromyography and and kinematic study', *International Journal Of Sports Medicine, 11(2) (1990), pp. 150–155*

14

TOP 10 EXERCISES FOR CYCLISTS

You know what's fun? Passing other athletes in a race. While RJ has never raced criteriums, cyclocross or stage races, he's done more than his fair share of triathlons and Fondos as well as a few off-road events. Passing people ... it just never gets old! You know what's even more satisfying? Passing other athletes on hills and watching them struggle and look hopeless while you ride by strong and confident. We know for a fact that we train differently than most of the other age-group triathletes. We know we're in the minority who regularly add resistance and mobility training to our endurance sport training. And you know what – it feels good being in that minority. Mentally, it gives us confidence on race day and physically, the results show when we ride past people. It's a real advantage.

Some of RJ's best cycling race performances at the half IRONMAN distance have come at IRONMAN 70.3 Mont-Tremblant. One thing he can say for sure is that it is not flat. It has about 3,000 feet (900m) of climbing over the 56-mile (90km) loop. Prior to the first time he did the event, he made sure he did his homework on the course by getting a report from a pro he's friendly with. He tends to favour courses with hills because that's what he's got in his "backyard" for training. He really focused on maintaining his leg and core strength leading up to the race so he'd be able to handle anything those hills threw at him. He averaged 20.5mph (33kph) on the bike, which tells us he nailed it.

It really shouldn't be a hard concept for a cyclist to understand that instituting regularly planned strength training into your aerobic sport training will make you a faster, more powerful athlete. If you're like RJ, you are training with a power meter and you're always eager to increase your functional threshold power (FTP). There are basically two ways to do this: 1) ride more (at strategic pacing – percentage of FTP); and 2) get your legs and core stronger so you can put more power to the pedals! Those of you who ride events that don't require as much steady state riding and where you need to attack (criteriums, Fondos, stage races) will really benefit greatly from having the improved leg strength. Triathletes, I'm sure you are racing more at a steady state; however, the improved strength will bump up your FTP, which in turn means you can ride at a higher percentage of FTP for your IRONMAN or other distance event.

We believe it's important to have a sound rationale for choosing strength and mobility exercises when it comes to specificity of training. Being academics, we turn to the research literature to help guide our exercise selections. Previous electromyography (EMG) research by Jorge and Hull[1] in the *Journal of Biomechanics* indicates that the hip extensor (gluteus maximus) is highly active during the 12–3 o'clock position during pedaling. The next most active muscles are the knee extensors (quadriceps) muscles, which fire mostly during the 3–6 o'clock position during the pedal stroke. Therefore, it should come as no surprise that our exercises have a focus on quads and glutes (think Squats, Squats, Squats!). If you remember back to the core/anti-rotation section in Chapter 10, having a strong core – the connection point between the right lower extremity and left upper extremity (and vice versa) – is critical for creating power when pedaling.

An additional issue that we need to address is whether the cyclist is focused on road, time trial or MTB. For obvious reasons, it is critical that MTB riders have a stronger upper body to stabilize and absorb forces when riding rough terrain. Similarly, a time trial rider or triathlete will need to have additional core stability to hold the aero position over time, as well as a strong upper back and neck.

As a quick reminder, these cycling-specific exercises should make up about 25 percent of your overall program. At this point, these exercises will be more complex in nature and will use a variety of apparatuses to keep you interested!

Throughout the years, we've developed our list of go-to exercises that we feel really meet the functional needs of cycling. We've got exercises that will help build the strength of the glutes and quads (Burpees, Lateral Lunge Press, Dumbbell Split Squat, Bench Pistol Squat and Kettlebell Clean and Press) as well as exercises that will help build stability between the trunk and pelvis to create that stable core (Dumbbell Renegade Row, Valslide Body Saw, Lateral Plate Drag, Half-kneel Downward Cable Chop). While each of the exercises on our list has a primary focus, they are complex exercises that will improve the strength of auxiliary stabilizing muscles as well. If you are ready to make your FTP larger and improve your age-group rankings, incorporate our cycling specific strength and mobility program and start flying by the competition.

1. Burpee
2. Valslide Body Saw
3. Dumbbell Renegade Row
4. Overhead Plate Circles
5. Lateral Lunge Press
6. Dumbbell Split Squat
7. Bench Pistol Squat
8. Single Arm Kettlebell Clean and Press
9. Lateral Plate Drag
10. Half-kneel Downward Cable Chop

BURPEE

Figure 14.1
Burpee phases 1–6 (A–F)

A   B   C   D   E   F

One of the best full-body exercises that doesn't require any gym equipment whatsoever is the Burpee. Your CrossFit friends have been on a steady diet of Burpees for a long time, and for good reason. Aside from working the muscles of your arms, back, chest, core, glutes and legs, it raises your heart rate, so it can be a valuable warm-up exercise. This bodyweight exercise has a plyometric or explosive component to it that allows the leg muscles to build more power. As with all exercises, however, when done to exhaustion, poor form sets in, which can have a more negative effect. Done at the correct dosage, though, these can really set you off in the right direction! Lifters new to this should focus on form. As you become more advanced, there are multiple ways to increase the level of difficulty.

START

Stand in an athletic stance with the knees slightly bent, the core tight and your shoulder blades retracted for good posture. Be sure that good posture and body positioning are maintained throughout the movement.

MOVEMENT

This is a complex movement with six parts to it. Start by squatting down to about a 90-degree bend at the hip. Quickly place the hands shoulder-width apart on the ground and kick the legs back into a Plank position while performing a Push-up at the upper extremity. At the conclusion of the Push-up, quickly jump your feet toward your hands (keep them in a shoulder-width position). Next, perform a vertical jump and extend the arms overhead. Land with soft knees to absorb the landing, finishing with arms at your side.

END

Move back to the starting position with both hands on the ground just outside the shoulders. Repeat for the required number of reps.

DOING IT RIGHT

- Start in an athletic position with the knees slightly bent and feet shoulder-width apart.
- The core should be tight and your posture should be rigid during the Push-up phase.
- Concentrate on driving upward on the jump.
- Land softly with no side-to-side movement of the knees.

TIPS

- Start out by doing Burpees in a slow and controlled manner before making it ballistic, so you can master the complexity of the movement before adding speed and power components.

SAFETY

- Always perform these on a firm surface. Soft surfaces may seem like a better choice but will be tough on your wrists.
- Make sure you can Squat and do a Push-up before doing Burpees.
- Keep an eye on your knees. If any side-to-side movement is occurring during your landing, you are fatigued and should stop.

VARIATIONS

- Box Jump Burpee – in the last phase of the Burpee (the vertical jump), jump up on to a box designed for plyometrics.
- Broad Jump Burpee – in the last phase of the Burpee (the vertical jump), rather than performing a vertical jump, jump forward a distance and land in an athletic position.
- Tuck Jump Burpee – in the last phase of the Burpee (the vertical jump), flex your hips and knees and quickly hug them with your hands before landing.

VALSLIDE BODY SAW

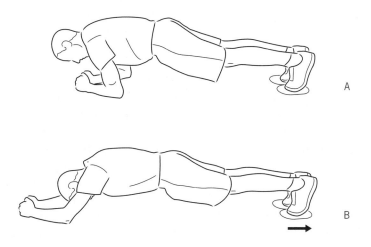

Figure 14.2 Valslide Body Saw start/finish (A) and midpoint (B)

Another challenging bodyweight exercise that will strengthen multiple body parts is the Valslide Body Saw. While the shoulders, chest and back help provide the movement, the rest of the body (especially the core) remains stable and rigid throughout the movement. The Valslides allow for a decreased resistance between your feet and the floor to allow them to glide forward and back.

START

Assume a Plank position on your elbows to initiate the exercise, with the forearms placed shoulder-width apart. Place your feet on the valslides, legs together and the body in an in-line rigid position, which it will maintain throughout. It is critical with all Planks to not pike up at your buttocks. As you gain experience and strength, you might choose to only use the valslide on one foot while extending the other leg straight, which adds an anti-rotation component.

MOVEMENT

The movement features a small push and pull but the forearms never leave their home position. It should be initiated with the chest, upper back and shoulders pulling the body forward approximately 3 inches (7.5cm) (try to picture the location of your feet moving forward this distance). The whole time this is occurring, you are still holding a perfect Plank by keeping your core tight and leg muscles rigid.

MIDPOINT

After providing the pulling motion forward, your chin is a little forward of your hands. It is now time to reverse the motion and push backward using your chest, upper back and shoulders.

END

At the conclusion of the push backward, your chin will be over the creases of your elbows. Repeat for the required number of reps.

DOING IT RIGHT

- Keep the ankles, knees, hips and shoulders in a single line with no piking of the hips.
- The core should be tight, and make sure to not hyperextend the lower back.
- There shouldn't be any bend at the knees, as this is not the goal of the exercise.

TIPS

- You don't need a Valslide. It is possible to use a towel on a hardwood or tile floor to achieve the same result. A slide board will also work.
- Work a small motion before making it larger. Moving 1 inch (2.5cm) forward and back may be hard enough when you start.
- The hands can be in a fist or the palms can be in contact with the ground. This may create greater contact surface area to initiate the pull and push of the upper extremity.

SAFETY

- This exercise requires a great deal of shoulder stability, so don't perform it if the shoulders can't handle it.
- The core must be active and tight otherwise the exercise may cause injury.

VARIATIONS

- Valslide Body Saw with Leg Lift – perform the movement as outlined above but elevate one of the legs just slightly off the ground. Going from four points of contact to three makes the exercise harder. It also creates an uneven load, which makes this variation an anti-rotation exercise.
- Straight Arm Valslide Body Saw – rather than supporting your forearms on the valslide, place your hands on the valslide. Keep the elbows locked out and slowly move the arms forward past your head. Only go as far as you are comfortable as this adds a great deal of stress to your shoulders.
- Valslide Body Saw with Weight Vest – one of the easiest ways to increase resistance is literally adding weight in the form of a vest. Perform the movement as described above.

DUMBBELL RENEGADE ROW

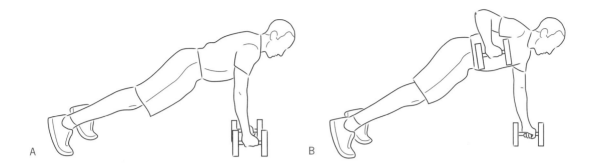

Figure 14.3 Dumbbell Renegade Row start/ finish (A) and midpoint right arm (B)

Whenever we hear the song 'Renegade' by Styx, it makes us want to get rowdy. Similarly, we like to use Renegade Rows to get the posterior kinetic chain, core and upper back muscles fired up. At this point, you've noticed a pattern with these specialized exercises – they are more advanced and we accomplish more than one goal by performing them. This exercise really capitalizes on the 'X' crossing pattern connection of the upper body and lower body as they meet in the core (think right shoulder and left glute). You don't want to be one of those riders with the wishy-washy S-shaped spine, do you? This exercise will really help you stabilize and produce more power.

START

Start by getting into a Plank position from your hands and feet. Your ankles, knees, hips and shoulders should be in line and your neck should be neutral. The hands are shoulder-width apart and feet should also be shoulder-width apart (the closer the feet come together, the less stable you become). Your shoulders should be hovering over your hands, which are holding the dumbbells with a neutral grip. This will keep the dumbbells in line with the body during the pull. The core is tight and active. In this exercise, you will be going from four points of contact to three, with the goal of creating as little movement at the core as possible.

MOVEMENT

Retract one scapula using the muscles of the upper back and perform the rowing motion. The motion isn't initiated by the arm musculature but rather by the scapula. Keep the elbow tight to the body (not flaring out) and bring the dumbbell up to the side of the chest. The torso should remain flat, with no rotation.

MIDPOINT

The dumbbell should come no further than the side of the chest. A common mistake is to pull the dumbbell up and then rotate the torso to the opposite side to seem like there is more range of motion. This is a critical mistake as this exercise is an anti-rotation exercise due to the unbalanced nature of it. The torso should be flat with no rotation.

END

Slowly lower the weight back to the ground to resume the Plank position with four points of contact. The shoulder blade will be moving from a retracted position to a protracted position. Repeat on the other side and for the required number of reps.

DOING IT RIGHT

- Perform the full range of motion of the Row, lifting the dumbbell from the ground to the ribcage.
- Fight the resistance all the way up and down for maximum muscle activation.

TIPS

- Try to minimize the amount of weight shifting from one side to the other.
- We like performing these with the midline of the body over a straight line on the ground so you can see if your weight is shifting.
- Keep the ankles, knees, hips and shoulders in a stacked position.
- Don't pike or hyperextend at the lower back.
- Don't over-row, which causes rotation in the trunk.

SAFETY

- If you feel an incredible amount of pressure in your lower back, you've selected a weight that is too much for you.
- Only use dumbbells that have squared-off ends. Ones with rounded ends make this incredibly unstable and dangerous.

VARIATIONS

- Kettlebell Renegade Row – swap out your dumbbells for a kettlebells. This makes the exercise harder because it decreases the stability of the weight as it contacts the ground.
- Renegade Row with Lateral Band Resistance – perform the Renegade Row as described above but add a resistance band around your waist attached to a stable object like a rack. Engage the band by setting up into the Push-up position just next to the rack.
- Renegade Row with Push-up – after each Row has been performed and the dumbbell has been returned to the ground, perform a Push-up, then perform the Row with the other arm. Rows are great for developing back strength and Push-ups are great for chest strength. This now becomes a push/pull exercise.

OVERHEAD PLATE CIRCLES (AKA AROUND THE WORLD)

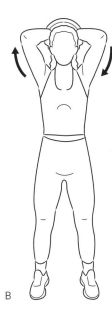

Figure 14.4 Overhead Plate Circles start/finish (A) and midpoint (B)

These have been a favorite of racecar drivers for a long time, to improve strength for steering. Since you're riding a bike, you are also steering. Yes, we're well aware that turning on a bike is done mostly at the hips by making a weight shift, unlike how a racecar driver would use his arms on the steering wheel, but seeing as this exercise is working both core and your shoulder group, it's perfect for a cyclist as well.

START

Begin standing in an athletic stance with your feet shoulder-width apart and a slight bend in your knees. The core should be active. Hold a plate out in front of you. The shoulders are neutral and the elbows are bent to 90 degrees (it's as if you are learning to drive and holding the steering wheel at 9 o'clock and 3 o'clock rather than 10 o'clock and 2 o'clock, much to your instructor's dismay). Grip the plate firmly to reduce the incidence of injuries.

MOVEMENT

Slowly make a circular motion with the plate, moving around your head in a clockwise manner. Allow a slight natural bend in the elbows to occur. You will pass your ear and then be at the midpoint, where the elbows will be flexed to 90 degrees. Minimize any pelvis or trunk rotation and/or sidebend that wants to occur (be the anti to the anti-rotation!). Maintain an athletic stance.

MIDPOINT

The plate will be behind your head but you won't be stopping here – instead, continue "around the world". Shoulders are fully extended with the scapulae squeezed together, elbows bent to 90 degrees with the triceps working to stabilize the plate. Continue on through past this midpoint and back to the start position. Maintain the tight core throughout.

END

End with your arms in the same position that horrified your driving instructor ... 3 o'clock and 9 o'clock. Repeat for the required number of reps.

DOING IT RIGHT

- The core must be tight and active throughout the movement.
- Move the plate slowly and be more like a Sunday driver than a racing car driver.
- There should be no side bend at the waist.
- Don't round or hyperextend the lower back.
- If you're using any of the variations, such as Half-kneel or Lunge Overhead Plate Circles, you will also have to make sure that the front knee doesn't go into a valgus position.

TIPS

If your lower back is hyperextended or rounded when you initially are holding the weight out at the 9 o'clock and 3 o'clock position, you've got too much resistance.

SAFETY

- We prefer using plates that have handles built in or rubber bumper plates, to reduce injury risk.
- Make sure you don't overflex the elbows as this will increase the likelihood of the weight hitting you in the head.

VARIATIONS

- Half-kneel Overhead Plate Circles – to decrease your base of support, drop into a half-kneeling position by bending the hip and knee of the front leg to 90 degrees, and dropping the back knee down to the ground below the body and curling your toes under. Then perform the movement.
- Lunge Overhead Plate Circles – to further decrease your base of support and make the exercise harder, step out into a Lunge (this position will be similar to the half-kneel, only the back knee will hover over the ground). Then perform the movement.

LATERAL LUNGE PRESS

Figure 14.5 Lateral Lunge Press start/ finish (A) and midpoint (B)

This exercise combines two great individual exercises to make for a more complex full body movement. Having strong glutes, scapular stabilizers and shoulders are all points of emphasis for cyclists – especially for MTB and time trial/triathlon riders. As soon as you add an upper extremity movement with the lower extremity, it begs for the core to be engaged for support. The lateral movement will help mimic the weight shift of your center of gravity used for steering into turns.

START
Begin by getting into an athletic stance with your feet shoulder-width apart and a slight bend in the knees. You will be holding a plate at the 3 o'clock and 9 o'clock position close to your body with your elbows bent to 90 degrees. The scapulae are retracted and the core is locked in, not allowing the lower back to hyperextend or round.

MOVEMENT
Using the foot on the side that you will be lunging to, take a lateral step about twice the distance that your feet were initially positioned apart, and keep the toes facing forward. Land on the midfoot or closer to the heel so that you sit back into the Lunge

and use your glutes. Simultanously push the plate away from your body by extending your elbows.

MIDPOINT
On the side you are lunging toward, the goal is to get the thigh parallel to the floor. If this is new to you, you may not go as deep initially. The hip, knee and ankle of the Lunge leg should be stacked over one another. It is important that you don't shift your weight forward as it will make your knee come over your toes (if this happens, it places extra pressure on your patellar tendon and you won't get the glute activation you are looking for). Fortunately, holding the plate in

front of you acts as a counterbalance so most people will sit back into the Lunge. The other leg should be fully extended and actively engaged, and the foot should remain in contact with the ground and remain pointing forward. If this leg is not actively engaged, it is common to see some knee valgus occur, which is not desirable. Continue to steady the plate at the 3 o'clock and 9 o'clock position and keep a good upright trunk posture by keeping the core active and scapulae locked in.

END

From the midpoint, use the lunging leg to press the body upward and toward the other leg, back to the start position while simultaneously pulling the plate back toward the chest. This should be done with control and by making a strong contraction with the glutes and quad muscles. Repeat for the required number of reps.

DOING IT RIGHT

- Keep your core neutral and locked in.
- Step out without pushing off from the planted leg.
- Sit back into the Lunge.
- Stack the hip, knee and ankle of the Lunge leg.

TIPS

- You might start this exercise without a plate and simply have the arms extended forward (again, this acts as a counterbalance to allow you to "trust" the Lunge and sit back into it.
- To add an additional core component, at the midpoint you can twist the plate side to side.

SAFETY

- There's no need to use a heavy plate… 10–25lb (4.5–11.5kg) is likely enough, depending on your size, strength and gender.
- Use a rubber bumper weight or plate with handles.
- If you are fatigued and can't maintain the stacked position or are shifting weight too far forward, switch to the basic forward or backward Lunge from the Foundation Exercise chapter.

VARIATIONS

- Lateral Lunge with Overhead Press – rather than pushing the plate forward from your chest, instead press the plate overhead. This will work some slightly different upper extremity muscles.
- Lateral Lunge Clean – perform the Lateral Lunge with a dumbbell in each hand. At the lowest point of the Lunge, flex the elbows and bring the dumbbells to the shoulder/collarbone area. Extend the elbows before returning the body to the starting position.
- Crossover Lunge (sometimes called a Curtsey Lunge) – bend the knee and hip of the stable leg while crossing the other leg behind it.
- Lateral Lunge and Twist – once you reach the midpoint position, slowly rotate your trunk to the left and to the right, then return to a neutral facing position and move to the end position.
- Valslide Lateral Lunge – rather than stepping laterally, slide your leg out with your foot on a Valslide while performing the rest of the motion.

DUMBBELL SPLIT SQUAT

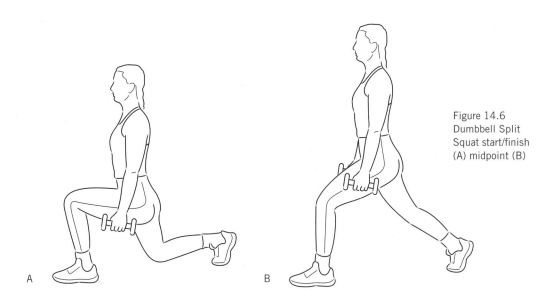

Figure 14.6
Dumbbell Split
Squat start/finish
(A) midpoint (B)

The name of this exercise can be misleading, because the movement is in fact a Lunge. The entire set-up is based around finding the 90/90 position of both the front and rear leg, like the midpoint position of a Lunge. This exercise focuses on building strength in the quads and glutes, which is vital for cycling. To make it more full body in nature, we add a dumbbell to lock in the scapular stabilizers and force the core to be a bit more active to stabilize the trunk, rather than using just the weight of the upper body.

START

It may seem unusual, but we will start this set-up at the bottom of the movement because getting the distance of the legs to create proper angles is critical. Position the legs so that both the front leg and rear leg are in the 90/90 position. Step out the front leg to achieve a 90-degree angle at the knee, and make sure the back thigh is in line with the trunk, the knee makes a 90-degree angle and the toes of the back leg are engaged with the ground. For the set-up, the rear knee may make contact with the ground; some people will even use a foam mat to gauge the distance from the floor. The trunk should be aligned vertically with the head up. Grasp the dumbbell with your scapulae engaged and the arms in a relaxed position at your sides.

MOVEMENT

Drive upward by straightening both legs at the same time by activating both the quad and glute of each leg simultaneously. Drive through the heel of the front leg and through the ball of the foot on the rear leg. There should be no twisting or side bending of the trunk. The core has to be active to maintain the neutral, perpendicular posture of the trunk. The arms remain at the side with the scapulae retracted.

MIDPOINT

Once in the upward position, the knees will still have a slight bend to them (approximately 20 degrees each). The feet should never leave their "home" position, so that they can maintain the proper 90/90 position at the bottom of the movement for the duration of the set.

END

Slowly lower the body in a controlled fashion back down to the 90/90 start position. The knee of the back leg should not touch the ground (hover approximately 1 inch (2.5cm) above the ground) between reps. The trunk should remain perfectly vertical and shouldn't fall forward, back or to one side. Switch sides and repeat the action for the required number of reps so that both legs have been in the forward/back positions an equal number of times.

DOING IT RIGHT

- Strive for the knees of both legs to be in the 90/90 position.
- Keep your chest up, head neutral and eyes slightly up to get the trunk vertically aligned.
- Keep your core tight to prevent rounding or hyperextension of the lower back.
- Keep your scapulae retracted and locked in to the rear of the ribs.
- Hold your arms down at your side with your elbows fully extended.

TIPS

- If you are new to the exercise, first practice this without any added resistance.
- If you can't rise up in a clean upward motion, you are using weights that are too heavy for you.

SAFETY

- If the front leg steps out too short, the knee will go over the toes and will place a great deal of strain on the patellar tendon.
- If the front leg steps out too far, the back leg may be extended at the hip, creating additional stress. You will also have a shorter range of motion for the exercise
- Be smart about how much resistance to use.

VARIATIONS

- Bulgarian Split Squat – perform the movement as indicated above but elevate the rear leg by placing the top of the foot on a bench with the knee hanging downward.
- Barbell Split Squat – the movement is the same, but you will be loaded with a barbell across your shoulders rather than using dumbbells.
- Split Squat Jump – perform the movement of the Dumbbell Split Squat but thrust upward and have the legs switch positions from front to back while in the air, and land in a balanced position. This should not be done with significant resistance.

BENCH PISTOL SQUAT

Figure 14.7
Bench Pistol Squat
start/finish (A)
and midpoint (B)

A

B

As we've explained, single leg exercises will build strength in the prime mover muscles while also creating stability of all the other muscles to provide balance. Additionally, as soon as we do a single leg exercise, an uneven load is created, which forces the core to work harder to stabilize – bonus! We really like this exercise for cycling because it mimics how a single leg produces the majority of the power (down stroke of the pedal cycle) while the other side is recovering.

START

Place a box, bench or stable chair that is approximately 18 inches (45cm) in height about 12 inches (30cm) from the back of your heels. Kick one leg out to about a 30-degree angle from the hip, keeping the knee extended and toes pointed upward. The foot of the leg making contact with the ground should be facing forward and the knee should have a slight bend with muscles actively engaged. Flex your shoulders forward slightly and slightly bend your elbow, while keeping the shoulder blades retracted. Engage the core to obtain a neutral upright trunk posture.

MOVEMENT

Slowly lower your hips to the box, bench or chair using the glute and quad muscles of the leg that is in contact with the ground. The weight of your body should be through your heel as your body won't be able to sit back if your bodyweight is over your toes. Your knee will go forward of your toes – that's to be expected with this exercise. Try to limit the side-to-side wobbling of your knee and keep your pelvis from rotating. Maintain an upright trunk posture (don't let it fall forward). Keep the shoulder blades retracted and don't let the arms fall forward. Be sure to keep the muscles active until your butt gently hits the box, bench or chair. Think of it as a plane landing – nobody likes a bumpy ride!

MIDPOINT

Just because the box, bench or chair is there doesn't mean it's time to sit down and relax. You should pause at this point of the exercise but keep all muscles actively engaged and ready to go. Don't let them turn off. The extended leg should remain straight and the heel may gently come in contact with the ground. The ears, shoulders and hips should be in line.

END

Engage the prime mover quads and glutes to slowly raise the body back to the start position. Movement at the trunk and pelvis and in the arms should be minimal. Repeat for the required number of reps. Be sure to work both sides equally.

DOING IT RIGHT

- Trust the Squat – the box, bench or chair will catch you.
- Keep the core tight to limit pelvis and trunk movement.
- Keep the trunk upright and resist the urge to fall forward.
- Minimize the side-to-side movement of the knee on the planted leg.

TIPS

- This exercise requires a great deal of balance. For this reason, it should not be the first single leg exercise that you try.
- You can start with an even taller box, bench or chair to make the exercise a bit easier.

SAFETY

- Never use a stool or chair that is on wheels or unstable in any way.
- Lower yourself to the box, bench or chair using both legs first to ensure you are standing the proper distance away from it.

VARIATIONS

- Full Pistol Squat – to progress, remove the box, bench or chair and go lower into the Full Pistol Squat. This will be a deep Squat on the loaded leg with the other leg straight out in front.
- Suspension Trainer Pistol Squat – to regress, perform the pistol squat while grasping the suspension trainer with your hands for stability.
- Counterweighted Pistol Squat – extend the arms in front of the chest and hold a dumbbell, kettlebell or sandbag to add resistance to the movement.

SINGLE ARM KETTLEBELL CLEAN AND PRESS

Figure 14.8
Single Arm
Kettlebell Clean
and Press start
(A), Clean (B),
Press (C)

A   B   C

Kettlebells can keep a workout interesting and that's one of the main reasons we like them. Swinging a kettlebell on one side creates the uneven load we are looking for that helps keep the core (especially the obliques) active. The Clean produces strength in the lower body via a Squat, and the Press builds strength in the shoulders, chest and upper back, all while featuring an uneven load.

START

Begin in an athletic stance with your feet shoulder-width apart and a slight bend in the knees. Place the kettlebell directly between both feet on the ground. The upper body should be in a strong, upright posture. Prepare to squat down and grab the kettlebell with one hand while throwing the other arm back as a counterbalance.

MOVEMENT

Using good Squat form, lower your body weight through your heels and extend one arm to grab the kettlebell while the other arm is fully extended from the shoulder in a backward position to provide counterbalance. The lower back should be flat and the chest

should be up. Drive through your heels and rotate the kettlebell, bringing it to the "racked" position in front of your shoulder. The elbow should be tight to the body. At this point, your other arm will be extended to the side of your body to provide counterbalance and you should be in an upright athletic stance. Next, press the kettlebell straight over your shoulder until your elbow is fully extended.

MIDPOINT

The body should be in a tall athletic stance with the kettlebell resting against the back of the forearm while the arm is fully extended at the elbow directly over the shoulder. The core should be tight, to hold the upright posture, and the scapula is locked in to create stability for the shoulder.

END

From the Press position, bring the kettlebell back to the racked position in front of the shoulder and tuck the elbow tight to the body. Next, lower the kettlebell back to the start position by performing a Squat. Repeat for the required number of reps, then switch sides.

DOING IT RIGHT

- Keep your back flat by maintaining an active core, keeping the chest tall and the shoulder blades retracted.
- Perform three separate movements (the Squat, the Clean, the Press), all with correct technique.

TIPS

- This exercise requires a bit of speed, but does not have to be plyometric in nature.

- If the exercise is too complex, break it into parts first by mastering the Squat, the Clean and the Press individually before putting them together into one exercise.

SAFETY

- Always use a closed grip on the kettlebell.
- There should be no rounding of the back or relaxing of the scapulae.
- The knees should stay behind the toes.

VARIATION

Double Arm Kettlebell Clean and Press – use two kettlebells and simultaneously perform the Clean and Press with both arms.

Single Arm Kettlebell Clean – perform the exercise listed above but without the "press" portion. If you lack shoulder stability, this may be a good option.

LATERAL PLATE DRAG

Figure 14.9
Lateral Plate Drag start (A) and midpoint (B)

This is a great go-to anti-rotation exercise, whether you are training at the gym or at home. Perhaps your home gym doesn't have a plate for you to drag... No problem! Simply take anything that is the desired weight and drag it across the floor (we've used an old backpack in the past without problems). The key to all anti-rotation exercises is to resist the turning or rotating that naturally wants to occur at the pelvis and trunk.

START

Start by getting into a Plank position from your hands and feet. Your ankles, knees, hips and shoulders should be in line and your neck should be neutral. The hands should be slightly wider than shoulder-width apart and the feet shoulder-width apart or wider (the closer the feet come together, the less stable you become). The shoulders should be hovering over your hands, which are firmly in contact with the floor, and the arms are fully extended. The plate to be dragged is slightly lower than one of the hands. The core should be tight and active. In this exercise, you will be going from four points of contact to three, with the goal of creating as little movement at the trunk and pelvis as possible.

MOVEMENT

Take the arm that doesn't have the plate near it and reach underneath, across the body, to grab the plate. Once that arm comes off the ground, the three points of contact will make stability a challenge. Typical compensations are piking up at the hips and allowing the trunk and pelvis to roll toward the plate. The goal is to limit all motion at the pelvis and trunk and only move at the shoulder to reach over and grab the plate.

MIDPOINT

The hand is in contact with the plate, the toes of both feet and the planted hand press firmly into the ground to provide stability. The shoulders, hips, knees and ankles are in line and the center of mass isn't shifting to the side of the plate. The torso should be flat, with no rotation.

END

Slowly drag the plate across the ground underneath the body until it is just down from where the hand will be placed. Resume the four points of contact Plank position. Repeat on the other side and for the required number of reps.

DOING IT RIGHT

- Dig in with the toes and hand to create full body tension and stability.
- Keep the core tight throughout the entire set.
- There should be no piking up at the hips.
- Resist the urge to roll at the trunk and pelvis.

TIPS

- To minimize the amount of weight shifting from one side, perform with the midline of the body over a line on the floor so you can see if your weight is shifting.
- Keep the ankles, knees, hips and shoulders in a stacked position.
- Don't pike or hyperextend at the lower back. Keep the upper body neutral.

VARIATIONS

- Valslide Lateral Drag – substitute the valslide for the plate to get used to the motion and reaching the arm underneath the body while in a three-point stance.
- Single Arm Valslide Forward Push – using the valslide, push the moving arm forward in line with the body. The weight shift of having your arm forward will force the muscles of the fixed shoulder and the core to stabilize the movement.

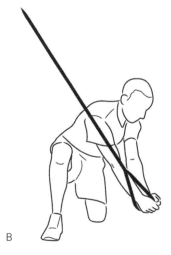

Figure 14.10
Half-kneel Downward
Cable Chop start/finish
(A) and midpoint (B)

A

B

This has to be our absolute favorite core/anti-rotation exercise. There is so much going on, and it features the classic 'X' crossing pattern that connects the upper and lower body as they meet at the core. Typically, anti-rotation exercises strengthen core stabilizers by having the person resist any movement at the trunk and pelvis. For this exercise, there will be trunk movement, but by slowly *resisting the eccentric component, it will achieve the results we're looking for. This is typically done with a cable stack but resistance bands can also be used.*

START

Place the cable pulley at a high anchor point and use a light weight. Start by getting into a half-kneeling position angled away from the cable stack at about a 45-degree angle. The leg closest to the cable stack should be out in front and should be bent to the 90/90 position. Drop down on to the knee of the back leg and curl the toes under to build tension through the back leg. Extend the arms forward so the shoulders are at 90 degrees and the elbows are fully extended. The arms should always stay in this same position in relation to the trunk when the trunk rotates. It's important that all movements are initiated at the core (oblique muscles) and not the arms

or shoulders. Rotate to the side of the front leg and grab the handle of the cable stack with both hands. The trunk should be rotated but upright, and tension should be built through both legs. The knee of the front leg is held neutral and the core is tight.

MOVEMENT

Use the core musculature and glute from the back leg to slowly rotate the cable across and down in front of the body, next to the front foot. The arms and trunk always move as one unit. Lead the movement by turning the eyes and head to the direction in which you will finish. The core must be tight and muscles of the shoulder blades should be retracted. The pattern of the movement is diagonal in nature so that it crosses the midline of the body.

MIDPOINT

Both hands are clasping the handle a few inches from the ground in front of the body, to the opposite side of where the front heel is placed. The downward motion should be a result of increased hip flexion of the front leg and extension of the back leg (meaning that the trunk and pelvis lean forward, but don't round out).

END

This is the most important part of this exercise. *Slowly* resist the rotation at the trunk and as the arms return to the position where they were over the shoulder of the front leg. The body needs to continue to have as little movement as possible; the recruitment of the core and glute resists the movement. Continue to move the arms and trunk as one solid unit. Look with your eyes and head to the direction where you wish to return your hands. Perform the desired number of repetitions on one side before switching to the opposite side.

DOING IT RIGHT

- The shoulders and trunk should move together as a single unit.
- Initiate the movement from your core instead of your elbows or shoulders.

- Keep your eyes on your hands throughout the movement to facilitate moving through the core.

TIPS

- Don't go too heavy as it will cause compensations and defeats the purpose of the exercise.
- Tucking the toes of the back foot under helps build tension and creates a more stable base of support.

SAFETY

- Only rotate as far as you are comfortable. We all have different ranges of motion and there is no need to use this as a stretch.

VARIATIONS

- Use resistance tubing – if you don't have a cable stack to work with, this exercise can easily be performed using resistance tubing fixed at a high attachment point. Perform the movement in the same way you would with a cable stack resistance.
- Standing Cable Chop – rather than performing the chop in a half-kneeling pose, position yourself in an athletic stance and perform the movement. You may have to raise the cable pulley slightly higher.
- Half-kneel Upward Cable Chop – move the pulley from a high position to a low position. Grab the handle and move the shoulders and trunk up and across the torso.

Cyclists should be the last endurance athletes to be scared to engage in strength and mobility training – even though watching riders in the Tour de France, such as Chris Froome, might make you crave a skinny body. When the overall goal is to improve your FTP, it should come as no surprise that having extra leg and core strength is beneficial. After all, the mathematical equation for power is *force* x distance/time. Strength will allow you to produce that force and therefore increase power. Furthermore, the true measure of a good rider is when the FTP is normalized to bodyweight – FTP/kg. Sure, we all want to be a badass like the guys in the Tour de France or pro triathletes and produce 6 W/kg, but honestly, for any of us age-group athletes looking to improve toward that, we need to gain strength. In a sport where we pay a lot to get the lightest bike, we the rider also want to be the lightest (while being the strongest we can be) to gain an advantage on courses with a great deal of climbing. There is a misconception that strength training will bulk you up and make you gain weight. The fact of the matter is that strength training will increase your lean body mass and reduce your fat mass. Therefore, the next time you're riding up a hill after doing an honest bit of resistance training (even if your bodyweight is unchanged), you won't be pushing up so much dead weight (fat). Additionally, in the triathlon world, those love handles aren't exactly aero, so becoming leaner by doing some resistance training will certainly help. Our point is simple: embrace resistance training – it will help you become a more powerful, faster rider.

MTB, gravel and cyclocross riders will also benefit from additional arm and shoulder exercises to help resist the shock when on bumpy terrain. Whether it's the Leadville Trail 100, UNBOUND Gravel or a more technical MTB course, the body is going to take a beating via vibrations. Whole-body vibration has been linked to a number of musculoskeletal injuries. In longer MTB and gravel races, our bodies (especially our upper bodies) are subjected to long bouts of vibration, which can leave us vulnerable. A 2002 study in the *European Journal of Applied Physiology*[2] found that long-bout vibrations to the hand led to decreased grip strength and could possibly result in injuries in the upper extremity. As a guy who once rode the VT50 MTB race on a broken front suspension of his hardtail, RJ can tell you that he was truly thankful for having a strong upper body to help mitigate all the vibrations that his front shocks should have been absorbing! Based on both the research and RJ's personal experience, it's clearly important to include more specific exercises to add stability to our upper bodies, which have to weather some tough conditions in certain races.

If you're looking to get to the next level with your bike racing performances, you need stronger legs to mash those pedals. By providing you with our list of go-to exercises, you no longer have an excuse to be going to the gym and randomly performing exercises you only vaguely think may help your performance. We've explained how each exercise will strengthen targeted muscle groups that are critical to producing powerful pedaling. We know that riding more and riding with specificity will help improve your cycling performance. The same goes for resistance training. Doing more resistance training, and using exercises that are specifically cycling focused, will help improve cycling performance.

Remember, our resistance training programs will provide you with a large dose of Foundation Exercises with the right amount of targeted cycling exercises. If there are ever weeks/days when you are really pressed for time, you can look at doing just the cycling-specific exercises and rest assured that you'll be making gains for your next race.

EXERCISES TO AVOID

Cycling is a lower extremity dominant exercise that does require total body strength to be performed well. There are no exercises that cyclists should universally avoid. As a general rule, as long as an exercise doesn't create pain and discomfort and you are using proper form, you should be able to do the exercise. Individuals with a history of injury should discuss with a physician or rehabilitation clinician the appropriateness of certain exercises. Incorporating the cycling specific mobility exercises with the foundation and cycling specific resistance exercises on a regular basis will help the body achieve balance and should help prevent injuries.

---

1. Jorge, M. and Hull, M. L., 'Analysis of EMG measurements during bicycle pedalling', *Journal of Biomechanics*, 19(9) (1986), pp. 683–694
2. Adamo, D. E., Martin, B. J. and Johnson P. W., 'Vibration-induced muscle fatigue, a possible contribution to musculoskeletal injury', *European Journal of Applied Physiology*, 88(1) (2002), pp. 134–140

15

TOP 10 EXERCISES FOR RUNNERS

Running is hard. Running long distances is harder. Running long distances consistently over the course of an endurance sports career is one of the hardest athletic feats possible. If you want proof, look at how "regular people" (aka non-runners) react when you tell them you have run a single marathon. They are normally a mixture of impressed and bewildered as to why anybody would subject themself to 26.2 miles (42.2km) of torture. Keep in mind, this person is probably only thinking about the miles you ran on race day. They are not even starting to consider the hundreds of miles you ran in preparation, the speed workouts on the track, the disciplined sleep/hydration/nutrition and the mental fortitude it took to get to the starting line and be ready to run that final stretch to the finish line.

Most people understand that distance running requires a great aerobic base, a high VO2 max and incredible discipline. Most people don't understand that successful distance running also requires the strength to withstand the rigours of training, have consistently good running technique and stay injury free. The ability to Finish Strong is largely predicated on having the strength to keep the body moving forward as fatigue sets in.

As a strength and conditioning coach with extensive weight training experience, Angelo is somewhat an anomaly in the endurance world. He didn't do cross country in high school or college. In fact, he was competitively powerlifting during his teens and early 20s – a sport that is literally the exact opposite of a road race. While doing single reps of the heaviest deadlifts possible doesn't really have a place in the training plans of most endurance athletes, the basic strength, structural integrity and muscular endurance developed during those early years have allowed him to have a racing career with consistent improvement and almost no injuries.

It's important to us that we are using sound rationale when choosing strength and mobility exercises that are specific to running. Providing you with exercises that target the right muscle groups will ensure you have purposeful resistance training sessions. Previous electromyography (EMG) research by Howard, Conway and Harrison[1] in *Sports Biomechanics* breaks down running gait into two main phases: 1) the stance phase (when the limb is in contact with the ground); and 2) the swing phase (when the limb is in the air). Stance has two critical instances – initial contact and toe off – which place different demands on the muscles. At initial contact, the muscles of the posterior chain act as a braking force and are recruited eccentrically as they control the mass of the body as it moves forward. Toe off features concentric activation of the muscles to create propulsive force. Propulsion occurs with hip and knee extension and with ankle plantarflexion, and thus the calves (gastrocnemius and soleus) as well as the hip extensors (glutes) and knee extensors (vastus lateralis) are highly active.

Another thing to discuss with regard to running gait is the activity of the tibialis anterior, which is the muscle on the front of the shin. This undergoes an eccentric contraction at initial contact and then is active concentrically during the swing phase, to prepare it for placement with the ground at initial contact. People who are hard-heel strikers will often experience pain here because of the demands they place on that muscle. Our sport-specific exercises will target these muscles, and all the key muscle groups used during running, so that they hold you in optimal posture and work the muscles in the way that is both powerful and efficient.

1. Step-ups
2. Leg Curls
3. Calf Raises
4. Dorsiflexion
5. Lat Pull-down
6. Barbell Inverted Row
7. Standing Overhead Press
8. Trap Bar Deadlift
9. Alternating Knee-to-chest
10. Rip Trainer March

STEP-UPS

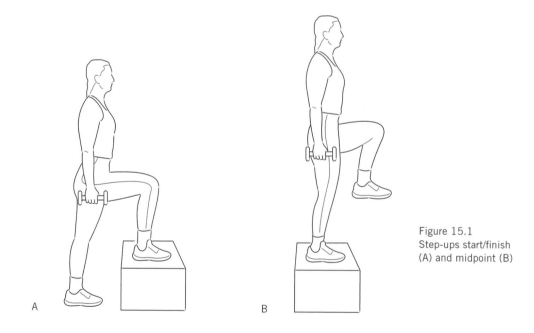

Figure 15.1
Step-ups start/finish
(A) and midpoint (B)

A

B

After Squats and Lunges have been mastered, Step-ups are a natural progression. They are a single leg movement that require more balance and stability because the body must negotiate moving upward onto an elevated platform while handling resistance. Step-ups can be performed weighted or with only bodyweight, and special care should be taken to ensure the trunk remains upright and the knee only flexes and extends and does not wobble from side to side during the movement. Regardless of the type of resistance chosen (barbell, dumbbells, medicine ball, weighted vest, etc.), be sure that the basic technique of the exercise remains the same and good posture and body positioning are maintained throughout the movement. Also, as lifters become more advanced, High Box Step-ups are a viable variation, but people new to the exercise should begin with a height just below the knee.

START

Stand about 12 inches (30cm) away from the box in an athletic stance with the knees slightly bent, core tight and shoulder blades retracted for good posture.

MOVEMENT

Flex the right hip until the thigh is parallel to the ground or 90 degrees at the hip. Place the entire right foot firmly on the box with the heel aligned with the back edge of the platform and drive up through the heel until the right knee is fully extended while driving the left (aka "free") leg upward until that thigh is parallel to the floor.

MIDPOINT

Stand on top of the box with the right foot firmly planted on the platform, with the right knee fully extended and the left knee flexed with the left thigh parallel to the ground.

END

Step down with the left leg, taking special care not to allow the right knee to move side to side. Once the left foot is firmly on the floor, remove the right foot from the box and return to the starting position to repeat the movement with the left leg. Repeat for the required number of reps.

DOING IT RIGHT

- Keep the whole foot on the box for each entire repetition.

- Drive through the heel on the way up.
- Move the "free" leg up until the thigh is parallel with the ground.
- Keep the core tight and continue to keep the trunk in an upright posture.

TIPS

- Select an appropriate-sized box that comes to right below the knee for beginners, and do not progress to higher boxes until this has been mastered.
- Start with bodyweight and then progress to dumbbells or a medicine ball before a barbell is attempted. Also, depending on how much spinal compression is being done in the rest of the program, using a barbell across the shoulders may not ever be necessary for Step-ups – other forms of resistance may be better options.

SAFETY

- Use weights that can be lifted safely.
- Make sure you can Squat and Lunge with good form before trying Step-ups.
- Keep an eye on knee movement and if any side-to-side movement is occurring, reduce either resistance or box height until it can be performed properly.

VARIATIONS

- Reverse Lunge to Step-up – stand with your toes about 6 inches (15cm) from a 2-inch (30cm) box (the height can vary once the exercise has been mastered). Step the right foot back and sink into a full Lunge position. Step the right foot from the Rear Lunge position to being planted firmly on the box and drive up through the heel until the right leg is fully extended and you are standing on top of the box.

- Step-up to Single Leg Romanian Deadlift – step up on to a box with the right leg and let the left leg trail behind as you bend at the waist until the upper body and left leg are both parallel to the ground.

- Lateral Step-ups – stand with a box to your left side. Step the right leg across the body until the foot is flat on the box. Extend the right knee until you are standing on top of the box. Cross the left leg behind the right and flex the right knee until the left foot is back on the ground. Return the right leg to the starting position.

LEG CURLS

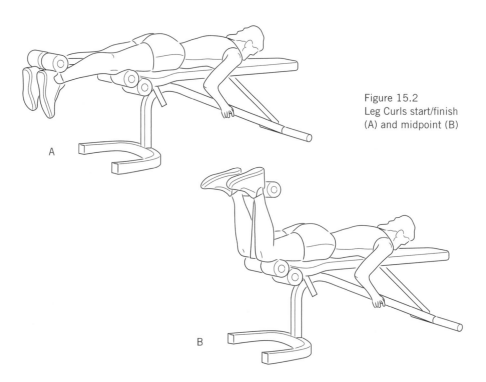

Figure 15.2
Leg Curls start/finish
(A) and midpoint (B)

Movements that incorporate the Hip Hinge represent the best way to develop posterior chain strength because they are performed in a standing position, require coordination of multiple muscle groups, and allow the body to handle the greatest loads. With that being said, there are still exercises that isolate the hamstrings and are valuable to the development of posterior chain size and strength.

There are multiple types of Leg Curl, including ones performed on seated machines, standing machines or prone (lying face down) machines, physioball, slide board, suspension trainer and partner assisted. All of these are quality options for accessory hamstring work and can be added as extra posterior chain training after the heavier Hip Hinge movements have been performed. They can also be used as alternatives during periods of high-volume endurance work to get the hamstrings activated and working.

START

Lie face down on the pad of the machine with the padding of the lever arm placed on both ankles. Grip the handles under the pad firmly to keep the upper body in place throughout the movement.

MOVEMENT

Use the hamstrings to flex the knees and bring the feet and lever arm of the machine forcefully toward the buttocks.

MIDPOINT

The knees are flexed as far as comfortable with the goal of full range of motion.

END

Slowly extend the knees while keeping tension on the hamstrings and returning to the starting position.

TIPS

- Learn and become proficient at several types of knee flexion exercises so that variety is always an option.
- Use multiple types of Leg Curl in order to stimulate the musculature differently and avoid boredom.
- Focus on achieving a full range of motion regardless of body position or resistance type.

SAFETY

- Use loads that can be handled safely.
- Anticipate soreness the day or two after a new variation is attempted and plan other workouts accordingly.
- Don't try anything new the day before a long/intense endurance workout or race.

VARIATIONS

- Physioball Leg Curls – place the upper back on the ground with the heels on a physioball. Elevate the hips so the body is in a straight line and use the hamstrings to flex the knees while rolling the ball closer to the hips. Keep the hips elevated while extending them to return to the starting position.
- Valslide Leg Curls – place the upper back on the ground with the heels on a towel or pad on a valslide or slide board. Bridge the hips and flex the knees to drag the heels across the slide board until they are as close to the hips as possible. Keep the hips bridged while extending the knees to return to the starting position.
- Suspension Trainer Leg Curls – place the upper back on the floor with the heels locked into a suspension trainer. Bridge the hips off the ground and flex the knees until the feet are as close as possible to the hips.
- Glute-ham Raises – use the prone position on a glute-ham bench with the ankles secured and the quads right on top of the main pads. Drive the knees into the pads while flexing the knees and forcing the body to go from parallel to perpendicular to the ground. Return to the starting position slowly and repeat for the desired number of reps.

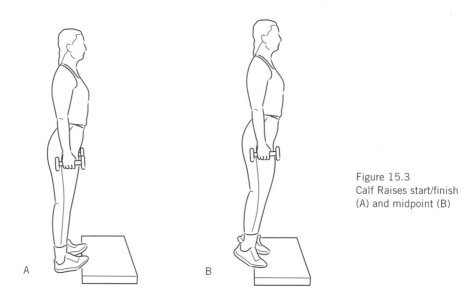

Figure 15.3
Calf Raises start/finish
(A) and midpoint (B)

It has become popular in the strength and conditioning world to discount most single joint and single muscle movements due to the prevailing thought that athletes' bodies should be trained as one cohesive unit because sports are played with the entire body at once. While there is absolutely some truth to this opinion, there is still room for some isolation exercises in a comprehensive training program. While most people would agree that spending a lot of time on a wide array of Biceps Curls is not optimal for an endurance athlete, taking the time to focus on a few key muscles that are active throughout the activity, and often get injured, will pay off in the long run (long run ... get it?).

The lower leg is often a site of discomfort for many runners; from shin splints to compartment syndrome and various other conditions, runners' calves and shins take a lot of abuse from hundreds of miles on hard, unrelenting terrain. In addition to controlling total mileage, selecting the proper footwear and being conscious of running surface, one way to make the lower leg more resilient to injury is by strengthening the muscles in the area.

The calf is comprised mainly of two muscles – the gastrocnemius and the soleus – both of which work to plantar flex the foot (point the toe) and are integral to almost all locomotion. There are several nuances to how each muscle works and how the unit functions together to propel the body forward, but to keep it simple and within the scope of this book, an easy way to think about the lower leg musculature is that the gastrocnemius fires when the knee is straight and the soleus fires when the knee is bent. With this in mind, make sure you perform calf raises with the knee both flexed and extended, to ensure strengthening of both muscles.

Also, there are multiple ways to apply resistance to calf raises and as long as the muscles of the area are firing to point the toe, they are all good options. Experiment with a few different types of resistance, such as holding dumbbells at your sides (this also improves grip strength), a barbell across your shoulders (this develops core and postural muscles) and the various machines available, to find the option that works best for you.

START

Place the balls of the feet on an elevated platform. The knees can be flexed (seated) or extended (standing) depending on the goal of the training session.

MOVEMENT

Begin by lowering the heels as low as possible while keeping the balls of the feet on the elevated platform. This will cause the calf musculature to stretch and improve range of motion and flexibility. Once this bottom position has been reached, forcefully plantar flex the foot and come up on your toes.

MIDPOINT

The ankle is fully extended and the heel is elevated as high as possible on the toes.

END

Lower the heels to the lowest possible position while keeping the balls of the feet on the elevated platform, and prepare for the next rep. Repeat for the required number of reps.

DOING IT RIGHT

- Use the full range of motion.
- Pause at the highest point to really stimulate the firing muscles.
- Emphasize going slowly on the way down and forcefully on the way up.

TIPS

- Use multiple variations of body position and resistance type over the course of a training program.
- Most people will be able to handle significant loads on this exercise (your calves fire constantly in most human movement, so they're probably pretty strong), but don't sacrifice full range of motion or good tempo for more weight.

SAFETY

- Be smart about how much weight is being lifted.
- Don't drop dumbbells when sets are finished (a triathlon is hard enough without a broken foot!).

VARIATIONS

- Seated Calf Raise – sit on a bench with your knees flexed to 90 degrees and resistance (plates, dumbbells, etc.) on the quads. Place the toes on a slightly elevated platform (just a few inches will work) and forcefully push up on to your toes so that your quads and the resistance are as high as possible. Slowly lower your lower body into the starting position with the toes on the elevated platform and your heels on the ground.
- Standing Calf Raise – stand with a barbell across your shoulders, dumbbells in your hands or holding a medicine ball under your chin and press your body up on to your toes by extending the muscles of the lower limb. This can also be done on an elevated platform to extend the range of motion.
- Machine Calf Raise (various types and angles of resistance) – there are various kinds of calf raise machines out there. Try the ones available where you train and decide if they should become part of your rotation of lower leg exercises.

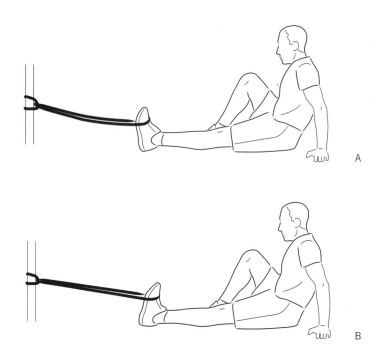

Figure 15.4 Dorsiflexion start/finish (A) and midpoint (B)

One of the most common complaints from novice runners all the way to experienced marathoners is the ugly, uncomfortable, downright nasty lower leg pain commonly called "shin splints". This condition can range from mild discomfort (possibly cured by ice, new shoes and some reduction in mileage) to a serious medical condition that may require you to stop running completely. Shin splints can seriously make even standing and watching a race too painful to enjoy.

There are multiple methods and theories about how to prevent shin splints, but one that is almost universally accepted as safe and effective is to strengthen the musculature of the lower limb to prevent the microtearing sometimes associated with high-mileage endurance training.

The first way to attack this issue is to strengthen the posterior muscles of the calf (aka the gastrocnemius and the soleus) with a variation of lower body resistance exercises including Calf Raises. Equally important to the complete development of and maintaining balance within the lower limb is the strengthening of the anterior muscles of the shin or the dorsiflexors (naming the individual muscles of the region and their functions is beyond the scope of this book and probably beyond your reason for reading it). These muscles pull the toe upward toward the knee and are incredibly important for any kind of locomotion.

The best way to strengthen these muscles is by applying resistance while trying to dorsiflex the ankle or pull the toes up. This can be done with specialized machines, bands or manual resistance and, much like Calf Raises, should be performed often and with a variety of resistance types.

START
Begin with the toes either flat on the ground or plantar flexed (toes pointed).

MOVEMENT
Work against the applied resistance to pull the toes upward toward the knee.

MIDPOINT
The foot is dorsiflexed as far as possible. This position will vary from person to person and will improve as flexibility and mobility are increased.

END
The foot returns to the starting position. Repeat on the other side and for the required number of reps.

DOING IT RIGHT
- Use the full range of motion. This might feel a little awkward because we naturally have a limited range of dorsiflexion motion.
- Fight the resistance all the way up and all the way down.

TIPS
Partner-assisted manual resistance is great for Seated Bent-knee Dorsiflexion while resistance bands are better for Seated Straight Leg Dorsiflexion. This is because there is less chance for miscommunication and injury when the ground naturally limits range of motion.

SAFETY
- Don't use excessive resistance.
- Good communication is incredibly important for all manual resistance exercises.

VARIATIONS
- Seated Bent-knee Dorsiflexion – perform the exercise from a sitting position with the knees bent – similar to the finishing position of a Sit-up.
- Seated Straight Leg Dorsiflexion – perform the exercise sitting on the floor with the upper body perpendicular to the ground and the legs fully extended.
- Band-resisted Dorsiflexion – wrap a band around the foot and pull the toes toward the knee as the band provides resistance to the range of motion.
- Partner-resisted Dorsiflexion – sitting with the knees bent, a partner places a hand on the top of the foot and provides resistance as you try to pull your toes closer to your knees.
- Machine-resisted Dorsiflexion – there are a few Dorsiflexion machines out there. Try them out and decide if they are for you.

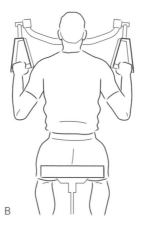

Figure 15.5
Lat Pull-down start/
finish (A) midpoint (B)

A

B

A strong back is incredibly important to both good posture (which aids in breathing) and proper running technique. There has been no shortage of literature ranging from research journal publications to clickbait online articles professing the importance of the core for proper human movement and functioning, but the musculature of the upper back is often overlooked. Without strong lats, rhomboids and scapular stabilization muscles maintaining good posture, efficient movement is almost impossible. What's more, poor posture leads to inefficient movement patterns, submaximal breathing and eventually premature fatigue.

Pull-ups and the associated variations are a great way to strengthen these muscles and improve core stability and body control (see the Foundation Exercise section in Chapter 11) but banging out sets of Pull-ups is not realistic for all endurance athletes. While eventually being able to do Pull-ups with ease is a great goal, Lat (latissimus dorsi, not lateral, as many people think) Pull-down machines are a good way to train a similar motor pattern while strengthening the same muscles. Also, Lat Pull-downs are not only for novice lifters; as strength is built and experience is gained, the exercise is still valuable to add variety and different angles of pull while training some of the most important muscles of the upper body.

Note: There are hundreds of different types of Lat Pull-down machines on the market. While all have their strengths, weaknesses and unique features, the following exercise description will work and the key principles will hold true for most of the popular versions.

START

Begin seated, facing the machine with the seat adjusted so the knees are bent to roughly 90 degrees and the feet are flat on the floor. The handles of the bar should be just out of arm's reach so that when the movement is being performed, full extension of the elbows is possible without the resistance hitting the top of the machine and limiting full range of motion. Grasp the handles slightly wider than shoulder-width apart with a pronated grip (palms out) and arms fully extended.

MOVEMENT

Begin pulling the bar toward the upper chest while retracting the scapulae and flexing the elbows, keeping them slightly in front of the torso or pulling down and into the chest.

MIDPOINT

The handles should be touching the upper chest with the scapulae retracted and the elbows in line with the torso.

END

Slowly extend the elbows until they are fully extended and the handles are directly overhead or slightly in front of the body with a slight posterior lean of the torso to keep the body in an ideal position for the next rep. Repeat for the required number of reps.

DOING IT RIGHT

- Keep the torso upright and keep the scapulae retracted for the duration of each set.
- Initiate the movement with the latissimus dorsi (aka the "back") and not the arms.
- There should be no swinging of the torso or using momentum to complete the movement.

TIPS

- Use loads that don't require any kind of cheating.
- Regularly do Lat Pull-downs and variations, especially if you are struggling to perform quality Pull-ups.

SAFETY

- If this exercise causes shoulder discomfort, experiment with different bars/handles, hand positioning and body positions before giving up.
- Keep the entire body stable. Movement should only come from the shoulders/arms.
- Make sure you are activating the latissimus dorsi and scapula movers/stabilizers every rep.
- Avoid pulling behind the head as it places undue stress on the shoulder without a significant differentiation in muscle activation. To put it another way, the risk isn't worth the reward.

VARIATIONS

- Reverse Grip Lat Pull-downs (palms facing in) – the movement is performed with the palms facing the face. Also known as an "underhand" or "chin-up" grip.
- V-Grip Lat Pull-down – the exercise is done with the palms facing each other on a bar that resembles an inverted letter "V".
- Close Grip Lat Pull-down – the hands are positioned inside the shoulders on the bar.
- Wide Grip Lat Pull-down – the movement is performed with the hands positioned outside the shoulders.
- Kneeling or Standing Lat Pull-down – get into a kneeling or standing position in front of the piece of equipment. This will engage the core musculature and develop balance and proprioception while strengthening the muscles of the back. These are good options once standard Lat Pull-downs have been mastered.

BARBELL INVERTED ROW

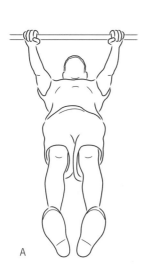

Figure 15.6
Inverted Row start/finish
(A) and midpoint (B)

A

B

If for every action there is an equal and opposite reaction, Inverted Rows are the equal and opposite reaction to Push-ups. While the Push-up is a great way to build upper body strength, especially for people new to resistance training and endurance athletes whose bodies are already incredibly fatigued from training, Inverted Rows work the opposing muscles that will promote good posture, proper breathing and prevent muscle imbalances.

Inverted Rows are a great exercise for beginners who may be struggling with Pull-ups, and provide another way to strengthen the upper back musculature without needing to move the entire weight of the body through a range of motion. Once you are strong enough for Pull-ups, this exercise provides a nice variation that works the lats, rhomboids and biceps in a slightly different manner, requires almost no equipment and is the right difficulty level to be performed during periods of intense endurance training without excessive fatigue.

START

Begin by setting a bar at roughly waist height. The most common way to do this is on a squat rack, but other equipment variations exist. If waist height is too difficult, place the bar higher to make the body more vertical and decrease the difficulty of the angle of pull. The lower the bar the harder the exercise becomes. This is because as the body is moved closer to horizontal, a higher percentage of the body's weight must be pulled toward the bar in order to perform the exercise correctly.

Sit under the bar and grasp it with the palms facing outward and the hands just about shoulder-width apart. Extend the legs in front with only the heels touching the ground, and contract the core musculature to raise the hips off the floor until the body is in a straight line from the ear to the ankle. Once the body is in this straight line, be conscious of keeping the core tight and the hips in line with the shoulders and ankles, as relaxing the core and bending at the waist will put the body in a weak position that will affect the integrity of the exercise and possibly cause injury.

Note: Keeping the body in a straight line is the ideal position for this exercise. However, if the full range of motion (bringing the chest to the bar) is impossible in this position, the knees can be bent to varying degrees with the feet flat on the floor to reduce the amount of bodyweight that needs to be moved in order to bring the chest to the bar. This is fine for beginners, but as the upper back gets stronger and body control is improved, the feet should be progressively moved away from the hips until a straight line from ear to ankle can be achieved.

MOVEMENT
Retract the shoulder blades and flex the shoulders and elbows to move the chest toward the bar while keeping the core tight and the body in a straight line from the ear to the ankle.

MIDPOINT
The body is in a straight line with the chest touching the bar. Emphasize stabilizing the body and "squeezing" this top position before beginning the descent or down phase.

END
Slowly extend the elbows while keeping the shoulder blades retracted and the body in a straight-line position until the body returns to the starting position. Repeat for the required number of reps.

DOING IT RIGHT
- Keep the hips high and in line with the feet and shoulders. While some athletes have

a tendency to overextend the hips and push them too far forward, the majority will not extend them far enough and will sag at the waist during this exercise. Both are examples of poor technique that could lead to potential injury and need to be addressed.
- If you are struggling, start with the knees bent and feet flat on the floor, but progressively extend the knees until the body is in a straight line from the ear to the ankle.
- Retract the shoulder blades before activating the lats and flexing the elbows to start the initial pull toward the bar.

TIPS
- Experiment with different bar heights until you find one that feels right.
- Use this relatively "easy" exercise when your body feels too fatigued for more strenuous back work.

SAFETY
- Always make sure the bar is secure.
- If a rep can't be completed due to fatigue, slowly lower yourself and sit on the floor below the bar instead of struggling to complete a rep with poor technique.

VARIATIONS
- Underhand Grip Inverted Row (palms in) – the movement is performed with palms facing the face.
- Suspension Trainer Inverted Row – using a suspension trainer creates instability, which improves the body's ability to perform in unstable conditions.
- Feet Elevated Inverted Row – having the feet elevated on a bench or box puts the body in a completely horizontal position and requires the entire bodyweight to be lifted. This move is for advanced athletes.

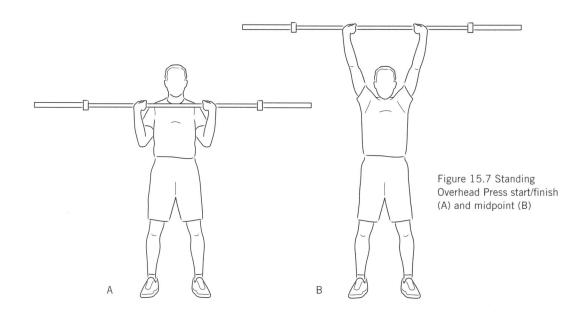

Figure 15.7 Standing Overhead Press start/finish (A) and midpoint (B)

Push-ups, Bench Press, Pull-ups and Lat Pull-downs are all great ways to develop strength in the upper body, but to really build the muscles of the shoulder, the Overhead Press is unmatched. The movement can be performed seated or standing, but endurance athletes should focus on standing presses if the goal is total body strength development for optimal performance instead of isolating the shoulder musculature like a bodybuilder. Also, the exercise is quite versatile as it can be performed with a barbell, dumbbells, kettlebells, machines, sandbags, resistance bands and multiple other modes of resistance, making it ideal for when your normal facility or equipment is not available. We will focus on Standing Barbell Presses, which are optimal for runners because they require core activation, the maintenance of good posture under stress and prepare the body to perform in a standing position while dealing with resistance.

START

Place the feet shoulder-width apart with the knees slightly bent to avoid undue stress on the lower back. Place your hands shoulder-width apart on the barbell and the bar at the upper chest or collarbones. Throughout the movement, keep the body in a straight line from the ear to the ankle with the only exception being a slight bend in the knees. The elbows should be pointed straight at the floor and the knuckles should be pointed straight up at the ceiling.

MOVEMENT

Forcefully drive the bar upward in a straight line directly overhead with no movement to the upper body or torso. As the bar passes the face, protrude the head forward so that when full extension is reached the biceps are in line with the ears and the bar is directly overhead. This aligns the centers of gravity of both the lifter and the bar and puts the lifter in the strongest position to move the most weight. It also reduces the risk of injury.

MIDPOINT

Feet should be flat on the floor with knees slightly bent. The hips are directly below the shoulders and the core is engaged to keep the upper body perpendicular to the ground. Shoulder blades are retracted against the posterior ribcage with arms fully extended overhead and biceps are in line with the ears.

END

Slowly lower the bar to the starting position with minimal movement to any part of the body except the shoulder girdle and upper extremity. Repeat for the required number of reps.

DOING IT RIGHT

- Lower the bar slowly and push upward with force and intensity on every single rep.
- The body should remain in a straight line from the ankle to the ear throughout the movement.
- When the elbows are fully extended, the biceps should be in line with the ears.
- Maintain a tight core and don't hyperextend the lower back by thrusting the hips forward.

TIPS

- Get good at Barbell Presses before moving on to more advanced modes of resistance like dumbbells, because it's harder to control two objects than one.
- Work to attain full range of motion and address the issues that are causing pain or discomfort instead of doing partial reps.

SAFETY

- Maintain proper body position throughout the movement. A lot of people new to weight training will push the bar forward and hyperextend their back to keep the bar moving upward. This is dangerous in both the short term (dropping the bar on your torso) and the long term (chronic lower back pain). Work hard to keep the torso erect and emphasize finishing each rep with the biceps and ears lined up, to keep the body in the strongest position possible.
- Keeping the elbows slightly in front of the body throughout the movement will keep the shoulder joint in a strong position and avoid future shoulder issues.
- Make sure you have enough space to do this exercise correctly and take precautions to keep others away from the bar as you are doing your sets.

VARIATIONS

- Seated Dumbbell Shoulder Press or Standing Dumbbell Shoulder Press – these are simply an Overhead Press with one dumbbell in each hand, in seated or standing.
- Push Press – start the movement by flexing the knees and pushing the hips backward, then forcefully extend the knees to initiate the bar moving upward. Finish the movement by using the upper body musculature to fully extend the elbows with the bar overhead. This has a definite value to endurance athletes but should be reserved for experienced men and women.
- Standing Land Mine Presses – while one end of the bar is secured in a landmine sleeve and the other end is held in one hand, the elbow is extended while one end of the bar moves upward until the elbow is fully extended. This forces the bar to move upward and slightly outward at the same time and provides a slight variation to regular overhead pressing.

Figure 15.8
Trap Bar Deadlift
start/finish (A) and
midpoint (B)

A

B

If we are talking about absolute strength, we are absolutely talking about the Deadlift. Few movements develop and demonstrate pure strength like picking up a heavy load off the ground. There are multiple Deadlift variations that are great for various types of training, but many of these require extensive coaching, demand near technical perfection and have a very thin line between a rep ending in glorious success and catastrophic injury. Using the trap bar (aka hex bar) puts the body in an ideal position to get all of the benefits of conventional deadlifting with less chance of injury and less time required to truly master the motor pattern.

Additionally, this exercise allows us to train the entire body with an emphasis on the lower extremity, much like squatting with a much lower amount of stress on the lower back, so it is ideal during periods of high-volume endurance training when the body may be too fatigued to squat properly.

START
Begin by standing inside the trap bar with the feet slightly wider than the hips and toes pointing slightly outward. Push the hips back while keeping the feet flat on the ground with the body's weight shifted toward the heels. Grasp the handles with the arms extended, back flat and head/eyes slightly upward.

MOVEMENT
Forcefully stand up, being careful to raise the hips and chest at the same time, until a fully erect standing position is achieved.

MIDPOINT
The body is standing tall with the arms fully extended at the sides and the trap bar around the mid-thighs.

END

Begin the descent or down phase by pushing the hips backward and keeping the feet flat with weight shifted toward the heels. Continue flexing the knees and keeping the lower back flat and shoulder blades retracted until the bar is returned to the ground and the body is in the starting position. Repeat for the required number of reps.

DOING IT RIGHT

- Keep the back and head in a neutral position with the eyes looking slightly upward.
- Squat with your legs by pushing the hips back before bending the knees. Avoid excessive bending at the waist and do not round the lower back.
- Envision pushing the ground away from you as you stand up.

TIPS

- Use Trap Bar Deadlifts as a total body or leg exercise.
- Don't be scared to put some plates on the bar but be reasonable and safe.

SAFETY

- There should be no rounding of the back or relaxing of the shoulder girdle.
- Knees should always stay behind the toes.
- Knees should stay stacked with the ankles and the hips and not wobble inside or outside the stance. If this problem persists, lower the resistance until the movement can be performed correctly or place a small resistance band around the knees that will fall off if tension is lost and the knees cave inward. This will force the lifter to push the knees away from each other and keep the lower extremity in a good position.
- The bar should remain level throughout the movement. If one side rises or lowers faster than the other, the back will be placed in a compromised position and injury could occur.

VARIATIONS

- Conventional Deadlifts – use a hip-width stance and a shoulder-width grip on a standard barbell to perform the Deadlift movement.
- Sumo Deadlifts – adopt a wider than hip-width stance and a narrow grip to perform the Deadlift movement.
- Dumbbell or Kettlebell Deadlifts – perform Deadlifts with a dumbbell or kettlebell in each hand.

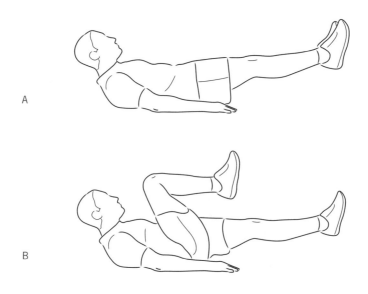

A

B

Figure 15.9 Alternating Knee-to-chest start/finish (A), and right leg (B)

Efficient running requires the core of the body (abdominals, obliques and lower back) to be strong enough that the force generated by the legs is transmitted through this solid foundation and used to propel the body forward. A weak core will inhibit proper running mechanics, contribute to poor posture (which will affect movement patterns and breathing) and cause the majority of force generated by the lower extremity to be absorbed by this weak midsection and not transferred to the outside environment.

There is an almost endless list of core exercises that will adequately strengthen the core muscles to allow the body to run efficiently, but the Alternating Knee-to-chest movement is one of the most effective at causing the core muscles to fire in the same way they operate while propelling the body in a forward motion.

START

The body is lying on the floor in a supine position with the knees fully extended, toes pointing straight up and arms on the floor right next to the sides, parallel with the body. The lower back is pushed into the floor, creating a flat back, with the head and shoulders elevated off the floor in a Crunch position. This starting position ensures a neutral back, eliminates undue stress on the lumbar spine and ensures the upper abdominal muscles are engaged throughout the movement.

Before each set begins, set the lower back into the floor by consciously elevating or crunching the head/shoulders off the ground and raising both legs about 6 inches (15cm) from the floor. This position will engage the core and may be challenging for some novices before the "real exercise" even starts.

MOVEMENT

While strictly maintaining the previously outlined body position, slowly flex the left knee and bring it as close to the chest as possible while maintaining contact between the lumbar vertebrae and the ground.

MIDPOINT

When the knee can no longer be pulled into the chest, slowly push it away from the body while maintaining the same upper body position and keeping the left leg fully extended and 6 inches (15cm) off the ground.

END

When both legs reach full extension, repeat the movement with the left leg and then alternate legs for the appropriate number of reps.

DOING IT RIGHT

- Keep the head and shoulder blades off the ground to maintain a Crunch position in the upper body.
- Flatten the lumbar vertebrae into a neutral position by pressing the lower back into the ground.
- While one knee is flexing, the "down" leg should remain 6 inches (15cm) off the floor.

SAFETY

- If keeping the lower back pushed into the floor is impossible, it may be smarter to work on holding this starting phase for several sets of 20–60 seconds until the core is strong enough to hold this position while the lower extremity is moving.
- Only do the number of sets/reps that can be performed properly.
- If technique breaks down over the course of a set, it might be better to do several shorter sets of fewer reps per set than one

or two longer sets. For example, if the end of each set of 20 gets ugly or starts to stress the lower back, more sets of 10 reps might be a good option until core strength has been increased.

VARIATIONS

- Weighted Alternating Knee-to-chest – perform the same motion while holding an implement (medicine ball, kettlebell, etc.) over the chest with arms extended to further stress the muscles of the upper abdomen.
- Resisted Alternating Knee-to-chest – perform the movement with bands anchored away from the body to make knee flexion more difficult.
- Unbalanced Alternating Knee-to-chest – perform the exercise on an unstable surface that will require the core to engage while stabilizing the body.

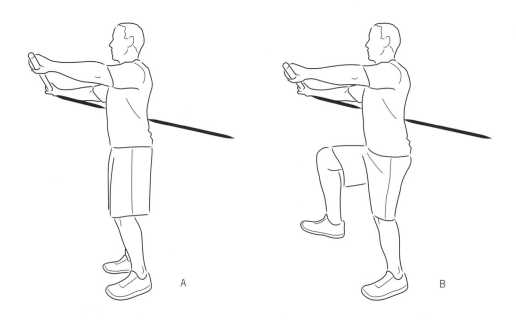

Figure 15.10 Rip Trainer March start/finish (A), midpoint on right side (B)

One of the best tools to use to perform anti-rotation exercises is the Rip Trainer from TRX. It features a solid bar that is loaded with a resistance band on one end, and anchors to many solid points (including doors). If your gym doesn't have Rip Trainers, look for a Keiser machine or you can achieve the same results with a cable stack attached to a solid bar. Using an unbalanced load like this requires the core muscles to brace against the rotation that naturally wants to occur. Marching simulates the leg-lifting phase of the run, which makes this exercise perfectly sport specific.

START

Attach the anchor approximately waist height to a solid object. Stand facing away from the anchor point, holding the bar out in front of your body by having your shoulders flexed to 90 degrees and the arms fully extended. The center of the bar should be in line with your sternum and the anchor point of the resistance band (this creates the uneven load). The body is in an athletic stance with the feet shoulder-width apart and slightly bent at the knee and hip. The core musculature should be engaged so that the pelvis and spine are held neutral throughout the entire set.

MOVEMENT

While keeping the core engaged, slowly lift one leg so that the hip flexes up to 90 degrees and the knee bends to 90 degrees. Keep the planted leg strong and in firm contact with the ground. Resist the desire to rotate the trunk toward the side with the resistance band. Continue to keep an active and tight core.

END

Lower the leg back to the ground while maintaining a neutral pelvis and trunk. Continue by performing the exact same movement with the other leg lifted and the opposite leg planted. You will lift both of the legs regardless of which side the resistance band is on. You must perform the exercises with the band on each side for the required number of reps so you don't develop a side dominance.

DOING IT RIGHT

- Line up the center of the bar, your sternum and the core's anchor point before starting each set.
- Keep your arms fully extended throughout each set.

- Maintain an active core and keep the pelvis and trunk neutral.
- Resist turning your body in either direction.

SAFETY

Don't step out too far to make for a large amount of resistance from the band. You will need less than you think for this to be an effective exercise.

VARIATIONS

If the exercise is too difficult with the elbows extended, you can hold the bar in tight to the body at the level of the shoulders and with the elbows flexed.

BONUS EXERCISE: SHORT FOOT EXERCISES

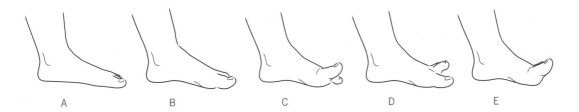

Figure 15.11 Short Foot Exercises flat foot (A), foot with arch (B), great toe extension (C), small toe extension (D), all toe extension and splay (E)

We know this chapter is called Top 10 Exercises for Runners, but we just couldn't leave out this super beneficial injury-prevention exercise, which we discussed in the Frank's Red Hot Exercises. For the runner who struggles with recurrent lower extremity injuries, and who has a flattened arch or pronated foot, it's quite possible that poor foot alignment is adversely affecting the alignment up the kinetic chain. This can cause anything from plantar fasciitis and Achilles tendinitis to shin splints and knee/hip pain. This exercise isn't really considered a resistance training exercise, but rather it's more of a rehabilitative exercise that clinicians use with patients who struggle with foot pronation. The goal is to restore a normal subtalar (rearfoot) neutral position to the foot and ankle complex, restore some "height" to the medial longitudinal arch and restore muscle firing patterns so that the smaller foot intrinsic muscles assist the larger muscles.

START

Remove your shoes and socks. Sit in a chair so that the foot and ankle are both at 90 degrees and the foot rests comfortably on the ground. If you have a greatly pronated foot, rock the weight of the foot slightly laterally while maintaining full contact of the heel and all toes with the ground (perhaps your medial foot is a bit more off the ground now). Focus on pulling the base of the great toe back toward the heel while keeping the toes in a straight forward position with no flexion or hyperextension. You should not see any tendons popping on the top of the foot.

MOVEMENT

Step 1 – Isolated great toe extension
While maintaining the same position described at the start, focus on only lifting the great toe and holding it in the air for five seconds. Keep toes two to five relaxed and in contact with ground while the great toe is lifted. Lower the great toe and repeat.

Step 2 – Combined little toe extension
While maintaining the same position described at the start, focus on only lifting toes two to five and holding them in the air for five seconds. Keep the first toe relaxed and in contact with the ground while the other toes are lifted. Lower the toes and repeat.

Step 3 – Toe splay
While maintaining the same position described at the start, focus on lifting toes one to five, then splay them apart. Hold the splayed position for five seconds. Keep the other portion of the foot in contact with the ground while the other toes are lifted and splayed. Lower the toes and repeat.

TIPS

- Perform the exercises in front of a mirror to ensure you have the proper start position.
- Visual feedback from your eyes is super important to speed up your learning of this unusual exercise.
- Don't be in a hurry to progress. This takes time!

PROGRESSIONS

Seated (non-weight bearing) -> double leg standing (weight bearing) -> single leg standing (weight bearing) -> incorporate into functional movements, such as Step-ups.

EXERCISES TO AVOID

Distance running is a total body activity and there are no exercises that should be universally avoided by the population. If the movement doesn't cause extreme pain/discomfort or exacerbate a pre-existing injury and it can be performed safely then it can be implemented in the training program around the six Foundation Exercises and Top 10 Exercises for Runners. Remember to always integrate resistance training with runs to avoid overtraining and soreness.

One thing all endurance runners can agree on is that as the miles pile up, the body takes a beating. Of the three disciplines (swim, bike, run), running results in the most injuries that keep athletes from making it to the start line. Over the course of long training sessions or races, muscles weaken and form breaks down, which not only affects running economy but also places stresses on vulnerable structures of the body. If you're looking to stay injury free and start gunning for new personal bests, then working at a stronger body with regularly planned resistance training will help you attain those goals. Our programs always include a steady dose of Foundation Exercises and just the right amount of the specialized exercises for runners. We've provided a rationale for how each of these targeted exercises will help improve your running performance and keep you injury free.

We know training for marathons, ultras and IRONMAN takes a lot of time and commitment. We also recognize the value of adding strength and mobility exercise to our training. Remember, performing regularly planned, purposeful resistance training doesn't have to be time-consuming. If you are ever feeling pressed for time during particularly busy weeks, you could consider just performing these go-to exercises for runners and know that you'll still be making strides toward reaching your goals. If you are tired of dealing with a body that feels broken down at the end of a season and you are ready to have a powerful "kick" all the way to the finish line, use these running-specific exercises and Finish Strong!

SECTION 3

THE
PLAN

16

INTRODUCTION TO OUR
TRAINING TEMPLATES

In the previous chapters we told you *why* you needed to add resistance and mobility exercise into your training routine and *how* to do it, now it's time to put that new knowledge into practice! We are hopeful that you are hungry to make those performance improvements we told you about and keep yourself from getting sidelined by chronic/overuse injuries by using the organized workouts. We also hope that you didn't just jump to this section of the book and start your strength and mobility training.

When we polled endurance athletes about why they weren't doing strength and mobility training, two major themes prevailed: 1) lack of time and 2) not knowing where to start. Don't worry – we've got you covered. Our goal is to empower you to take the next step to either untap that hidden performance potential or get away from the therapy clinic and back in the race.

Fact: there are 1,440 minutes in each day and 10,080 minutes in each week. Most people are great at wasting a lot of these minutes scrolling through social media or watching television (yes – even you – the guys and gals who are busting their ass training for their respective endurance sport). Surely you can find 45 minutes a few times a week to do some strength training! You've successfully made your aerobic training a habit, now you just have to commit to this and let strength and mobility training also become a habit. We were fed up reading through triathlon and marathon training books and training plans on TrainingPeaks and seeing some haphazard attempt to "cram" in strength training one day a week. Heck, there are lots of you paying big bucks for coaches who aren't coming through with a well-developed plan to keep you strong and mobile (most just focus on aerobic training). What if we explained that the American College of Sports Medicine recommends performing resistance training a *minimum* of two to three times per week for every major muscle group.[1] When you think about it, it really isn't that much. If you've been the misguided athlete who randomly did one day of strength training in the past, we've just given you an important bit of information that will empower you to take your performance to the next level. Now, let's get that healthy new habit started!

Two common questions we get are: 1) 'Should I do the strength training before or after aerobic training?' and 2) 'How do I structure the strength days with high volume and rest days?' As early risers, our personal preference is to get our aerobic training done before work and hit the gym for strength training after work. If you work an untraditional schedule or have family demands and need to stack your strength training and aerobic workout back to back, we'd recommend getting the strength and mobility training done first. On the days when you do your high-volume aerobic work, we don't recommend also strength training. Your body has been stressed enough and could probably use a break. As a triathlete, should you ever do a triple session (brick workout and resistance training)? Sure! RJ has done it countless times. We'd suggest performing the training brick in the early morning, taking a break through the day and then doing your resistance training in the late afternoon. You may just have to opt for some slightly lower-intensity (lighter weights) training, but there will still be benefits to the workout. As far as honouring the sacred rest day, that is up to you. We've used the rest day as a strength training day for years without problems (quite simply, you aren't making the same demands on the muscles that the aerobic training does). The take-home message here is: listen to your body – it will let you know if it can handle it.

Over the years, we've used our athletes and ourselves as guinea pigs to test what works and what doesn't work. The keys to a good resistance training program are that it can be fit into our busy life/aerobic sport training schedules, can keep a person interested and engaged and, most importantly, yields the big results we are looking for! To fit your busy schedule, we've opted for full body workouts that feature supersets and last a total of about 45 minutes. Why? Because that's achievable for the busy athlete. If our program split days by upper body and lower body exercises, you'd have to work out for a minimum of four days a week and if you missed a day you'd be in trouble (because a muscle has to be stressed at least two days a week to achieve the desired gains). Full body workouts fix that issue. Supersets allow you to move from exercise to exercise quickly without sitting around looking awkward at the gym, though they do feature built-in rest periods. If you do an upper body push exercise (such as a Bench Press), you can easily move to a lower body pull exercise (Leg Curl) and your chest can rest while you do the lower body exercise. It's all about efficiency – and this allows us to keep the sessions to 45 minutes.

In our program, we've given you the Foundation Exercises and sport-specific exercises and have included progressions and regressions that will help you individualize the program to your needs based on your ability (see page 20). This is our recipe for success. Ready, set, go!

HALLMARKS OF OUR SYSTEM

- Full body workouts
- Upper push/lower pull, upper pull/lower push supersets, with core work
- Minimal rest between sets
- Never last more than 45 minutes
- Ability to regress or progress exercises as needed
- Ability to individualize to fit your specific needs as an athlete

Step 1 is to take our training templates with you to the gym and follow a single day's plan. See for yourself that in a short period of time you'll get a fantastic full body workout that will hit all the target strength and mobility exercises for someone in your sport. Experience first-hand the flow that we have set up and start reaping the rewards with stronger, leaner muscles that will propel you to new personal bests.

Step 2 is to start making a habit of doing the workouts a minimum of three times per week. As you gain more confidence, don't be afraid to mix in some of the progressions for each of the exercises.

Step 3 is to make this new-found habit stick and follow the program through the different phases of your season. Lather, rinse, repeat!

HOW TO USE THE TRAINING TEMPLATES

Each week features four full body workouts with changes to sets/reps/exercises/resistance, depending on the training phase. During the off-season, you might go to the gym four days a week but during taper you might choose to do two bodyweight sessions to facilitate recovery. To achieve optimal results, you should perform the resistance and mobility training each of these designated days. However, we are realists and do understand that sometimes our weeks can be a bit time crunched with other obligations, and that's OK. If you only have time to get two workouts in, you've at least hit every muscle group twice (and have met ACSM minimum standards). While it might be a minimalist approach, you're still getting stronger and more powerful.

Each daily template starts with about 10 minutes of mobility exercises. These should be highly individualized based on your sport and quite possibly your movement assessment (if you have had one performed by a trained individual). Previously, in the mobility section in Chapter 9, we identified common problem areas by sport (i.e. – swimmers should work on thoracic spine and shoulder mobility), and we outlined the exercises that will help address those common problem areas. Feel free to do a few more if your body has other spots worthy of addressing. Self-myofascial release exercises such as foam rolling are also suggested in this part of the program. Remember, take your time to hit those trigger points in the muscles and let the muscles and fascia become more supple. By starting with the mobility exercises and self-myofascial release, we are priming your muscles to be at their optimal length for the strength training exercises.

The next portion of the daily template features the Foundation Exercises. Remember that these make up about 75 percent of the program. They are split into upper body push/lower body pull and vice versa supersets, and are meant to be a time-saver. We've seen people waste countless precious minutes resting between sets by sitting on equipment and exercising their thumbs checking social media. It's madness. By moving on directly from an upper body push exercise to a lower body pull exercise, you have an automatic built-in rest for that muscle group. By the time you finish your lower body pull exercise, your upper body has recovered and is ready for the next set. Remember, when we are out for a one-hour swim, three-hour bike ride or two-hour run, our muscles don't get a chance to rest.

Each day will have two supersets that include three exercises and they should be performed for four sets (one core/anti-rotation, one upper body pull, one lower body push, one core/anti-rotation, one upper body push, one lower body pull). You will also notice that we've included core/anti-rotation exercises as the first exercise prior to the push/pull sequence. This will ensure that your core musculature is ready and active for the push/pull exercises. As we stressed in the core/anti-rotation chapter, all of the body's kinetic chains cross at the core, making it critical that this area is strong and stable. By including these exercises at the start of each superset, they should reinforce proper muscle recruitment patterns for the Foundation Exercises in those sets.

When looking through the Foundation Exercises in the supersets, if there's something you're not comfortable with, no problem. Our progression/regression chart allows you to find an appropriate regression of the Foundation Exercise so you can do it safely. Conversely, for those of you who have experience in resistance training, you might be looking for options to progress the exercise and make it more difficult, and our chart has that information for you too!

After you've worked through the supersets, we finish off each day with sport-specific exercises. Based on your sport, you will use the exercises that will help you specifically from our Top 10 Lists. Whether you are an avid marathon runner, competitive OWS, experienced criterium rider or a triathlete, we've got you covered. That's right, we've got separate training templates for our multisport friends! The triathlon templates feature a blend of the sport-specific resistance and mobility exercises. Different exercise session templates have also been provided for each of the different training phases to account for the subtle differences in each. Lastly, we encourage you to always record your weights so you can track your progress.

THE TRAINING PHASES

We've included weekly programs for all of the different training phases: off-season, base & build, peak mileage and taper. Can't make it to the gym? No problem, we've got you covered with our home gym/travel program.

In our periodization chapter, we identified the goals of the four main phases of training throughout the year. To recap: the off-season is the time to try new things in the gym and really commit to increasing strength and mobility; base & build is the time to continue resistance training while covering more miles and building a solid aerobic base; peak mileage is when you should maintain the strength you've developed while running/biking/swimming longer distances than any other time of the year; and taper is when you can take your "foot off the gas" and let your body recover for peak performance on race day.

Training in each of these four distinct phases will be determined by where your body is physically in relation to the biggest events of your competition year. The sets/reps/weights/exercises will be radically different six days before your biggest event than they were six months beforehand. Sticking to this plan and knowing how to modify certain exercises to match your particular training emphasis will be of utmost importance when putting together a yearly training plan.

Also, as fellow endurance athletes, we realize that not everybody has access to all equipment at all times. Travel, training at odd hours and life commitments may render training in a full service health club impossible at times. To make some kind of resistance training available at all times and under all circumstances, we've included many exercises that require no equipment and can be performed almost anywhere. These bodyweight-resisted movements are not meant to replace barbells, dumbbells and resistance bands on a regular basis, but rather provide a viable option to maintain strength until traditional modalities are available again.

The following abbreviations are used throughout the training programs:

BW: bodyweight
DB: dumbbell
KB: kettlebell
MB: medicine ball
PB: physioball
OH: overhand grip
UH: underhand grip
RDL: Romanian deadlift

OFF-SEASON PLAN

During the off-season plan, we snuck in an extra superset in case you have more time since you aren't doing so much aerobic training. This is the one example where the training session may take longer than 45 minutes (more like 55 minutes).

The aim of the off-season plan is to build lean body mass. Endurance sports can be brutal on the body and even with extreme care taken to maintain nutrition and hydration status, some weight loss occurs throughout most training periods. For a non-competitive fitness enthusiast, this weight loss is one of the best perks of regular cardiovascular training. However, for endurance athletes who are already at a healthy bodyweight and aspire to continually improve their performance, this loss of muscle mass can be potentially devastating for performance and injury prevention. This is the time of the year to get as strong as possible by trying progressively more difficult exercises and pushing some weight around the gym.

Even when you're doing exercises that you have previously mastered there are always ways to tweak the program and make it more challenging. More weight on the bar, less rest time between sets and changes to your grip or angle of pull are all good options.

This is also the best phase in which to try new things because any increased fatigue will not impact big runs, bikes or swims. If you normally stick to Medicine Ball Squats, now's the time to find out what a barbell across your shoulders feels like. If you normally stay on the light end of the dumbbell rack, now's the time to move toward the heavier weights. If you've never picked up a kettlebell, now's your chance!

BASE & BUILD PLAN

This is the most traditional plan, which features four 45-minute full body gym workouts per week. If you put in the time to work on strength and mobility here, it won't hurt so much to cut back when you are in peak mileage phase.

In traditional endurance training programs, building a base refers to covering progressively more miles while your body adapts by establishing a solid base of aerobic endurance. Building your resistance training base involves the same concept for developing muscular strength and endurance. During this phase of training, you are moving progressively heavier loads in an effort to make the body as strong as possible before the distances really ramp up during the peak mileage phase.

It's now that you want to lock in and perfect your Foundation Exercises. Doing every movement with great technique, laser beam-like focus and through a full range of motion is key to staying strong when your body is running, cycling and swimming potentially hundreds of miles per week. Scheduling training sessions and individual exercises around your longer endurance sessions is also incredibly important to being able to train both strength and endurance during the same phase of training. This plan consists of four sessions per week that should last about 45 minutes each. This will require additional time and energy, but the long-term results will be worth it. Developing strength here is like putting fuel in your gas tank, money into long-term investments or eating a good meal the night before a race. The results might not be immediately apparent, but going into the peak mileage phase as strong as possible will put you in the best position to reach the starting line heathy and the finish line happy.

PEAK MILEAGE PLAN

During the peak mileage weeks, we understand that the body can start to feel beaten up and tired. Additionally, your aerobic training is demanding a great deal of your time. For this reason, we feature two traditional gym workouts and two workouts that can be done from home with minimal equipment. This will work both physically and practically. It will give your body a chance to maintain strength and mobility without the rigorous nature of gym equipment and it will open up some hours in your week by requiring fewer trips to the gym. Doing a bodyweight circuit at home can be physically beneficial without the driving, parking, locker room, waiting for equipment, talking to your friends etc. normally associated with going to the gym.

Sometimes when you are covering peak mileage your body feels anything but peak condition. Running, biking and/or swimming serious distances takes a toll on the body. A lot of high school and college programs actually stop weight training or make it optional during this time of the season. While we're not here to tell successful coaches that they are doing it all wrong, most research and our experience tells us that continuing to perform some level of resistance training during the most strenuous training time of year will yield big long-term results. Training through this phase and making sure you maintain or even increase strength and mobility will pay off when you show up at the starting line strong, confident and ready to set a new personal best.

TAPER PLAN

The key feature to this is our 80 percent rule. Resistance and repetitions of all exercises should be knocked down to 80 percent of what you were doing most recently. The rationale behind less resistance is to keep the muscles active and the motor program intact for race day. We have kept this as four 45-minute full body gym workouts for the week, although since you're only doing 80% of the reps, we're confident you can finish more quickly. If you are traveling to an event, consider trying to get two gym workouts in and then using a couple of the workouts from the home gym/travel plan once you are there. These workouts are not necessarily "easier" but they will place less stress on the joints and musculature and aid in recovery for race day.

Devising a proper taper for a race is incredibly important. Too much work results in you getting to the starting line overtrained, exhausted and looking forward to the end of the event to let your body recover. Too little work results in the body feeling OK, but being ultimately undertrained for the event. The right level of tapering, both on the road and in the weight room, will have you showing up ready to Finish Strong!

HOME GYM/TRAVEL PLAN

We get it ... sometimes you just can't make it to the gym. Or perhaps you travel frequently for work, or events. We've got a plan for this, too. With minimal equipment, you can get a great workout done in the comfort of your own home or hotel room. These are typically only going to take about 30 minutes.

If something is not important to you, you will find an excuse not to do it. If something is important to you, you will find a way. Find a way to make resistance training happen! If the Covid-19 pandemic taught us anything, it's that effective training without access to health clubs is absolutely possible. As training facilities were forced to shut their doors, trainers, coaches and athletes took to social media in droves to show people how to train from home. These workouts vary greatly in terms of quality and difficulty, but it has become abundantly clear that if you want to train, there's always a way.

Our home gym workouts are pretty straightforward. We're not asking you to carry a gallon of milk up a hill or do Lunges with your dog draped over your shoulders. They consist of slight variations on our six Foundation Exercises and a few sport-specific movements that can be done with little or no equipment. Training at home or in your hotel room is not ideal, but with a little effort and ingenuity it can be key in maintaining basic levels of strength and mobility when the universe conspires to keep you out of the gym.

If you are a runner, are you ready to cross the finish line feeling strong and confident? If you are a cyclist, are you ready to cover mile after mile with less fatigue than ever before? If you are a swimmer, are you ready to maintain stroke efficiency well into your longest swims? If you are a triathlete, are you ready to Finish Strong? This is where to start!

The templates in this section are the blueprint for taking your training to the next level. Much like a blueprint lays out the plans of the basic structure of the building, these plans will lay out the basic structure of your training. Once that basic framework is in place, changes can be made to the building (painting, flooring, interior design, etc.) to suit the needs of the inhabitant, but the basic structure never really changes. The templates are similar in that there is plenty of "wiggle room" to accommodate for different times of the year, fatigue, time constraints, travel, etc., but the basic framework remains fairly consistent.

Maintaining this consistency in your training will prove invaluable for long-term athletic development. Sure, there should be some modifications when necessary, but constantly changing plans or going to the gym with no plan at all is arguably worse than not hitting the weight room at all. Treat the gym like your endurance workouts: be consistent, be methodical and believe that the path you are on will take you where you want to go.

Let's go!

17

TRAINING SESSION TEMPLATES

The following templates are the blueprint for your resistance training program. There is one week of training for each phase of the year included and each is formatted for an individual training session with predetermined exercise selection, sets and reps. There are also spaces provided to record the weights you are lifting to track your progress. Once you are comfortable with the basic workout format you can begin to make exercise substitutions from the Top 10 Lists earlier in the book.

OFF-SEASON TEMPLATE

This is the training session format to use when your big races are still several months away and you are trying to build strength, mobility and lean muscle mass before entering another season of long endurance training sessions. These workouts are slightly longer than those for other parts of the year, include more challenging exercises and require you to add enough resistance that your body is forced to respond with increased strength. These are the most challenging gym workouts of the year because you should be focused on getting as strong as possible during this time.

SWIMMER'S OFF-SEASON TEMPLATE

TYPE	EXERCISE	WEIGHT	REPS	WEIGHT	REPS	WEIGHT	REPS
Individualized Mobility							
Soft Tissue Release / Foam Roll	As needed						
Mobility Exercise 1	Bretzel		x30 Sec.		x30 Sec.		x30 Sec.
Mobility Exercise 2	Book Openers		x10		x10		x10
Foundation Superset 1							
Traditional Core Exercise	Plank		x60 Sec.		x60 Sec.		x60 Sec.
Lower Body Push	Barbell Back Squats or Front Squats		x10		x10		x10
Upper Body Pull	Pull-Up		x5 to 8		x5 to 8		x5 to 8
Foundation Superset 2							
Anti-Rotation Exercise	Shoulder Taps		x10		x10		x10
Lower Body Pull	Barbell Romanian Deadlift		x10		x10		x10
Upper Body Push	Barbell Bench Press or Dumbbell Chest Press		x10		x10		x10
Foundation Superset 3							
Traditional Core Exercise	Crunch		x15		x15		x15
Upper Body Push or Pull	Lat Pull-Down		x10		x10		x10
Lower Body Push or Pull	Kettlebell Swing		x10		x10		x10
Sport-Specific Exercises							
	Single Arm Dumbbell Reverse Fly		x10		x10		
	Cable Push/Pull		x10		x10		
	Clam Shell		x10		x10		
	Hip Thrust March		x10		x10		

TYPE	EXERCISE	WEIGHT	REPS	WEIGHT	REPS	WEIGHT	REPS
Individualized Mobility							
Soft Tissue Release / Foam Roll	As needed						
Mobility Exercise 1	Side-Lying Thoracic Spine Rotation		x10		x10		x10
Mobility Exercise 2	Thread the Needle		x10		x10		x10
Foundation Superset 1							
Traditional Core Exercise	Side Plank		x30 Sec.		x30 Sec.		x30 Sec.
Lower Body Push	Barbell Lunges or Front Squats		x10		x10		x10
Upper Body Pull	Chin-Up		x5 to 8		x5 to 8		x5 to 8
Foundation Superset 2							
Anti-Rotation Exercise	Dumbbell Windshield Wipers		x10		x10		x10
Lower Body Pull	Glute-Ham Raises		x5		x5		x5
Upper Body Push	Hands Elevated Push-Ups		x10 to 15		x10 to 15		x10 to 15
Foundation Superset 3							
Traditional Core Exercise	Crossover Crunch		x10		x10		x10
Upper Body Push or Pull	Alternating Dumbbell Chest Press		x10		x10		x10
Lower Body Push or Pull	Trap Bar Deadlift		x10		x10		x10
Sport-Specific Exercises							
	Cable Cross-Pull Low to High		x10		x10		
	Physioball Flutter Kicks		x10		x10		
	V-Grip Lat Pull-Down		x10		x10		
	Resisted Hip Bridge		x10		x10		

TYPE	EXERCISE	WEIGHT	REPS	WEIGHT	REPS	WEIGHT	REPS
Individualized Mobility							
Soft Tissue Release / Foam Roll	As needed						
Mobility Exercise 1	Cross-Body Stretch		x30 Sec.		x30 Sec.		x30 Sec.
Mobility Exercise 2	Sleeper Stretch		x30 Sec.		x30 Sec.		x30 Sec.
Foundation Superset 1							
Traditional Core Exercise	High Side Plank		x60 Sec.		x60 Sec.		x60 Sec.
Lower Body Push	Dumbbell Goblet Squat		x10		x10		x10
Upper Body Pull	Inverted Row on Suspension Trainer		x10		x10		x10
Foundation Superset 2							
Anti-Rotation Exercise	Dead Bug Paloff Press		x10		x10		x10
Lower Body Pull	Dumbbell Romanian Deadlift		x10		x10		x10
Upper Body Push	Barbell Incline Press or Dumbbell Alternating Incline Press		x10		x10		x10
Foundation Superset 3							
Traditional Core Exercise	Butterfly Crunch		x15		x15		x15
Upper Body Push or Pull	Lat Pull-Down		x10		x10		x10
Lower Body Push or Pull	Single Leg Hip Bridge		x10		x10		x10
Sport-Specific Exercises							
	Reverse Fly on Physioball		x10		x10		
	Cable Push/Pull		x10		x10		
	Clam Shell		x10		x10		
	Resisted Hip Thrust March		x10		x10		

TYPE	EXERCISE	WEIGHT	REPS	WEIGHT	REPS	WEIGHT	REPS
Individualized Mobility							
Soft Tissue Release / Foam Roll	As needed						
Mobility Exercise 1	Doorway Stretch		x30 Sec.		x30 Sec.		x30 Sec.
Mobility Exercise 2	Bretzel		x30 Sec.		x30 Sec.		x30 Sec.
Foundation Superset 1							
Traditional Core Exercise	Alternating Limb Dead Bug		x10		x10		x10
Lower Body Push	Walking Lunge		x10		x10		x10
Upper Body Pull	Pull-Ups or Chin-Ups		x5 to 8		x5 to 8		x5 to 8
Foundation Superset 2							
Anti-Rotation Exercise	Overhead Plate Circles		x10		x10		x10
Lower Body Pull	Slide Board or Towel Leg Curls		x10		x10		x10
Upper Body Push	Push-Ups		x10		x10		x10
Foundation Super Set 3							
Traditional Core Exercise	Alternating Knee-to-Chest		x10		x10		x10
Upper Body Push or Pull	Resisted Push-Ups		x10		x10		x10
Lower Body Push or Pull	Shrugs		x10		x10		x10
Sport-Specific Exercises							
	Cable Cross-Pull – Low to High		x10		x10		
	BOSU Ball Flutter Kicks		x10		x10		
	Close Grip Lat Pull-Down		x10		x10		
	Resisted Hip Bridge		x10		x10		

CYCLIST'S OFF-SEASON TEMPLATE

TYPE	EXERCISE	WEIGHT	REPS	WEIGHT	REPS	WEIGHT	REPS
Individualized Mobility							
Soft Tissue Release / Foam Roll	As needed						
Mobility Exercise 1	World's Greatest Stretch		x30 Sec.		x30 Sec.		x30 Sec.
Mobility Exercise 2	Down Dog		x30 Sec.		x30 Sec.		x30 Sec.
Foundation Superset 1							
Traditional Core Exercise	Plank		x60 Sec.		x60 Sec.		x60 Sec.
Lower Body Push	Barbell Back Squats		x10		x10		x10
Upper Body Pull	Pull-Up		x5 to 8		x5 to 8		x5 to 8
Foundation Superset 2							
Anti-Rotation Exercise	Shoulder Taps		x10		x10		x10
Lower Body Pull	Barbell Romanian Deadlift		x10		x10		x10
Upper Body Push	Barbell Bench Press		x10		x10		x10
Foundation Superset 3							
Traditional Core Exercise	Crunch		x15		x15		x15
Upper Body Push or Pull	Lat Pull-Down		x10		x10		x10
Lower Body Push or Pull	Kettlebell Swing		x10		x10		x10
Sport-Specific Exercises							
	Lateral Lunge with Overhead Press		x10		x10		
	Half-Kneel Downward Cable Chop		x10		x10		
	Lateral Plate Drag		x10		x10		
	Valslide Body Saw		x10		x10		

TYPE	EXERCISE	WEIGHT	REPS	WEIGHT	REPS	WEIGHT	REPS
Individualized Mobility							
Soft Tissue Release / Foam Roll	As needed						
Mobility Exercise 1	Foam Roller Back Extension		x30 Sec.		x30 Sec.		x30 Sec.
Mobility Exercise 2	90/90 Hip Rotations		x10		x10		x10
Foundation Superset 1							
Traditional Core Exercise	Side Plank		x30 Sec.		x30 Sec.		x30 Sec.
Lower Body Push	Barbell Lunges		x10		x10		x10
Upper Body Pull	Chin-Ups		x5 to 8		x5 to 8		x5 to 8
Foundation Superset 2							
Anti-Rotation Exercise	Dumbbell Windshield Wipers		x10		x10		x10
Lower Body Pull	Glute-Ham Raises		x5		x5		x5
Upper Body Push	Hands Elevated Push-Ups		x10 to 15		x10 to 15		x10 to 15
Foundation Superset 3							
Traditional Core Exercise	Crossover Crunch		x10		x10		x10
Upper Body Push or Pull	Alternating Dumbbell Chest Press		x10		x10		x10
Lower Body Push or Pull	Trap Bar Deadlift		x10		x10		x10
Sport-Specific Exercises							
	Overhead Plate Circles		x10		x10		
	Renegade Row with Push-Up		x10		x10		
	Tuck Jump Burpee		x10		x10		
	Single Arm Kettlebell Clean		x10		x10		

TYPE	EXERCISE	WEIGHT	REPS	WEIGHT	REPS	WEIGHT	REPS
Individualized Mobility							
Soft Tissue Release / Foam Roll	As needed						
Mobility Exercise 1	Lateral Hip Distraction		x30 Sec.		x30 Sec.		x30 Sec.
Mobility Exercise 2	Down Dog		x30 Sec.		x30 Sec.		x30 Sec.
Foundation Superset 1							
Traditional Core Exercise	High Side Plank		x30 Sec.		x30 Sec.		x30 Sec.
Lower Body Push	Dumbbell Goblet Squat		x10		x10		x10
Upper Body Pull	Pull-Ups		x5 to 8		x5 to 8		x5 to 8
Foundation Superset 2							
Anti-Rotation Exercise	Dead Bug Paloff Press		x10		x10		x10
Lower Body Pull	Dumbbell Romanian/Deadlift		x10		x10		x10
Upper Body Push	Barbell Incline Press		x10		x10		x10
Foundation Super Set 3							
Traditional Core Exercise	Butterfly Crunch		x15		x15		x15
Upper Body Push or Pull	Lat Pull-Down		x10		x10		x10
Lower Body Push or Pull	Single Leg Hip Bridge		x10		x10		x10
Sport-Specific Exercises							
	Full Pistol Squat		x10		x10		
	Standing Cable Chop		x10		x10		
	Split Squat Jump		x10		x10		
	Kettlebell Renegade Row		x10		x10		

TYPE	EXERCISE	WEIGHT	REPS	WEIGHT	REPS	WEIGHT	REPS
Individualized Mobility							
Soft Tissue Release / Foam Roll	As needed						
Mobility Exercise 1	World's Greatest Stretch		x30 Sec.		x30 Sec.		x30 Sec.
Mobility Exercise 2	Foam Roller Back Extension		x30 Sec.		x30 Sec.		x30 Sec.
Foundation Superset 1							
Traditional Core Exercise	Alternating Limb Dead Bug		x10		x10		x10
Lower Body Push	Walking Lunge		x10		x10		x10
Upper Body Pull	Pull-Ups or Chin-Ups		x5 to 8		x5 to 8		x5 to 8
Foundation Superset 2							
Anti-Rotation Exercise	Overhead Plate Circles		x10		x10		x10
Lower Body Pull	Slide Board or Towel Leg Curls		x10		x10		x10
Upper Body Push	Push-Ups		x10		x10		x10
Foundation Superset 3							
Traditional Core Exercise	Alternating Knee-to-Chest		x10		x10		x10
Upper Body Push or Pull	Resisted Push-Ups		x10		x10		x10
Lower Body Push or Pull	Shrugs		x10		x10		x10
Sport-Specific Exercises							
	Burpee		x10		x10		
	Valslide Body Saw with Leg Lift		x10		x10		
	Lateral Lunge with Overhead Press		x10		x10		
	Single Arm Kettlebell Clean and Press		x10		x10		

RUNNER'S OFF-SEASON TEMPLATE

TYPE	EXERCISE	WEIGHT	REPS	WEIGHT	REPS	WEIGHT	REPS
Individualized Mobility							
Soft Tissue Release / Foam Roll	As needed						
Mobility Exercise 1	90/90 Hip Rotation		x10		x10		x10
Mobility Exercise 2	Lateral Hip Distraction		x30 Sec.		x30 Sec.		x30 Sec.
Foundation Superset 1							
Traditional Core Exercise	Plank		x60 Sec.		x60 Sec.		x60 Sec.
Lower Body Push	Barbell Back Squat		x10		x10		x10
Upper Body Pull	Pull-Up		x5 to 8		x5 to 8		x5 to 8
Foundation Superset 2							
Anti-Rotation Exercise	Shoulder Taps		x10		x10		x10
Lower Body Pull	Barbell Romanian Deadlift		x10		x10		x10
Upper Body Push	Barbell Bench Press		x10		x10		x10
Foundation Superset 3							
Traditional Core Exercise	Crunch		x15		x15		x15
Upper Body Push or Pull	Lat Pull-Down		x10		x10		x10
Lower Body Push or Pull	Kettlebell Swing		x10		x10		x10
Sport-Specific Exercises							
	Dumbbell Step-Ups		x10		x10		
	Machine Leg Curl		x10		x10		
	Standing Overhead Press		x10		x10		
	Barbell Inverted Row		x10		x10		

TYPE	EXERCISE	WEIGHT	REPS	WEIGHT	REPS	WEIGHT	REPS
Individualized Mobility							
Soft Tissue Release / Foam Roll	As needed						
Mobility Exercise 1	Posterior Hip Distraction		x30 Sec.		x30 Sec.		x30 Sec.
Mobility Exercise 2	Band Distraction Dorsiflexion		x30 Sec.		x30 Sec.		x30 Sec.
Foundation Superset 1							
Traditional Core Exercise	Side Plank		x30 Sec.		x30 Sec.		x30 Sec.
Lower Body Push	Barbell Lunges		x10		x10		x10
Upper Body Pull	Chin-Up		x5 to 8		x5 to 8		x5 to 8
Foundation Superset 2							
Anti-Rotation Exercise	Dumbbell Windshield Wipers		x10		x10		x10
Lower Body Pull	Glute-Ham Raises		x5		x5		x5
Upper Body Push	Hands Elevated Push-Up		x10 to 15		x10 to 15		x10 to 15
Foundation Superset 3							
Traditional Core Exercise	Crossover Crunch		x10		x10		x10
Upper Body Push or Pull	Alternating Dumbbell Chest Press		x10		x10		x10
Lower Body Push or Pull	Trap Bar Deadlift		x10		x10		x10
Sport-Specific Exercises							
	Standing Calf Raises		x15		x15		
	Body Weight Dorisflexion		x10		x10		
	Alternating Knee-to-Chest		x10		x10		
	Rip Trainer March		x10		x10		

TYPE	EXERCISE	WEIGHT	REPS	WEIGHT	REPS	WEIGHT	REPS
Individualized Mobility							
Soft Tissue Release / Foam Roll	As needed						
Mobility Exercise 1	Slant Board Dorsiflexion		x30 Sec.		x30 Sec.		x30 Sec.
Mobility Exercise 2	90/90 Hip Rotations		x10		x10		x10
Foundation Superset 1							
Traditional Core Exercise	High Side Plank		x60 Sec.		x60 Sec.		x60 Sec.
Lower Body Push	Dumbbell Goblet Squat		x10		x10		x10
Upper Body Pull	Inverted Row on Suspension Trainer		x10		x10		x10
Foundation Superset 2							
Anti-Rotation Exercise	Dead Bug Paloff Press		x10		x10		x10
Lower Body Pull	Dumbbell Romanian Deadlift		x10		x10		x10
Upper Body Push	Barbell Incline Press		x10		x10		x10
Foundation Superset 3							
Traditional Core Exercise	Butterfly Crunch		x15		x15		x15
Upper Body Push or Pull	Lat Pull-Down		x10		x10		x10
Lower Body Push or Pull	Single Leg Hip Bridge		x10		x10		x10
Sport-Specific Exercises							
	Dumbbell Step-Ups		x10		x10		
	Physioball Leg Curls		x10		x10		
	Standing Overhead Press		x10		x10		
	Underhand Grip Inverted Row		x10		x10		

TYPE	EXERCISE	WEIGHT	REPS	WEIGHT	REPS	WEIGHT	REPS
Individualized Mobility							
Soft Tissue Release / Foam Roll	As needed						
Mobility Exercise 1	Lateral Hip Distraction		x30 Sec.		x30 Sec.		x30 Sec.
Mobility Exercise 2	Posterior Hip Distraction		x30 Sec.		x30 Sec.		x30 Sec.
Foundation Superset 1							
Traditional Core Exercise	Alternating Limb Dead Bug		x10		x10		x10
Lower Body Push	Walking Lunge		x10		x10		x10
Upper Body Pull	Pull-Ups or Chin-Ups		x5 to 8		x5 to 8		x5 to 8
Foundation Superset 2							
Anti-Rotation Exercise	Overhead Plate Circles		x10		x10		x10
Lower Body Pull	Slide Board or Towel Leg Curls		x10		x10		x10
Upper Body Push	Push-Ups		x10		x10		x10
Foundation Superset 3							
Traditional Core Exercise	Alternating Knee-to-Chest		x10		x10		x10
Upper Body Push or Pull	Resisted Push-Ups		x10		x10		x10
Lower Body Push or Pull	Shrugs		x10		x10		x10
Sport-Specific Exercises							
	Standing Calf Raises		x15		x15		
	Body Weight Dorisflexion		x10		x10		
	V-Grip Lat Pull-Down		x10		x10		
	Standing Dumbbell Shoulder Press		x10		x10		

TRIATHLETE'S OFF-SEASON TEMPLATE

TYPE	EXERCISE	WEIGHT	REPS	WEIGHT	REPS	WEIGHT	REPS
Individualized Mobility							
Soft Tissue Release / Foam Roll	As needed						
Mobility Exercise 1	Book Opener		x10		x10		x10
Mobility Exercise 2	90/90 Hip Rotation		x10		x10		x10
Foundation Superset 1							
Traditional Core Exercise	Plank		x60 Sec.		x60 Sec.		x60 Sec.
Lower Body Push	Barbell Back Squat		x10		x10		x10
Upper Body Pull	Pull-Up		x5 to 8		x5 to 8		x5 to 8
Foundation Superset 2							
Anti-Rotation Exercise	Shoulder Taps		x10		x10		x10
Lower Body Pull	Barbell Romanian Deadlift		x10		x10		x10
Upper Body Push	Barbell Bench Press		x10		x10		x10
Foundation Superset 3							
Traditional Core Exercise	Crunch		x15		x15		x15
Upper Body Push or Pull	Lat Pull-Down		x10		x10		x10
Lower Body Push or Pull	Kettlebell Swing		x10		x10		x10
Sport-Specific Exercises							
	Hip Thrust March		x10		x10		
	Dumbbell Windshield Wipers		x10		x10		
	Dumbbell Renegade Row		x10		x10		
	Rip Trainer March		x10		x10		

TYPE	EXERCISE	WEIGHT	REPS	WEIGHT	REPS	WEIGHT	REPS
Individualized Mobility							
Soft Tissue Release / Foam Roll	As needed						
Mobility Exercise 1	World's Greatest Stretch		x30 Sec.		x30 Sec.		x30 Sec.
Mobility Exercise 2	Slant Board Dorsiflexion		x30 Sec.		x30 Sec.		x30 Sec.
Foundation Superset 1							
Traditional Core Exercise	Side Plank		x30 Sec.		x30 Sec.		x30 Sec.
Lower Body Push	Barbell Lunges		x10		x10		x10
Upper Body Pull	Chin-Up		x5 to 8		x5 to 8		x5 to 8
Foundation Superset 2							
Anti-Rotation Exercise	Dumbbell Windshield Wipers		x10		x10		x10
Lower Body Pull	Glute-Ham Raises		x5		x5		x5
Upper Body Push	Hands Elevated Push-Up		x10 to 15		x10 to 15		x10 to 15
Foundation Superset 3							
Traditional Core Exercise	Crossover Crunch		x15		x15		x15
Upper Body Push or Pull	Alternating Dumbbell Chest Press		x10		x10		x10
Lower Body Push or Pull	Trap Bar Deadlift		x10		x10		x10
Sport-Specific Exercises							
	Standing Overhead Press		x10		x10		
	Lateral Plate Drag		x10		x10		
	Physioball Flutter Kicks		x10		x10		
	Cable Push/Pull		x10		x10		

TYPE	EXERCISE	WEIGHT	REPS	WEIGHT	REPS	WEIGHT	REPS
Individualized Mobility							
Soft Tissue Release / Foam Roll	As needed						
Mobility Exercise 1	Foam Roller Back Extension		x30 Sec.		x30 Sec.		x30 Sec.
Mobility Exercise 2	Bretzel		x30 Sec.		x30 Sec.		x30 Sec.
Foundation Superset 1							
Traditional Core Exercise	High Side Plank		x60 Sec.		x60 Sec.		x60 Sec.
Lower Body Push	Dumbbell Goblet Squat		x10		x10		x10
Upper Body Pull	Inverted Row on Suspension Trainer		x10		x10		x10
Foundation Superset 2							
Anti-Rotation Exercise	Dead Bug Paloff Press		x10		x10		x10
Lower Body Pull	Dumbbell Romanian Dead Lift		x10		x10		x10
Upper Body Push	Barbell Incline Press		x10		x10		x10
Foundation Superset 3							
Traditional Core Exercise	Butterfly Crunch		x15		x15		x15
Upper Body Push or Pull	Lat Pull-Down		x10		x10		x10
Lower Body Push or Pull	Single Leg Hip Bridge		x10		x10		x10
Sport-Specific Exercises							
	Cable Cross-Pull – Low to High		x10		x10		
	Tuck Jump Burpee		x10		x10		
	Lateral Lunge with Overhead Press		x10		x10		
	Seated Calf Raise		x10		x10		

TYPE	EXERCISE	WEIGHT	REPS	WEIGHT	REPS	WEIGHT	REPS
Individualized Mobility							
Soft Tissue Release / Foam Roll	As needed						
Mobility Exercise 1	Posterior Hip Distraction		x30 Sec.		x30 Sec.		x30 Sec.
Mobility Exercise 2	Doorway Stretch		x30 Sec.		x30 Sec.		x30 Sec.
Foundation Superset 1							
Traditional Core Exercise	Alternating Limb Dead Bug		x10		x10		x10
Lower Body Push	Walking Lunge		x10		x10		x10
Upper Body Pull	Pull-Ups or Chin-Ups		x5 to 8		x5 to 8		x5 to 8
Foundation Superset 2							
Anti-Rotation Exercise	Overhead Plate Circles		x10		x10		x10
Lower Body Pull	Slide Board or Towel Leg Curls		x10		x10		x10
Upper Body Push	Push-Ups		x10		x10		x10
Foundation Superset 3							
Traditional Core Exercise	Alternating Knee-to-Chest		x10		x10		x10
Upper Body Push or Pull	Resisted Push-Ups		x10		x10		x10
Lower Body Push or Pull	Shrugs		x10		x10		x10
Sport-Specific Exercises							
	Seated Bent-Knee Dorsiflexion		x15		x15		
	Trap Bar Deadlift		x10		x10		
	Valslide Body Saw		x10		x10		
	Dumbbell Standing Reverse Fly		x10		x10		

BASE & BUILD TEMPLATE

The base & build templates are used when you are steadily increasing your mileage on runs, rides or swims. The intensity remains fairly high and the length of each workout is still about 45 minutes. Continuing to get stronger during this time of the year will be pivotal when distances really increase and strength and mobility are a real factor in your ability to keep up with your training and competition plan later in the year.

SWIMMER'S BASE & BUILD TEMPLATE

TYPE	EXERCISE	WEIGHT	REPS	WEIGHT	REPS	WEIGHT	REPS
Individualized Mobility							
Soft Tissue Release / Foam Roll	As needed						
Mobility Exercise 1	Bretzel		x30 Sec.		x30 Sec.		x30 Sec.
Mobility Exercise 2	Book Openers		x10		x10		x10
Foundation Superset 1							
Traditional Core Exercise	Plank		x60 Sec.		x60 Sec.		x60 Sec.
Lower Body Push	Barbell Back Squats or Barbell Front Squats		x8		x8		x8
Upper Body Pull	Pull-Up		x8 to 12		x8 to 12		x8 to 12
Foundation Superset 2							
Anti-Rotation Exercise	Hip Taps		x10		x10		x10
Lower Body Pull	Barbell Romanian Deadlift		x8		x8		x8
Upper Body Push	Barbell Bench Press		x8		x8		x8
Sport-Specific Exercises							
	Single Arm Dumbbell Reverse Fly		x10		x10		
	Cable Push/Pull Prone on Bench		x10		x10		
	Clam Shell with Heels Elevated		x10		x10		
	Glute Bridge March		x10		x10		

TYPE	EXERCISE	WEIGHT	REPS	WEIGHT	REPS	WEIGHT	REPS
Individualized Mobility							
Soft Tissue Release / Foam Roll	As needed						
Mobility Exercise 1	Side-Lying Thoracic Spine Rotation		x10		x10		x10
Mobility Exercise 2	Sleeper Stretch		x30 Sec.		x30 Sec.		x30 Sec.
Foundation Superset 1							
Traditional Core Exercise	Side Plank		x30 Sec.		x30 Sec.		x30 Sec.
Lower Body Push	Barbell Reverse Lunge		x8		x8		x8
Upper Body Pull	Chin-Up		x8 to 12		x8 to 12		x8 to 12
Foundation Superset 2							
Anti-Rotation Exercise	Medicine Ball Windshield Wipers		x10		x10		x10
Lower Body Pull	Glute-Ham Raises		x8		x8		x8
Upper Body Push	Negative Push-Ups (5 Sec. Each)		x5 to 8		x5 to 8		x5 to 8
Sport-Specific Exercises							
	Cable Cross-Pull – High to Low		x10		x10		
	Physioball Flutter Kicks		x10		x10		
	V-Grip Pull-Down		x10		x10		
	Resisted Hip Bridge		x10		x10		

TYPE	EXERCISE	WEIGHT	REPS	WEIGHT	REPS	WEIGHT	REPS
Individualized Mobility							
Soft Tissue Release / Foam Roll	As needed						
Mobility Exercise 1	Cross-Body Stretch		x30 Sec.		x30 Sec.		x30 Sec.
Mobility Exercise 2	Thread the Needle		x10		x10		x10
Foundation Superset 1							
Traditional Core Exercise	High Side Plank		x60 Sec.		x60 Sec.		x60 Sec.
Lower Body Push	Barbell Back Squat or Barbell Front Squat		x8		x8		x8
Upper Body Pull	Chin-Up		x12		x12		x12
Foundation Superset 2							
Anti-Rotation Exercise	Dead Bug Paloff Press		x10		x10		x10
Lower Body Pull	Single Leg Dumbbell Romanian Deadlift		x8		x8		x8
Upper Body Push	Alternating Dumbbell Incline Press		x8		x8		x8
Sport-Specific Exercises							
	Dumbbell Standing Reverse Fly		x10		x10		
	Cable Push/Pull		x10		x10		
	Clam Shell		x10		x10		
	Hip Thrust March		x10		x10		

TYPE	EXERCISE	WEIGHT	REPS	WEIGHT	REPS	WEIGHT	REPS
Individualized Mobility							
Soft Tissue Release / Foam Roll	As needed						
Mobility Exercise 1	Doorway Stretch		x30 Sec.		x30 Sec.		x30 Sec.
Mobility Exercise 2	Book Openers		x10		x10		x10
Foundation Superset 1							
Traditional Core Exercise	Alternating Limb Dead Bug		x10		x10		x10
Lower Body Push	Walking Lunge		x10		x10		x10
Upper Body Pull	Pull-Ups or Chin-Ups		x8 to 12		x8 to 12		x8 to 12
Foundation Superset 2							
Anti-Rotation Exercise	Half-Kneel Overhead Plate Circles		x10		x10		x10
Lower Body Pull	Slide Board or Towel Leg Curls		x15		x15		x15
Upper Body Push	Resisted Push-Up		x10		x10		x10
Sport-Specific Exercises							
	Cable Cross-Pull – Low to High		x10		x10		
	BOSU Ball Flutter Kicks		x10		x10		
	Close Grip Lat Pull-Down		x10		x10		
	Resisted Hip Bridge		x10		x10		

CYCLIST'S BASE & BUILD TEMPLATE

TYPE	EXERCISE	WEIGHT	REPS	WEIGHT	REPS	WEIGHT	REPS
Individualized Mobility							
Soft Tissue Release / Foam Roll	As needed						
Mobility Exercise 1	Bretzel		x30 Sec.		x30 Sec.		x30 Sec.
Mobility Exercise 2	Foam Roller Back Extension		x30 Sec.		x30 Sec.		x30 Sec.
Foundation Superset 1							
Traditional Core Exercise	Plank		x60 Sec.		x60 Sec.		x60 Sec.
Lower Body Push	Barbell Back Squats or Barbell Front Squats		x8		x8		x8
Upper Body Pull	Pull-Up		x8 to 12		x8 to 12		x8 to 12
Foundation Superset 2							
Anti-Rotation Exercise	Hip Taps		x10		x10		x10
Lower Body Pull	Barbell Romanian Deadlift		x8		x8		x8
Upper Body Push	Barbell Bench Press		x8		x8		x8
Sport-Specific Exercises							
	Standing Cable Chop		x10		x10		
	Lateral Lunge Clean		x10		x10		
	Dumbbell Split Squat		x10		x10		
	Half-Kneel Overhead Plate Circles		x10		x10		

TYPE	EXERCISE	WEIGHT	REPS	WEIGHT	REPS	WEIGHT	REPS
Individualized Mobility							
Soft Tissue Release / Foam Roll	As needed						
Mobility Exercise 1	World's Greatest Stretch		x30 Sec.		x30 Sec.		x30 Sec.
Mobility Exercise 2	Posterior Hip Distraction		x30 Sec.		x30 Sec.		x30 Sec.
Foundation Superset 1							
Traditional Core Exercise	Side Plank		x60 Sec.		x60 Sec.		x60 Sec.
Lower Body Push	Barbell Reverse Lunge		x8		x8		x8
Upper Body Pull	Chin-Up		x8 to 12		x8 to 12		x8 to 12
Foundation Superset 2							
Anti-Rotation Exercise	Medicine Ball Windshield Wipers		x10		x10		x10
Lower Body Pull	Glute-Ham Raises		x5		x5		x5
Upper Body Push	Negative Push-Ups (5 Sec. Each)		x5 to 8		x5 to 8		x5 to 8
Sport-Specific Exercises							
	Renegade Row		x10		x10		
	Broad Jump Burpee		x10		x10		
	Valslide Body Saw with Leg Lift		x10		x10		
	Lateral Lunge Press		x10		x10		

TYPE	EXERCISE	WEIGHT	REPS	WEIGHT	REPS	WEIGHT	REPS
Individualized Mobility							
Soft Tissue Release / Foam Roll	As needed						
Mobility Exercise 1	Down Dog		x30 Sec.		x30 Sec.		x30 Sec.
Mobility Exercise 2	Foam Roller Back Extension		x30 Sec.		x30 Sec.		x30 Sec.
Foundation Superset 1							
Traditional Core Exercise	High Side Plank		x60 Sec.		x60 Sec.		x60 Sec.
Lower Body Push	Barbell Back Squat or Barbell Front Squat		x8		x8		x8
Upper Body Pull	Inverted Row on Suspension Trainer		x12		x12		x12
Foundation Superset 2							
Anti-Rotation Exercise	Dead Bug Paloff Press		x10		x10		x10
Lower Body Pull	Single Leg Dumbbell Romanian Deadlift		x8		x8		x8
Upper Body Push	Alternating Dumbbell Incline Press		x8		x8		x8
Sport-Specific Exercises							
	Crossover Lunge		x10		x10		
	Lateral Plate Drag		x10		x10		
	Suspension Trainer Pistol Squat		x10		x10		
	Single Arm Kettlebell Clean and Press		x10		x10		

TYPE	EXERCISE	WEIGHT	REPS	WEIGHT	REPS	WEIGHT	REPS
Individualized Mobility							
Soft Tissue Release / Foam Roll	As needed						
Mobility Exercise 1	World's Greatest Stretch		x30 Sec.		x30 Sec.		x30 Sec.
Mobility Exercise 2	Thread the Needle		x30 Sec.		x30 Sec.		x30 Sec.
Foundation Superset 1							
Traditional Core Exercise	Alternating Limb Dead Bug		x10		x10		x10
Lower Body Push	Walking Lunge		x10		x10		x10
Upper Body Pull	Pull-Ups or Chin-Ups		x8 to 12		x8 to 12		x8 to 12
Foundation Superset 2							
Anti-Rotation Exercise	Half-Kneel Overhead Plate Circles		x10		x10		x10
Lower Body Pull	Slide Board or Towel Leg Curls		x15		x15		x15
Upper Body Push	Resisted Push-Up		x10		x10		x10
Sport-Specific Exercises							
	Valslide Body Saw		x10		x10		
	Lateral Lunge and Twist		x10		x10		
	Bulgarian Split Squat		x10		x10		
	Half-Kneel Upward Cable Chop		x10		x10		

RUNNER'S BASE & BUILD TEMPLATE

TYPE	EXERCISE	WEIGHT	REPS	WEIGHT	REPS	WEIGHT	REPS
Individualized Mobility							
Soft Tissue Release / Foam Roll	As needed						
Mobility Exercise 1	90/90 Hip Rotation		x10		x10		x10
Mobility Exercise 2	Lateral Hip Distraction		x30 Sec.		x30 Sec.		x30 Sec.
Foundation Superset 1							
Traditional Core Exercise	Plank		x60 Sec.		x60 Sec.		x60 Sec.
Lower Body Push	Barbell Back Squats or Barbell Front Squats		x8		x8		x8
Upper Body Pull	Pull-Up		x8 to 12		x8 to 12		x8 to 12
Foundation Superset 2							
Anti-Rotation Exercise	Hip Taps		x10		x10		x10
Lower Body Pull	Barbell Romanian Deadlift		x8		x8		x8
Upper Body Push	Barbell Bench Press		x8		x8		x8
Sport-Specific Exercises							
	Lateral Step-Ups		x10		x10		
	Machine Leg Curl		x10		x10		
	Standing Overhead Press		x10		x10		
	Feet Elevated Inverted Row		x10		x10		

TYPE	EXERCISE	WEIGHT	REPS	WEIGHT	REPS	WEIGHT	REPS
Individualized Mobility							
Soft Tissue Release / Foam Roll	As needed						
Mobility Exercise 1	Posterior Hip Distraction		x30 Sec.		x30 Sec.		x30 Sec.
Mobility Exercise 2	Band Distraction Dorsiflexion		x30 Sec.		x30 Sec.		x30 Sec.
Foundation Superset 1							
Traditional Core Exercise	Side Plank		x30 Sec.		x30 Sec.		x30 Sec.
Lower Body Push	Barbell Reverse Lunge		x8		x8		x8
Upper Body Pull	Chin-Up		x8 to 12		x8 to 12		x8 to 12
Foundation Superset 2							
Anti-Rotation Exercise	Medicine Ball Windshield Wipers		x10		x10		x10
Lower Body Pull	Glute-Ham Raises		x5		x5		x5
Upper Body Push	Negative Push-Ups (5 Sec. Each)		x5 to 8		x5 to 8		x5 to 8
Sport-Specific Exercises							
	Seated Calf Raises		x15		x15		
	Band Resisted Dorisflexion		x10		x10		
	Weighted Alternating Knee-to-Chest		x10		x10		
	Rip Trainer March		x10		x10		

TYPE	EXERCISE	WEIGHT	REPS	WEIGHT	REPS	WEIGHT	REPS
Individualized Mobility							
Soft Tissue Release / Foam Roll	As needed						
Mobility Exercise 1	Slant Board Dorsiflexion		x30 Sec.		x30 Sec.		x30 Sec.
Mobility Exercise 2	90/90 Hip Rotations		x10		x10		x10
Foundation Superset 1							
Traditional Core Exercise	High Side Plank		x60 Sec.		x60 Sec.		x60 Sec.
Lower Body Push	Barbell Back Squat or Barbell Front Squat		x8		x8		x8
Upper Body Pull	Inverted Row on Suspension Trainer		x12		x12		x12
Foundation Superset 2							
Anti-Rotation Exercise	Dead Bug Paloff Press		x10		x10		x10
Lower Body Pull	Single Leg Dumbbell Romanian Deadlift		x8		x8		x8
Upper Body Push	Alternating Dumbbell Incline Press		x8		x8		x8
Sport-Specific Exercises							
	Reverse Lunge to Step-Up		x10		x10		
	Physioball Leg Curls		x15		x15		
	Standing Overhead Press		x10		x10		
	Underhand Grip Inverted Row		x10		x10		

TYPE	EXERCISE	WEIGHT	REPS	WEIGHT	REPS	WEIGHT	REPS
Individualized Mobility							
Soft Tissue Release / Foam Roll	As needed						
Mobility Exercise 1	Lateral Hip Distraction		x30 Sec.		x30 Sec.		x30 Sec.
Mobility Exercise 2	Posterior Hip Distraction		x30 Sec.		x30 Sec.		x30 Sec.
Foundation Superset 1							
Traditional Core Exercise	Alternating Limb Dead Bug		x10		x10		x10
Lower Body Push	Walking Lunge		x10		x10		x10
Upper Body Pull	Pull-Ups or Chin-Ups		x8 to 12		x8 to 12		x8 to 12
Foundation Superset 2							
Anti-Rotation Exercise	Half-Kneel Overhead Plate Circles		x10		x10		x10
Lower Body Pull	Slide Board or Towel Leg Curls		x15		x15		x15
Upper Body Push	Resisted Push-Up		x10		x10		x10
Sport-Specific Exercises							
	Standing Calf Raises		x15		x15		
	Body Weight Dorisflexion		x10		x10		
	Close Grip Lat Pull-Down		x10		x10		
	Standing Dumbbell Shoulder Press		x10		x10		

TRIATHLETE'S BASE & BUILD TEMPLATE

TYPE	EXERCISE	WEIGHT	REPS	WEIGHT	REPS	WEIGHT	REPS
Individualized Mobility							
Soft Tissue Release / Foam Roll	As needed						
Mobility Exercise 1	Side-Lying Thoracic Spine Rotation		x10		x10		x10
Mobility Exercise 2	Band Distraction Dorsiflexion		x30 Sec.		x30 Sec.		x30 Sec.
Foundation Superset 1							
Traditional Core Exercise	Plank		x60 Sec.		x60 Sec.		x60 Sec.
Lower Body Push	Barbell Back Squats or Barbell Front Squats		x8		x8		x8
Upper Body Pull	Pull-Up		x8 to 12		x8 to 12		x8 to 12
Foundation Superset 2							
Anti-Rotation Exercise	Hip Taps		x10		x10		x10
Lower Body Pull	Barbell Romanian Deadlift		x8		x8		x8
Upper Body Push	Barbell Bench Press		x8		x8		x8
Sport-Specific Exercises							
	Suspension Trainer Inverted Row		x10		x10		
	Single Arm Kettlebell Clean and Press		x10		x10		
	Clam Shells		x10		x10		
	Cable Push/Pull		x10		x10		

TYPE	EXERCISE	WEIGHT	REPS	WEIGHT	REPS	WEIGHT	REPS
Individualized Mobility							
Soft Tissue Release / Foam Roll	As needed						
Mobility Exercise 1	Bretzel		x30 Sec.		x30 Sec.		x30 Sec.
Mobility Exercise 2	90/90 Hip Rotations		x10		x10		x10
Foundation Superset 1							
Traditional Core Exercise	Side Plank		x30 Sec.		x30 Sec.		x30 Sec.
Lower Body Push	Barbell Reverse Lunge		x8		x8		x8
Upper Body Pull	Chin-Up		x8 to 12		x8 to 12		x8 to 12
Foundation Superset 2							
Anti-Rotation Exercise	Medicine Ball Windshield Wipers		x10		x10		x10
Lower Body Pull	Glute-Ham Raises		x5		x5		x5
Upper Body Push	Negative Push-Ups (5 Sec. Each)		x5 to 8		x5 to 8		x5 to 8
Sport-Specific Exercises							
	Deadbug Paloff Press		x10		x10		
	Split Squat Jump		x10		x10		
	Half-Kneel Upward Cable Chop		x10		x10		
	Wide Grip Lat Pull-Down		x10		x10		

TYPE	EXERCISE	WEIGHT	REPS	WEIGHT	REPS	WEIGHT	REPS
Individualized Mobility							
Soft Tissue Release / Foam Roll	As needed						
Mobility Exercise 1	Foam Roller Back Extension		x30 Sec.		x30 Sec.		x30 Sec.
Mobility Exercise 2	Posterior Hip Distraction		x30 Sec.		x30 Sec.		x30Sec.
Foundation Superset 1							
Traditional Core Exercise	High Side Plank		x60 Sec.		x60 Sec.		x60 Sec.
Lower Body Push	Barbell Back Squat or Barbell Front Squat		x8		x8		x8
Upper Body Pull	Inverted Row on Suspension Trainer		x12		x12		x12
Foundation Superset 2							
Anti-Rotation Exercise	Dead Bug Paloff Press		x10		x10		x10
Lower Body Pull	Single Leg Dumbbell Romanian Deadlift		x8		x8		x8
Upper Body Push	Alternating Dumbbell Incline Press		x8		x8		x8
Sport-Specific Exercises							
	Valslide Leg Curls		x10		x10		
	Bench Pistol Squat		x10		x10		
	Lateral Lunge Clean		x10		x10		
	Dumbbell Windshield Wipers		x10		x10		

TYPE	EXERCISE	WEIGHT	REPS	WEIGHT	REPS	WEIGHT	REPS
Individualized Mobility							
Soft Tissue Release / Foam Roll	As needed						
Mobility Exercise 1	Sleeper Stretch		x30 Sec.		x30 Sec.		x30 Sec.
Mobility Exercise 2	World's Greatest Stretch		x30 Sec.		x30 Sec.		x30Sec.
Foundation Superset 1							
Traditional Core Exercise	Alternating Limb Dead Bug		x10		x10		x10
Lower Body Push	Walking Lunge		x10		x10		x10
Upper Body Pull	Pull-Up or Chin-Up		x8 to 12		x8 to 12		x8 to 12
Foundation Superset 2							
Anti-Rotation Exercise	Half-Kneel Overhead Plate Circles		x10		x10		x10
Lower Body Pull	Slide Board or Towel Leg Curls		x15		x15		x15
Upper Body Push	Resisted Push-Up		x10		x10		x10
Sport-Specific Exercises							
	Rip Trainer March		x10		x10		
	Lateral Step-Ups		x10		x10		
	Barbell Inverted Row		x10		x10		
	Dumbbell Renegade Row		x10		x10		

PEAK MILEAGE TEMPLATE

The peak mileage templates are designed for when you are doing the most intense endurance workouts of the year. The amount of time you spend in the gym will be slightly reduced to account for increased fatigue and amount of time you are spending on your endurance sessions. These sessions should still be done with intensity and purpose, but your main focus should be on getting as much quality aerobic training as possible every day and pushing your body to achieve further distances or faster times.

SWIMMER'S PEAK MILEAGE TEMPLATE

TYPE	EXERCISE	WEIGHT	REPS	WEIGHT	REPS	WEIGHT	REPS
Individualized Mobility							
Soft Tissue Release / Foam Roll	As needed						
Mobility Exercise 1	Book Openers		x10		x10		x10
Mobility Exercise 2	Bretzel		x30 Sec.		x30 Sec.		x30 Sec.
Foundation Superset 1							
Traditional Core Exercise	Plank		x60 Sec.		x60 Sec.		x60 Sec.
Lower Body Push	Barbell Back Squat		x10		x10		x10
Upper Body Pull	Pull-Up		x8 to 12		x8 to 12		x8 to 12
Foundation Superset 2							
Anti-Rotation Exercise	Lateral Plate Drag		x10		x10		x10
Lower Body Pull	Barbell Romanian Deadlift		x10		x10		x10
Upper Body Push	Barbell Bench Press		x10		x10		x10
Sport-Specific Exercises							
	Dumbbell Standing Reverse Fly		x10		x10		
	Cable Push/Pull		x10		x10		
	Clam Shells		x10		x10		
	Hip Thrust March		x10		x10		

TYPE	EXERCISE	WEIGHT	REPS	WEIGHT	REPS	WEIGHT	REPS
Individualized Mobility							
Soft Tissue Release / Foam Roll	As needed						
Mobility Exercise 1	Side-Lying Thoracic Spine Rotations		x10		x10		x10
Mobility Exercise 2	Sleeper Stretch		x30 Sec.		x30 Sec.		x30 Sec.
Foundation Superset 1							
Traditional Core Exercise	Side Plank		x30 Sec.		x30 Sec.		x30 Sec.
Lower Body Push	Barbell Lunge		x8		x8		x8
Upper Body Pull	Chin-Up		x8 to 12		x8 to 12		x8 to 12
Foundation Superset 2							
Anti-Rotation Exercise	Straight Leg Dumbbell Windshield Wipers		x10		x10		x10
Lower Body Pull	Glute-Ham Raises		x8		x8		x8
Upper Body Push	Negative Push-Ups (5 Sec. Each)		x5 to 8		x5 to 8		x5 to 8
Sport-Specific Exercises							
	Cable Cross-Pull – Low to High		x10		x10		
	Physioball Flutter Kicks		x10		x10		
	V-Grip Pull-Down		x10		x10		
	Resisted Hip Bridge		x10		x10		

TYPE	EXERCISE	WEIGHT	REPS	WEIGHT	REPS	WEIGHT	REPS
Individualized Mobility							
Soft Tissue Release / Foam Roll	As needed						
Mobility Exercise 1	Cross-Body Stretch		x30 Sec.		x30 Sec.		x30 Sec.
Mobility Exercise 2	Thread the Needle		x10		x10.		x10
Foundation Superset 1							
Traditional Core Exercise	High Side Plank		x60 Sec.		x60 Sec.		x60 Sec.
Lower Body Push	Barbell Back Squat or Barbell Front Squat		x10		x10		x10
Upper Body Pull	Inverted Row on Suspension Trainer		x12		x12		x12
Foundation Superset 2							
Anti-Rotation Exercise	Dead Bug Paloff Press		x10		x10		x10
Lower Body Pull	Dumbbell Romanian Deadlift		x10		x10		x10
Upper Body Push	Alternating Dumbbell Chest Press		x10		x10		x10
Sport-Specific Exercises							
	Reverse Fly on Incline Bench		x10		x10		
	Cable Push/Pull on Bench		x10		x10		
	Clam Shell		x10		x10		
	Resisted Hip Thrust March		x10		x10		

TYPE	EXERCISE	WEIGHT	REPS	WEIGHT	REPS	WEIGHT	REPS
Individualized Mobility							
Soft Tissue Release / Foam Roll	As needed						
Mobility Exercise 1	Doorway Stretch		x30 Sec.		x30 Sec.		x30 Sec.
Mobility Exercise 2	Thread the Needle		x10		x10		x10
Foundation Superset 1							
Traditional Core Exercise	Alternating Limb Dead Bug		x10		x10		x10
Lower Body Push	Walking Lunge		x8		x8		x8
Upper Body Pull	Pull-Ups or Chin-Ups		x8 to 12		x8 to 12		x8 to 12
Foundation Superset 2							
Anti-Rotation Exercise	Overhead Plate Circles		x10		x10		x10
Lower Body Pull	Slide Board or Towel Leg Curls		x15		x15		x15
Upper Body Push	Resisted Push-Up		x8 to 12		x8 to 12		x8 to 12
Sport-Specific Exercises							
	Cable Cross-Pull – High to Low		x10		x10		
	Floor Flutter Kicks		x10		x10		
	Close Grip Lat Pull-Down		x10		x10		
	Hip Bridge		x10		x10		

CYCLIST'S PEAK MILEAGE TEMPLATE

TYPE	EXERCISE	WEIGHT	REPS	WEIGHT	REPS	WEIGHT	REPS
Individualized Mobility							
Soft Tissue Release / Foam Roll	As needed						
Mobility Exercise 1	90/90 Hip Rotations		x10		x10		x10
Mobility Exercise 2	Down Dog		x30 Sec.		x30 Sec.		x30 Sec.
Foundation Superset 1							
Traditional Core Exercise	Plank		x60 Sec.		x60 Sec.		x60 Sec.
Lower Body Push	Barbell Back Squat		x10		x8		x6
Upper Body Pull	Pull-Up		x8 to 12		x8 to 12		x8 to 12
Foundation Superset 2							
Anti-Rotation Exercise	Lateral Plate Drag		x10		x10		x10
Lower Body Pull	Barbell Romanian Deadlift		x10		x8		x6
Upper Body Push	Barbell Bench Press		x10		x8		x6
Sport-Specific Exercises							
	Barbell Split Squat		x10		x10		
	Renegade Row		x10		x10		
	Valslide Body Saw with Leg Lift		x10		x10		
	Standing Cable Chop		x10		x10		

TYPE	EXERCISE	WEIGHT	REPS	WEIGHT	REPS	WEIGHT	REPS
Individualized Mobility							
Soft Tissue Release / Foam Roll	As needed						
Mobility Exercise 1	Foam Roller Back Extension		x30 Sec.		x30 Sec.		x30 Sec.
Mobility Exercise 2	World's Greatest Stretch		x30 Sec.		x30 Sec.		x30 Sec.
Foundation Superset 1							
Traditional Core Exercise	Side Plank		x30 Sec.		x30 Sec.		x30 Sec.
Lower Body Push	Barbell Lunge		x8		x8		x8
Upper Body Pull	Chin-Up		x8 to 12		x8 to 12		x8 to 12
Foundation Superset 2							
Anti-Rotation Exercise	Straight Leg Dumbbell Windshield Wipers		x10		x10		x10
Lower Body Pull	Glute-Ham Raises		x8		x8		x8
Upper Body Push	Negative Push-Ups (5 Sec. Each)		x5 to 8		x5 to 8		x5 to 8
Sport-Specific Exercises							
	Split Squat Jump		x10		x10		
	Half-Kneel Overhead Plate Circles		x10		x10		
	Valslide Lateral Lunge		x10		x10		
	Double Arm Kettlebell Clean and Press		x10		x10		

TYPE	EXERCISE	WEIGHT	REPS	WEIGHT	REPS	WEIGHT	REPS
Individualized Mobility							
Soft Tissue Release / Foam Roll	As needed						
Mobility Exercise 1	Bretzel		x30 Sec.		x30 Sec.		x30 Sec.
Mobility Exercise 2	Lateral Hip Distraction		x30 Sec.		x30 Sec.		x30 Sec.
Foundation Superset 1							
Traditional Core Exercise	High Side Plank		x60 Sec.		x60 Sec.		x60 Sec.
Lower Body Push	Barbell Back Squat or Barbell Front Squat		x10		x8		x6
Upper Body Pull	Inverted Row on Suspension Trainer		x12		x12		x12
Foundation Superset 2							
Anti-Rotation Exercise	Dead Bug Paloff Press		x10		x10		x10
Lower Body Pull	Dumbbell Romanian Deadlift		x10		x8		x6
Upper Body Push	Alternating Dumbbell Chest Press		x10		x8		x6
Sport-Specific Exercises							
	Suspension Trainer Pistol Squat		x10		x10		
	Valslide Body Saw		x10		x10		
	Half-Kneel Upward Cable Chop		x10		x10		
	Overhead Plate Circles		x10		x10		

TYPE	EXERCISE	WEIGHT	REPS	WEIGHT	REPS	WEIGHT	REPS
Individualized Mobility							
Soft Tissue Release / Foam Roll	As needed						
Mobility Exercise 1	Foam Roller Back Extension		x30 Sec.		x30 Sec.		x30 Sec.
Mobility Exercise 2	Posterior Hip Distraction		x30 Sec.		x30 Sec.		x30 Sec.
Foundation Superset 1							
Traditional Core Exercise	Alternating Limb Dead Bug		x10		x10		x10
Lower Body Push	Walking Lunge		x8		x8		x8
Upper Body Pull	Pull-Ups or Chin-Ups		x8 to 12		x8 to 12		x8 to 12
Foundation Superset 2							
Anti-Rotation Exercise	Overhead Plate Circles		x10		x10		x10
Lower Body Pull	Slide Board or Towel Leg Curls		x15		x15		x15
Upper Body Push	Resisted Push-Up		x8 to 12		x8 to 12		x8 to 12
Sport-Specific Exercises							
	Burpee		x10		x10		
	Lateral Plate Drag		x10		x10		
	Full Pistol Squat		x10		x10		
	Lateral Lunge Press		x10		x10		

RUNNER'S PEAK MILEAGE TEMPLATE

TYPE	EXERCISE	WEIGHT	REPS	WEIGHT	REPS	WEIGHT	REPS
Individualized Mobility							
Soft Tissue Release / Foam Roll	As needed						
Mobility Exercise 1	90/90 Hip Rotations		x10		x10		x10
Mobility Exercise 2	Lateral Hip Distraction		x30 Sec.		x30 Sec.		x30 Sec.
Foundation Superset 1							
Traditional Core Exercise	Plank		x60 Sec.		x60 Sec.		x60 Sec.
Lower Body Push	Barbell Back Squat		x10		x8		x6
Upper Body Pull	Pull-Up		x8 to 12		x8 to 12		x8 to 12
Foundation Superset 2							
Anti-Rotation Exercise	Lateral Plate Drag		x10		x10		x10
Lower Body Pull	Barbell Romanian Deadlift		x10		x8		x6
Upper Body Push	Barbell Bench Press		x10		x8		x6
Sport-Specific Exercises							
	Step-Ups		x10		x10		
	Machine Leg Curl		x10		x10		
	Standing Overhead Press		x10		x10		
	Inverted Row		x10		x10		

TYPE	EXERCISE	WEIGHT	REPS	WEIGHT	REPS	WEIGHT	REPS
Individualized Mobility							
Soft Tissue Release / Foam Roll	As needed						
Mobility Exercise 1	Posterior Hip Distraction		x30 Sec.		x30 Sec.		x30 Sec.
Mobility Exercise 2	Band Distraction Dorsiflexion		x30 Sec.		x30 Sec.		x30 Sec.
Foundation Superset 1							
Traditional Core Exercise	Side Plank		x30 Sec.		x30 Sec.		x30 Sec.
Lower Body Push	Barbell Lunge		x8		x8		x8
Upper Body Pull	Chin-Up		x8 to 12		x8 to 12		x8 to 12
Foundation Superset 2							
Anti-Rotation Exercise	Straight Leg Dumbbell Windshield Wipers		x10		x10		x10
Lower Body Pull	Glute-Ham Raises		x8		x8		x8
Upper Body Push	Negative Push-Ups (5 Sec. Each)		x5 to 8		x5 to 8		x5 to 8
Sport-Specific Exercises							
	Seated Calf Raises		x10		x10		
	Partner-Resisted Dorsiflexion		x10		x10		
	Resisted Alternating Knee-to-Chest		x10		x10		
	Rip Trainer March		x10		x10		

TYPE	EXERCISE	WEIGHT	REPS	WEIGHT	REPS	WEIGHT	REPS
Individualized Mobility							
Soft Tissue Release / Foam Roll	As needed						
Mobility Exercise 1	Slant Board Dorsiflexion		x30 Sec.		x30 Sec.		x30 Sec.
Mobility Exercise 2	90/90 Hip Rotations		x10		x10		x10
Foundation Superset 1							
Traditional Core Exercise	High Side Plank		x60 Sec.		x60 Sec.		x60 Sec.
Lower Body Push	Barbell Back Squat or Barbell Front Squat		x10		x8		x6
Upper Body Pull	Inverted Row on Suspension Trainer		x12		x12		x12
Foundation Superset 2							
Anti-Rotation Exercise	Dead Bug Paloff Press		x10		x10		x10
Lower Body Pull	Dumbbell Romanian Deadlift		x10		x8		x6
Upper Body Push	Alternating Dumbbell Chest Press		x10		x8		x6
Sport-Specific Exercises							
	Step-Up to Single Leg Romanian Deadlift		x10		x10		
	Physioball Leg Curls		x10		x10		
	Standing Overhead Press		x10		x10		
	Underhand Grip Inverted Row		x10		x10		

TYPE	EXERCISE	WEIGHT	REPS	WEIGHT	REPS	WEIGHT	REPS
Individualized Mobility							
Soft Tissue Release / Foam Roll	As needed						
Mobility Exercise 1	Lateral Hip Distraction		x30 Sec.		x30 Sec.		x30 Sec.
Mobility Exercise 2	Posterior Hip Distraction		x30 Sec.		x30 Sec.		x30 Sec.
Foundation Superset 1							
Traditional Core Exercise	Alternating Limb Dead Bug		x10		x10		x10
Lower Body Push	Walking Lunge		x8		x8		x8
Upper Body Pull	Pull-Ups or Chin-Ups		x8 to 12		x8 to 12		x8 to 12
Foundation Superset 2							
Anti-Rotation Exercise	Overhead Plate Circles		x10		x10		x10
Lower Body Pull	Slide Board or Towel Leg Curls		x15		x15		x15
Upper Body Push	Resisted Push-Up		x8 to 12		x8 to 12		x8 to 12
Sport-Specific Exercises							
	Standing Calf Raises		x15		x15		
	Band-Resisted Dorisflexion		x10		x10		
	Wide Grip Lat Pull-Down		x10		x10		
	Standing Dumbbell Shoulder Press		x10		x10		

TRIATHLETE'S PEAK MILEAGE TEMPLATE

TYPE	EXERCISE	WEIGHT	REPS	WEIGHT	REPS	WEIGHT	REPS
Individualized Mobility							
Soft Tissue Release / Foam Roll	As needed						
Mobility Exercise 1	Thread the Needle		x10		x10		x10
Mobility Exercise 2	Band Distraction Dorsiflexion		x30 Sec.		x30 Sec.		x30 Sec.
Foundation Superset 1							
Traditional Core Exercise	Plank		x60 Sec.		x60 Sec.		x60 Sec.
Lower Body Push	Barbell Back Squat		x10		x8		x6
Upper Body Pull	Pull-Up		x8 to 12		x8 to 12		x8 to 12
Foundation Superset 2							
Anti-Rotation Exercise	Lateral Plate Drag		x10		x10		x10
Lower Body Pull	Barbell Romanian Deadlift		x10		x8		x6
Upper Body Push	Barbell Bench Press		x10		x8		x6
Sport-Specific Exercises							
	Standing Overhead Press		x10		x10		
	Paloff Press		x10		x10		
	Cable Cross-Pull – High to Low		x10		x10		
	Lateral Lunge and Twist		x10		x10		

TYPE	EXERCISE	WEIGHT	REPS	WEIGHT	REPS	WEIGHT	REPS
Individualized Mobility							
Soft Tissue Release / Foam Roll	As needed						
Mobility Exercise 1	90/90 Hip Rotations		x10		x10		x10
Mobility Exercise 2	Doorway Stretch		x30 Sec.		x30 Sec.		x30 Sec.
Foundation Superset 1							
Traditional Core Exercise	Side Plank		x30 Sec.		x30 Sec.		x30 Sec.
Lower Body Push	Barbell Lunge		x8		x8		x8
Upper Body Pull	Chin-Up		x8 to 12		x8 to 12		x8 to 12
Foundation Superset 2							
Anti-Rotation Exercise	Straight Leg Dumbbell Windshield Wipers		x10		x10		x10
Lower Body Pull	Glute-Ham Raises		x8		x8		x8
Upper Body Push	Negative Push-Up (5 Sec. Each)		x5 to 8		x5 to 8		x5 to 8
Sport-Specific Exercises							
	Barbell Inverted Row		x10		x10		
	Alternating Knee-to-Chest		x10		x10		
	Step-Up		x10		x10		
	Valslide Body Saw with Leg Lift		x10		x10		

TYPE	EXERCISE	WEIGHT	REPS	WEIGHT	REPS	WEIGHT	REPS
Individualized Mobility							
Soft Tissue Release / Foam Roll	As needed						
Mobility Exercise 1	World's Greatest Stretch		x30 Sec.		x30 Sec.		x30 Sec.
Mobility Exercise 2	Slant Board Dorsiflexion		x30 Sec.		x30 Sec.		x30 Sec.
Foundation Superset 1							
Traditional Core Exercise	High Side Plank		x60 Sec.		x60 Sec.		x60 Sec.
Lower Body Push	Barbell Back Squat or Barbell Front Squat		x10		x8		x6
Upper Body Pull	Inverted Row on Suspension Trainer		x12		x12		x12
Foundation Superset 2							
Anti-Rotation Exercise	Dead Bug Paloff Press		x10		x10		x10
Lower Body Pull	Dumbbell Romanian Deadlift		x10		x8		x6
Upper Body Push	Alternating Dumbbell Chest Press		x10		x8		x6
Sport-Specific Exercises							
	Crossover Lunge		x10		x10		
	Suspension Trainer Pistol Squat		x10		x10		
	Single Arm Kettlebell Clean		x10		x10		
	Half-Kneel Overhead Plate Circles		x10		x10		

TYPE	EXERCISE	WEIGHT	REPS	WEIGHT	REPS	WEIGHT	REPS
Individualized Mobility							
Soft Tissue Release / Foam Roll	As needed						
Mobility Exercise 1	Foam Roller Back Extension		x30 Sec.		x30 Sec.		x30 Sec.
Mobility Exercise 2	Bretzel		x30 Sec.		x30 Sec.		x30 Sec.
Foundation Superset 1							
Traditional Core Exercise	Alternating Limb Dead Bug		x10		x10		x10
Lower Body Push	Walking Lunge		x8		x8		x8
Upper Body Pull	Pull-Ups or Chin-Ups		x8 to 12		x8 to 12		x8 to 12
Foundation Superset 2							
Anti-Rotation Exercise	Overhead Plate Circles		x10		x10		x10
Lower Body Pull	Slide Board or Towel Leg Curls		x12		x12		x12
Upper Body Push	Resisted Push-Up		x8 to 12		x8 to 12		x8 to 12
Sport-Specific Exercises							
	Standing Cable Chop		x10		x10		
	V-Grip Lat Pull-Down		x10		x10		
	Renegade Row with Push-Up		x10		x10		
	Hip Thrust March		x10		x10		

TAPER TEMPLATE

The taper templates should be used when you are in the final weeks leading up to your biggest events. During these few weeks, your endurance training should be reduced to allow your musculoskeletal system to recover while your cardiovascular system remains functioning at a highly trained level, meaning you show up at the starting line with the absolute best chance for success. Keep in mind that we will continue to use the philosophy that resistance training should be tapered to the same degree as endurance training. So, if total mileage is reduced by 20 percent during a taper, the number or reps per set and the amount of weight being lifted should also be reduced by 20 percent.

Additional sessions during a taper phase can be taken from the home gym/travel templates or individual bodyweight exercises can be selected based on equipment availability and personal preference.

SWIMMER'S TAPER TEMPLATE

TYPE	EXERCISE	WEIGHT	REPS	WEIGHT	REPS	WEIGHT	REPS
Individualized Mobility							
Soft Tissue Release / Foam Roll	As needed						
Mobility Exercise 1	Bretzel		x30 Sec.		x30 Sec.		x30 Sec.
Mobility Exercise 2	Book Openers		x10		x10		x10
Foundation Superset 1							
Traditional Core Exercise	Plank		x45 Sec.		x45 Sec.		x45 Sec.
Lower Body Push	Squat (Variation Based on Individual Fatigue)		x8		x8		x8
Upper Body Pull	Pull-Up		x5 to 8		x5 to 8		x5 to 8
Foundation Superset 2							
Anti-Rotation Exercise	Hip Taps		x8		x8		x8
Lower Body Pull	Barbell Romanian Deadlift		x8		x8		x8
Upper Body Push	Barbell Bench Press		x8		x8		x8
Sport-Specific Exercises							
	Single Arm Dumbbell Reverse Fly		x8		x8		
	Cable Push/Pull Prone on Bench		x8		x8		
	Clam Shell with Heels Elevated		x8		x8		
	Glute Bridge March		x8		x8		

TYPE	EXERCISE	WEIGHT	REPS	WEIGHT	REPS	WEIGHT	REPS
Individualized Mobility							
Soft Tissue Release / Foam Roll	As needed						
Mobility Exercise 1	90/90 Hip Rotations		x10		x10		x10
Mobility Exercise 2	Doorway Stretch		x30 Sec.		x30 Sec.		x30 Sec.
Foundation Superset 1							
Traditional Core Exercise	Side Plank		x25 Sec.		x25 Sec.		x25 Sec.
Lower Body Push	Barbell Lunge		x8		x8		x8
Upper Body Pull	Chin-Up		x5 to 8		x5 to 8		x5 to 8
Foundation Superset 2							
Anti-Rotation Exercise	Dumbbell Windshield Wipers		x8		x8		x8
Lower Body Pull	Glute-Ham Raises		x8		x8		x8
Upper Body Push	Negative Push-Ups (5 Sec. Each)		x5 to 8		x5 to 8		x5 to 8
Sport-Specific Exercises							
	Cable Cross-Pull – High to Low		x8		x8		
	Physioball Flutter Kicks		x8		x8		
	V-Grip Pull-Down		x8		x8		
	Resisted Hip Bridge		x8		x8		

TYPE	EXERCISE	WEIGHT	REPS	WEIGHT	REPS	WEIGHT	REPS
Individualized Mobility							
Soft Tissue Release / Foam Roll	As needed						
Mobility Exercise 1	Cross-Body Stretch		x30 Sec.		x30 Sec.		x30 Sec.
Mobility Exercise 2	Thread the Needle		x10		x10		x10
Foundation Supeset 1							
Traditional Core Exercise	High Side Plank		x45 Sec.		x45 Sec.		x45 Sec.
Lower Body Push	Squat (Variation Based on Individual Fatigue)		x8		x8		x8
Upper Body Pull	Inverted Row on Suspension Trainer		x8		x8		x8
Foundation Superset 2							
Anti-Rotation Exercise	Dead Bug Paloff Press		x8		x8		x8
Lower Body Pull	Dumbbell Romanian Deadlift		x8		x8		x8
Upper Body Push	Alternating Dumbbell Incline Press		x8		x8		x8
Sport-Specific Exercises							
	Dumbbell Standing Reverse Fly		x8		x8		
	Cable Push/Pull		x8		x8		
	Clam Shells		x8		x8		
	Hip Thrust March		x8		x8		

TYPE	EXERCISE	WEIGHT	REPS	WEIGHT	REPS	WEIGHT	REPS
Individualized Mobility							
Soft Tissue Release / Foam Roll	As needed						
Mobility Exercise 1	Doorway Stretch		x30 Sec.		x30 Sec.		x30 Sec.
Mobility Exercise 2	Book Opener		x10		x10		x1 0
Foundation Superset 1							
Traditional Core Exercise	Alternating Limb Dead Bug		x8		x8		x8
Lower Body Push	Walking Lunge		x8		x8		x8
Upper Body Pull	Pull-Ups or Chin-Ups		x5 to 8		x5 to 8		x5 to 8
Foundation Superset 2							
Anti-Rotation Exercise	Half-Kneel Overhead Plate Circles		x8		x8		x8
Lower Body Pull	Slide Board or Towel Leg Curls		x10		x10		x10
Upper Body Push	Resisted Push-Up		x8		x8		x8
Sport-Specific Exercises							
	Cable Cross-Pull – Low to High		x8		x8		
	BOSU Ball Flutter Kicks		x8		x8		
	Close Grip Lat Pull-Down		x8		x8		
	Resisted Hip Bridge		x8		x8		

CYCLIST'S TAPER TEMPLATE

TYPE	EXERCISE	WEIGHT	REPS	WEIGHT	REPS	WEIGHT	REPS
Individualized Mobility							
Soft Tissue Release / Foam Roll	As needed						
Mobility Exercise 1	Bretzel		x30 Sec.		x30 Sec.		x30 Sec.
Mobility Exercise 2	Down Dog		x30 Sec.		x30 Sec.		x30 Sec.
Foundation Superset 1							
Traditional Core Exercise	Plank		x45 Sec.		x45 Sec.		x45 Sec.
Lower Body Push	Squat (Variation Based on Individual Fatigue)		x8		x8		x8
Upper Body Pull	Pull-Up		x5 to 8		x5 to 8		x5 to 8
Foundation Superset 2							
Anti-Rotation Exercise	Hip Taps		x8		x8		x8
Lower Body Pull	Barbell Romanian Deadlift		x8		x8		x8
Upper Body Push	Barbell Bench Press		x8		x8		x8
Sport-Specific Exercises							
	Dumbbell Split Squat		x8		x8		
	Lateral Lunge and Twist		x8		x8		
	Single Arm Kettlebell Clean and Press		x8		x8		
	Lateral Plate Drag		x8		x8		

TYPE	EXERCISE	WEIGHT	REPS	WEIGHT	REPS	WEIGHT	REPS
Individualized Mobility							
Soft Tissue Release / Foam Roll	As needed						
Mobility Exercise 1	World's Greatest Stretch		x30 Sec.		x30 Sec.		x30 Sec.
Mobility Exercise 2	Foam Roller Back Extension		x30 Sec.		x30 Sec.		x30 Sec.
Foundation Superset 1							
Traditional Core Exercise	Side Plank		x25 Sec.		x25 Sec.		x25 Sec.
Lower Body Push	Lunge (Variation Based on Individual Fatigue)		x8		x8		x8
Upper Body Pull	Chin-Up		x5 to 8		x5 to 8		x5 to 8
Foundation Superset 2							
Anti-Rotation Exercise	Dumbbell Windshield Wipers		x8		x8		x8
Lower Body Pull	Glute-Ham Raises		x4 to 6		x4 to 6		x4 to 6
Upper Body Push	Negative Push-Ups (5 Sec. Each)		x5 to 8		x5 to 8		x5 to 8
Sport-Specific Exercises							
	Burpee Tuck Jump		x8		x8		
	Renegade Row with Push-Up		x8		x8		
	Lateral Lunge Press		x8		x8		
	Half-Kneel Overhead Plate Circles		x8		x8		

TYPE	EXERCISE	WEIGHT	REPS	WEIGHT	REPS	WEIGHT	REPS
Individualized Mobility							
Soft Tissue Release / Foam Roll	As needed						
Mobility Exercise 1	Foam Roller Back Extension		x30 Sec.		x30 Sec.		x30 Sec.
Mobility Exercise 2	90/90 Hip Rotations		x10		x10		x10
Foundation Superset 1							
Traditional Core Exercise	High Side Plank		x45 Sec.		x45 Sec.		x45 Sec.
Lower Body Push	Squat (Variation Based on Individual Fatigue)		x8		x8		x8
Upper Body Pull	Inverted Row on Suspension Trainer		x8		x8		x8
Foundation Superset 2							
Anti-Rotation Exercise	Dead Bug Paloff Press		x8		x8		x8
Lower Body Pull	Dumbbell Romanian Deadlift		x8		x8		x8
Upper Body Push	Alternating Dumbbell Incline Press		x8		x8		x8
Sport-Specific Exercises							
	Suspension Trainer Pistol Squat		x8		x8		
	Half-Kneel Upward Cable Chop		x8		x8		
	Valslide Body Saw		x8		x8		
	Dumbbell Split Squat		x8		x8		

TYPE	EXERCISE	WEIGHT	REPS	WEIGHT	REPS	WEIGHT	REPS
Individualized Mobility							
Soft Tissue Release / Foam Roll	As needed						
Mobility Exercise 1	World's Greatest Stretch		x30 Sec.		x30 Sec.		x30 Sec.
Mobility Exercise 2	Down Dog		x30 Sec.		x30 Sec.		x30 Sec.
Foundation Superset 1							
Traditional Core Exercise	Alternating Limb Dead Bug		x8		x8		x8
Lower Body Push	Walking Lunge		x8		x8		x8
Upper Body Pull	Pull-Ups or Chin-Ups		x5 to 8		x5 to 8		x5 to 8
Foundation Superset 2							
Anti-Rotation Exercise	Half-Kneel Overhead Plate Circles		x8		x8		x8
Lower Body Pull	Slide Board or Towel Leg Curls		x8		x8		x8
Upper Body Push	Resisted Push-Up		x8		x8		x8
Sport-Specific Exercises							
	Dumbbell Renegade Row		x8		x8		
	Lateral Plate Drag		x8		x8		
	Single Arm Kettlebell Clean		x8		x8		
	Standing Cable Chop		x8		x8		

RUNNER'S TAPER TEMPLATE

TYPE	EXERCISE	WEIGHT	REPS	WEIGHT	REPS	WEIGHT	REPS
Individualized Mobility							
Soft Tissue Release / Foam Roll	As needed						
Mobility Exercise 1	90/90 Hip Rotation		x10		x10		x10
Mobility Exercise 2	Lateral Hip Distraction		x30 Sec.		x30 Sec.		x30 Sec.
Foundation Superset 1							
Traditional Core Exercise	Plank		x45 Sec.		x45 Sec.		x45 Sec.
Lower Body Push	Squat (Variation Based on Individual Fatigue)		x8		x8		x8
Upper Body Pull	Pull-Up		x5 to 8		x5 to 8		x5 to 8
Foundation Superset 2							
Anti-Rotation Exercise	Hip Taps		x8		x8		x8
Lower Body Pull	Barbell Romanian Deadlift		x8		x8		x8
Upper Body Push	Barbell Bench Press		x8		x8		x8
Sport-Specific Exercises							
	Lateral Step-Ups		x8		x8		
	Machine Leg Curl		x8		x8		
	Standing Overhead Press		x8		x8		
	Inverted Row		x8		x8		

TYPE	EXERCISE	WEIGHT	REPS	WEIGHT	REPS	WEIGHT	REPS
Individualized Mobility							
Soft Tissue Release / Foam Roll	As needed						
Mobility Exercise 1	Posterior Hip Distraction		x30 Sec.		x30 Sec.		x30 Sec.
Mobility Exercise 2	Band Distraction Dorsiflexion		x30 Sec.		x30 Sec.		x30 Sec.
Foundation Superset 1							
Traditional Core Exercise	Side Plank		x25 Sec.		x25 Sec.		x25 Sec.
Lower Body Push	Lunge (Variation Based on Individual Fatigue)		x8		x8		x8
Upper Body Pull	Chin-Up		x5 to 8		x5 to 8		x5 to 8
Foundation Superset 2							
Anti-Rotation Exercise	Dumbbell Windshield Wipers		x8		x8		x8
Lower Body Pull	Glute-Ham Raises		x4 to 6		x4 to 6		x4 to 6
Upper Body Push	Negative Push-Ups (5 Sec. Each)		x5 to 8		x5 to 8		x5 to 8
Sport-Specific Exercises							
	Seated Calf Raises		x12		x12		
	Band-Resisted Dorsiflexion		x8		x8		
	Alternating Knee-to-Chest		x8		x8		
	Rip Trainer March		x8		x8		

TYPE	EXERCISE	WEIGHT	REPS	WEIGHT	REPS	WEIGHT	REPS
Individualized Mobility							
Soft Tissue Release / Foam Roll	As needed						
Mobility Exercise 1	Slant Board Dorsiflexion		x30 Sec.		x30 Sec.		x30 Sec.
Mobility Exercise 2	90/90 Hip Rotations		x10		x10		x10
Foundation Superset 1							
Traditional Core Exercise	High Side Plank		x45 Sec.		x45 Sec.		x45 Sec.
Lower Body Push	Squat (Variation Based on Individual Fatigue)		x8		x8		x8
Upper Body Pull	Inverted Row on Suspension Trainer		x8		x8		x8
Foundation Superset 2							
Anti-Rotation Exercise	Dead Bug Paloff Press		x8		x8		x8
Lower Body Pull	Dumbbell Romanian Deadlift		x8		x8		x8
Upper Body Push	Alternating Dumbbell Incline Press		x8		x8		x8
Sport-Specific Exercises							
	Reverse Lunge to Step-Up		x8		x8		
	Physioball Leg Curls		x12		x12		
	Standing Overhead Press		x8		x8		
	Underhand Grip Inverted Row		x8		x8		

TYPE	EXERCISE	WEIGHT	REPS	WEIGHT	REPS	WEIGHT	REPS
Individualized Mobility							
Soft Tissue Release / Foam Roll	As needed						
Mobility Exercise 1	Lateral Hip Distraction		x30 Sec.		x30 Sec.		x30 Sec.
Mobility Exercise 2	Posterior Hip Distraction		x30 Sec.		x30 Sec.		x30 Sec.
Foundation Superset 1							
Traditional Core Exercise	Alternating Limb Dead Bug		x8		x8		x8
Lower Body Push	Walking Lunge		x8		x8		x8
Upper Body Pull	Pull-Ups or Chin-Ups		x5 to 8		x5 to 8		x5 to 8
Foundation Superset 2							
Anti-Rotation Exercise	Half-Kneel Overhead Plate Circles		x8		x8		x8
Lower Body Pull	Slide Board or Towel Leg Curls		x10		x10		x10
Upper Body Push	Resisted Push-Up		x8		x8		x8
Sport-Specific Exercises							
	Standing Calf Raises		x12		x12		
	Body Weight Dorisflexion		x8		x8		
	Close Grip Lat Pull-Down		x8		x8		
	Standing Dumbbell Shoulder Press		x8		x8		

TRIATHLETE'S TAPER TEMPLATE

TYPE	EXERCISE	WEIGHT	REPS	WEIGHT	REPS	WEIGHT	REPS
Individualized Mobility							
Soft Tissue Release / Foam Roll	As needed						
Mobility Exercise 1	Cross-Body Stretch		x30 Sec.		x30 Sec.		x30 Sec.
Mobility Exercise 2	Down Dog		x30 Sec.		x30 Sec.		x30 Sec.
Foundation Superset 1							
Traditional Core Exercise	Plank		x45 Sec.		x45 Sec.		x45 Sec.
Lower Body Push	Squat (Variation Based on Individual Fatigue)		x8		x8		x8
Upper Body Pull	Pull-Up		x5 to 8		x5 to 8		x5 to 8
Foundation Superset 2							
Anti-Rotation Exercise	Hip Taps		x8		x8		x8
Lower Body Pull	Barbell Romanian Deadlift		x8		x8		x8
Upper Body Push	Barbell Bench Press		x8		x8		x8
Sport-Specific Exercises							
	Reverse Fly on Physioball		x8		x8		
	Cable Cross-Pull – Low to High		x8		x8		
	Lunge Overhead Plate Circles		x8		x8		
	Single Arm Kettlebell Clean and Press		x8		x8		

TYPE	EXERCISE	WEIGHT	REPS	WEIGHT	REPS	WEIGHT	REPS
Individualized Mobility							
Soft Tissue Release / Foam Roll	As needed						
Mobility Exercise 1	Slant Board Dorsiflexion		x30 Sec.		x30 Sec.		x30 Sec.
Mobility Exercise 2	Bretzel		x30 Sec.		x30 Sec.		x30 Sec.
Foundation Superset 1							
Traditional Core Exercise	Side Plank		x25 Sec.		x25 Sec.		x25 Sec.
Lower Body Push	Lunge (Variation Based on Individual Fatigue)		x8		x8		x8
Upper Body Pull	Chin-Up		x5 to 8		x5 to 8		x5 to 8
Foundation Superset 2							
Anti-Rotation Exercise	Dumbbell Windshield Wipers		x8		x8		x8
Lower Body Pull	Glute-Ham Raises		x4 to 6		x4 to 6		x4 to 6
Upper Body Push	Negative Push-Ups (5 Sec. Each)		x5 to 8		x5 to 8		x5 to 8
Sport-Specific Exercises							
	Physioball Leg Curl		x8		x8		
	Close Grip Lat Pull-Down		x8		x8		
	Rip Trainer March		x8		x8		
	Physioball Alternating Chest Press		x8		x8		

TYPE	EXERCISE	WEIGHT	REPS	WEIGHT	REPS	WEIGHT	REPS
Individualized Mobility							
Soft Tissue Release / Foam Roll	As needed						
Mobility Exercise 1	World's Greatest Stretch		x30 Sec.		x30 Sec.		x30 Sec.
Mobility Exercise 2	Foam Roller Back Extension		x30 Sec.		x30 Sec.		x30 Sec.
Foundation Superset 1							
Traditional Core Exercise	High Side Plank		x45 Sec.		x45 Sec.		x45 Sec.
Lower Body Push	Squat (Variation Based on Individual Fatigue)		x8		x8		x8
Upper Body Pull	Inverted Row on Suspension Trainer		x8		x8		x8
Foundation Superset 2							
Anti-Rotation Exercise	Dead Bug Paloff Press		x8		x8		x8
Lower Body Pull	Dumbbell Romanian Deadlift		x8		x8		x8
Upper Body Push	Alternating Dumbbell Incline Press		x8		x8		x8
Sport-Specific Exercises							
	BOSU Ball Flutter Kick		x8		x8		
	Clam Shells		x8		x8		
	Lateral Step-Up		x8		x8		
	Standing Calf Raise		x8		x8		

TYPE	EXERCISE	WEIGHT	REPS	WEIGHT	REPS	WEIGHT	REPS
Individualized Mobility							
Soft Tissue Release / Foam Roll	As needed						
Mobility Exercise 1	Book Openers		x10		x10		x10
Mobility Exercise 2	90/90 Hip Rotations		x10		x10		x10
Foundation Superset 1							
Traditional Core Exercise	Alternating Limb Dead Bug		x8		x8		x8
Lower Body Push	Walking Lunge		x8		x8		x8
Upper Body Pull	Pull-Ups or Chin-Ups		x5 to 8		x5 to 8		x5 to 8
Foundation Superset 2							
Anti-Rotation Exercise	Half-Kneel Overhead Plate Circles		x8		x8		x8
Lower Body Pull	Slide Board or Towel Leg Curls		x10		x10		x10
Upper Body Push	Resisted Push-Up		x8		x8		x8
Sport-Specific Exercises							
	Trap Bar Deadlift		x8		x8		
	Alternating Knee-to-Chest		x8		x8		
	Lateral Lunge with Overhead Press		x8		x8		
	Cable Cross-Pull – High to Low		x8		x8		

HOME GYM/TRAVEL TEMPLATE

The home gym/travel template is meant to be used when you are crunched for time (as in the peak mileage phase). If you've decided to make resistance training a priority, don't let lack of time or having to travel become an excuse for not getting some quality work done. We encourage everyone to have some basic equipment on hand so that you can maintain mobility, continually stress the muscles and reinforce an optimal motor program.

HOME GYM/TRAVEL TEMPLATE

TYPE	EXERCISE	WEIGHT	REPS	WEIGHT	REPS	WEIGHT	REPS
Individualized Mobility							
Soft Tissue Release / Foam Roll	As needed						
Mobility Exercise 1	Foam Roller Back Extension		x30 Sec.		x30 Sec.		x30 Sec.
Mobility Exercise 2	Bretzel		x30 Sec.		x30 Sec.		x30 Sec.
Foundation Superset 1							
Traditional Core Exercise	Bird Dog		x10		x10		x10
Lower Body Push	Valslide Leg Curl		x10		x10		x10
Upper Body Pull	Push-Up		x10		x10		x10
Foundation Superset 2							
Anti-Rotation Exercise	Shoulder Taps		x10		x10		x10
Lower Body Pull	Valslide Lateral Lunge		x10		x10		x10
Upper Body Push	Inverted Row on Suspension Trainer		x10		x10		x10

TYPE	EXERCISE	WEIGHT	REPS	WEIGHT	REPS	WEIGHT	REPS
Individualized Mobility							
Soft Tissue Release / Foam Roll	As needed						
Mobility Exercise 1	Hip 90/90 Rotations		x10		x10		x10
Mobility Exercise 2	World's Greatest Stretch		x30 Sec.		x30 Sec.		x30 Sec.
Foundation Superset 1							
Traditional Core Exercise	High Side Plank		x10		x10		x10
Lower Body Push	Banded Hip Bridge		x10		x10		x10
Upper Body Pull	Suspension Trainer Push-Up		x10		x10		x10
Foundation Superset 2							
Anti-Rotation Exercise	Dead Bug Paloff Press		x10		x10		x10
Lower Body Pull	Burpee		x10		x10		x10
Upper Body Push	Suspension Trainer Inverted Row		x10		x10		x10

TYPE	EXERCISE	WEIGHT	REPS	WEIGHT	REPS	WEIGHT	REPS
Individualized Mobility							
Soft Tissue Release / Foam Roll	As needed						
Mobility Exercise 1	Doorway Stretch		x30 Sec.		x30 Sec.		x30 Sec.
Mobility Exercise 2	Banded Hip Lateral Distraction		x30 Sec.		x30 Sec.		x30 Sec.
Foundation Superset 1							
Traditional Core Exercise	Crossover Crunch		x10		x10		x10
Lower Body Push	Suspension Trainer Leg Curl		x10		x10		x10
Upper Body Pull	Split Squat Jump		x10		x10		x10
Foundation Superset 2							
Anti-Rotation Exercise	Dumbbell Windshield Wiper		x10		x10		x10
Lower Body Pull	Split Squat Jump		x10		x10		x10
Upper Body Push	Suspension Trainer Leg Curl		x10		x10		x10

TYPE	EXERCISE	WEIGHT	REPS	WEIGHT	REPS	WEIGHT	REPS
Individualized Mobility							
Soft Tissue Release / Foam Roll	As needed						
Mobility Exercise 1	Dorsiflexion Stretch		x30 Sec.		x30 Sec.		x30 Sec.
Mobility Exercise 2	Book Openers		x10		x10		x10
Foundation Superset 1							
Traditional Core Exercise	Crunch		x10		x10		x10
Lower Body Push	Body Weight Good Morning		x10		x10		x10
Upper Body Pull	Inverted Push-Up		x10		x10		x10
Foundation Superset 2							
Anti-Rotation Exercise	Rip Trainer March		x10		x10		x10
Lower Body Pull	Bodyweight Walking Lunge		x10		x10		x10
Upper Body Push	Resistance Tubing Cross-Pull – High to Low		x10		x10		x10

The templates in this section provide the road map to incorporating resistance training into your endurance training calendar. If you follow the plan that's right for you, commit to the process and realize when slight modifications need to be made, you will be on the path to stronger finishes and a more successful racing career.

Strength training on a regular basis is like competing in an IRONMAN in that you have to stay vigilant in your commitment to completing the task when the goal seems far away. At the starting line, 140.6 miles (226.3km) seems like an insurmountable distance, but if you commit to putting one foot in front of the other, the next thing you know the swim is done and you're moving on to the bike. If you can consistently stay focused, before you know it you're halfway to your goal. As you continue to chip away at that massive 140.6 (226.3) number, the distance to your goal will steadily decrease and eventually you will be at the finish line.

Resistance training is similar. On your first day in the gym, movements such as Squats and Pull-ups may seem impossible and using heavy plates may seem like a pipe dream. However, if you stay consistent, keep showing up, keep challenging yourself to be better and stick to the plan, you will eventually be stronger than you may have thought possible.

These templates lay out the path to your goal the same way the race director maps out the route during a marathon. There are parts that require you to push as hard as possible and parts that allow you to recover. There are also times you have to stay with the pack and times to make your move. Finally, there are times when you have to trust the process, your coaches and yourself that you will make it to the end and Finish Strong!

---

1. *ACSM's Guidelines for Exercise Testing and Prescription,* 10th ed. (Wolters Kluwer, 2018)

TRAINING LOAD CHART

Max reps (RM)	1	2	3	4	5	6	7	8	9	10	12
% 1RM	100%	95%	93%	90%	87%	85%	83%	80%	77%	75%	70%
Load											
10	9.5	9.3	9	8.7	8.5	8.3	8	7.7	7.5	7
20	19	18.6	18	17.4	17	16.6	16	15.4	15	14
30	28.5	27.9	27	26.1	25.5	24.9	24	23.1	22.5	21
40	38	37.2	36	34.8	34	33.2	32	30.8	30	28
50	47.5	46.5	45	43.5	42.5	41.5	40	38.5	37.5	35
60	57	55.8	54	52.2	51	49.8	48	46.2	45	42
70	66.5	65.1	63	60.9	59.5	58.1	56	53.9	52.5	49
80	76	74.4	72	69.6	68	66.4	64	61.6	60	56
90	85.5	83.7	81	78.3	76.5	74.7	72	69.3	67.5	63
100	95	93	90	87	85	83	80	77	75	70
110	104.5	102.3	99	95.7	93.5	91.3	88	84.7	82.5	77
120	114	111.6	108	104.4	102	99.6	96	92.4	90	84
130	123.5	120.9	117	113.1	110.5	107.9	104	11.1	97.5	91
140	133	130.2	126	121.8	119	116.2	112	107.8	105	98
150	142.5	139.5	135	130.5	127.5	124.5	120	115.5	112.5	105
160	152	148.8	144	139.2	136	132.8	128	123.2	120	112
170	161.5	158.1	153	147.9	144.5	141.1	136	130.9	127.5	119
180	171	167.4	162	156.6	153	149.4	144	138.6	135	126
190	180.5	176.7	171	165.3	161.5	157.7	152	146.3	142.5	133
200	190	156	180	174	170	166	160	154	150	140
210	199.5	195.3	189	182.7	178.5	174.3	168	161.7	157.5	147
220	209	204.6	198	191.4	187	182.6	176	169.4	165	154
230	218.5	213.9	207	200.1	195.5	190.9	184	177.1	172.5	161
240	228	223.2	216	208.8	204	199.2	192	184.8	180	168
250	237.5	232.5	225	217.5	212.5	207.5	200	192.5	187.5	175
260	247	241.8	234	226.2	221	215.8	208	200.2	195	182
270	256.5	251.1	243	234.9	229.5	224.1	216	207.9	202.5	189
280	266	260.4	252	243.6	238	232.4	224	215.6	210	196
290	275.5	269.7	261	252.3	246.5	240.7	232	223.3	217.5	203
300	285	279	270	261	255	249	240	231	225	210
310	294.5	288.3	279	269.7	263.5	257.3	248	238.7	232.5	217
320	304	297.6	288	278.4	272	265.6	256	246.4	240	224
330	313.5	306.9	297	287.1	280.5	273.9	264	254.1	247.5	231
340	323	316.2	306	295.8	289	282.2	272	261.8	255	238
350	332.5	325.5	315	304.5	297.5	290.5	280	269.5	262.5	245
360	342	334.8	324	313.2	306	298.8	288	277.2	270	252
370	351.5	344.1	333	321.9	314.5	307.1	396	284.9	277.5	259
380	361	353.4	342	330.6	323	315.4	304	292.6	285	266
390	370.5	362.7	351	339.3	331.5	323.7	312	300.3	292.5	273
400	380	372	360	348	340	332	320	308	300	280
410	389.5	381.3	369	356.7	348.5	340.3	328	315.7	307.5	287
420	399	390.6	378	365.4	357	348.6	336	323.4	315	294
430	408.5	399.9	387	374.1	365.5	356.9	344	331.1	322.5	301
440	418	409.2	396	382.8	374	365.2	352	338.8	330	308
450	427.5	418.5	405	391.5	382.5	373.5	360	346.5	337.5	315
460	437	427.8	414	400.2	391	381.8	368	354.2	345	322
470	446.5	437.1	423	408.9	399.5	390.1	376	361.9	352.5	329
480	456	446.4	432	417.6	408	398.4	384	369.6	360	336
490	465.5	455.7	441	426.3	416.5	406.7	392	377.3	367.5	343
500	475	465	450	435	425	415	400	385	375	350

Adapted from Landers © 2012

AFTERWORD

Being comfortable with being uncomfortable is a concept familiar to all endurance athletes. In the book *Mindset* by Dr. Carol Dweck (which we believe every athlete should read), the author describes the growth mindset as the attitude we apply when we leave our comfort and fear zones and enter the learning and growth zones to acquire new skills and set new goals. It is our sincere hope that you are willing to get uncomfortable with us and that after reading this book you are primed for a major growth spurt in your sporting career.

When we first met each other over a decade ago, we were just a young athletic trainer and a strength and conditioning coach with a passion for our respective professions and a goal of being life-long learners. We certainly didn't know everything, but we were determined to keep a growth mindset and learn from others as well as each other. Interestingly, our endurance sports careers have been a similar journey. We both started resistance training at a fairly young age, pursued careers around it and have "lifted weights" in some capacity regularly ever since. Given our knowledge from our professional careers, there wasn't ever a thought given to not doing resistance training while we were training and conditioning for our endurance sport events. Instead, we had so many questions as to why other endurance athletes weren't doing it.

Aside from the general misconceptions that strength training will slow you down and the lack of role models who speak openly of creating body balance through strength and mobility, we've heard countless stories of athletes who just didn't know where to start or have been doing the wrong things when they did actually make it to the gym, which was troubling for us to hear, and was the reason for writing this book. We want to empower you to execute a planned, purposeful, sport-specific program that will make you stronger, faster and less prone to injury.

To help with this, we've shared the idea of the 4 x 4 matrix (remember, you can always change how stable the body is for the exercise and you can change the load in more ways than just adding a few extra plates). We've also shared our progression and regression chart of the Foundation Exercises so you'll easily be able to "plug and play" these as you get stronger, or need to regress because of an injury (hopefully not) before progressing again.

Performing planned, progressive resistance and mobility exercise from the programs that this book provides will help you unlock your potential. We have no doubt that you're willing to make the sacrifices and put the time in training for your sport; it's our wish that now you're ready to join us in adding resistance and mobility training into your training program so that you can Finish Strong.

We hope that you finish reading this book feeling shaved and tapered! Whether you are an IRONMAN triathlete, swimming Alcatraz, competing off-road, or running an ultra or your local marathon, we sincerely want you to add regularly planned strength and mobility work into your training so that you can achieve your next personal best. In other words, swim like you are going to drown, ride it like you stole it and run like you're being chased!

All kidding aside, we thank you for taking this journey with us and hope you put our lessons and programs to good use. Like you, we've been humbled during some races where we failed to execute a nutrition plan or didn't take into account course elevation and didn't reach our goals. As much as it sucks to fail, it's in these humbling moments that we learn the most. One thing to always remember is to practice self-forgiveness when you make these sport-related mistakes. If you'd never made the mistake, you never would have gained the new knowledge from it. And knowledge is empowering.

In closing, we would like to acknowledge all the people who have helped us to get to this point. Without the experiences and interactions with the many patients, clients, student-athletes, coaches, teammates, training partners and colleagues whom we've been fortunate to work with, we wouldn't have been able to write this book. It's our teammates and training partners who keep us excited about continuing training and competing and chasing new personal bests. We especially thank the individuals who have encouraged us to come out of our comfort zones and consider some different treatment and training techniques, which has made us vastly better in our professional careers.

See you at the finish line...

EXERCISE INDEX

INDEX